THE GENOCIDE DEBATE

THE GENOCIDE DEBATE

POLITICIANS, ACADEMICS, AND VICTIMS

DONALD W. BEACHLER

THE GENOCIDE DEBATE
Copyright © Donald W. Beachler, 2011.

All rights reserved.

First published in 2011 by
PALGRAVE MACMILLAN®
in the United States—a division of St. Martin's Press LLC,
175 Fifth Avenue, New York, NY 10010.

Where this book is distributed in the UK, Europe and the rest of the world,
this is by Palgrave Macmillan, a division of Macmillan Publishers Limited,
registered in England, company number 785998, of Houndmills,
Basingstoke, Hampshire RG21 6XS.

Palgrave Macmillan is the global academic imprint of the above companies
and has companies and representatives throughout the world.

Palgrave® and Macmillan® are registered trademarks in the United States,
the United Kingdom, Europe and other countries.

ISBN: 978–0–230–11414–2

Library of Congress Cataloging-in-Publication Data

Beachler, Donald W., 1957–
    The genocide debate : politicians, academics, and victims / Donald W.
Beachler.
      p. cm.
    ISBN 978–0–230–11414–2 (hardback)
     1. Genocide—Research. 2. Ethnic groups. 3. Identity (Philosophical
concept) I. Title.

HV6322.7.B427 2011
364.15′1—dc22   2011007449

A catalogue record of the book is available from the British Library.

Design by Newgen Imaging Systems (P) Ltd., Chennai, India.

First edition: September 2011

10 9 8 7 6 5 4 3 2 1

Printed in the United States of America.

For Brigid

CONTENTS

Acknowledgments

The Jewish Studies program at Ithaca College has encouraged and aided my teaching and research on the Holocaust and on other genocides. In addition to much needed moral support, the program has provided funds for journal subscriptions, books, and travel. I am grateful to its founder, Barbara Johnson, and the current director, Rebecca Lesses.

Ithaca College has, on several occasions, supported my research endeavors. With a grant from the Provost's Office at Ithaca College, I presented an early version of chapter 2 at the International Association of Genocide Scholars Conference in Galway, Ireland, in 2003. A Faculty Development Grant from the Provost's Office allowed me to deepen my knowledge on this topic by traveling to Holocaust-related sites in Poland and Germany. Drafts of chapters 4 and 6 were presented at the International Studies Association annual conferences in San Francisco in 2008 and New Orleans in 2010. These presentations were made possible by travel funds from the School of Humanities and Sciences at Ithaca College.

A prior version of chapter 2 was published in the journal *Patterns of Prejudice* in 2007. I am deeply indebted to Barbara Rosenbaum for her patience and editorial guidance in improving the article.

Chapter 3 on Cambodia appeared in *Holocaust and Genocide Studies* in 2009. It was a pleasure to work with Michael Gelb, assistant editor, on this project. His intelligence, knowledge, and sharp editorial eye improved the style and substance of my arguments about the political disputes that surround the Cambodian genocide.

Naeem Inayatullah, of the Politics Department at Ithaca College, has been an interesting and engaging critic of my universalist worldview. He has not convinced me (nor I, him), but he often induced me to ponder further my assumptions and ideas.

Kevin McMahon, of the Political Science Department at Trinity College, does not delve into the field of genocides studies, but we have collaborated on occasion on publications in American Politics. I have valued greatly his friendship and advice as I have proceeded with this project.

Most of all, I have enjoyed our discussions about so many aspects of politics, policy, and life.

My debts to my wife Brigid, personal and professional, are far too extensive to fully enumerate here. I would not have completed this book or much else without her love, patience, and persistence. Above anything else, she taught me to love snorkeling off the beaches of Maui. Our annual two-week trips to swim with turtles and beautiful fish off that lovely island are the highlight of my year. I would not have taken them without Brigid's initial interest. Unlike many academics in the United States, I am proud to take vacations and holidays (and admit that pleasure is the purpose of my trip), and Brigid has made so many trips to Maui and many other places more fun.

CHAPTER 1

A MOST SENSITIVE MATTER

IN DECEMBER 2008, several films that explored themes related to various aspects of Nazi Germany were released. Among the most discussed films was *The Reader*, based on the novel of the same title by German author Bernhard Schlink. The film attracted considerable attention, and Kate Winslet won the Academy Award for Best Actress for her portrayal of Hanna Schmitz, the film's protagonist.[1] A working-class woman, Schmitz was a former guard at an Auschwitz subcamp who was complicit in the deaths of many Jewish inmates. Especially horrifying was Schmitz's role in the deaths of female Jews who perished when she and other guards refused to unlock the door of a burning church where the prisoners had been shuttered for the night as they proceeded toward Germany on one of the death marches that occurred in the waning months of the war. In the 1960s, Schmitz and a number of other women guards were placed on trial for the crimes they committed during the Holocaust. In response to the judge's question as to why she did not unlock the door of the burning church, Schmitz responds that it was her duty to ensure that the prisoners did not escape. When the judge inquires as to why she could not defy an order under such extreme circumstances, Schmitz responds by asking him what he would have done under similar circumstances. The judge is unable to answer this query.

Writing in the *New York Times* in 2008, Jacob Heilbrunn attacks the film version of the *The Reader* because the judge is unable to give a clear answer as to how he might have acted in response to orders from Nazi superiors two decades earlier, and because Schmitz is presented as "an unthinking tool of the Nazi regime rather than a fervent anti-Semite."[2] Thus for Heilbrunn, as for many who write about the Holocaust, the Germans who participated in the Holocaust must be depicted as rabid anti-Semites rather than as mere ordinary, compliant human beings.[3] There has of course been a long-standing scholarly debate about perpetrators' motives, whether they are major figures in the implementation of the Holocaust such as Adolf Eichmann, or the middle-aged reservists from Hamburg who served as occupation police in Police Battalion 101 and whose actions in Poland have been the source of considerable academic controversy.[4] For Heilbrunn, it seems that in this complex and probably irresolvable debate, there can be only one morally acceptable answer: all Germans of the Nazi era must be presented as vicious anti-Semites. Furthermore, it should have been possible to say in good faith and without doubt, two decades after the war that one would have defied the orders of the Nazi authorities with regard to the treatment of the Jews.

There is, of course, no doubt that the Nazis were murderous anti-Semites and genocidal racists. The Holocaust and the German plan for the murder of tens of millions of Slavs in Eastern Europe, especially in the USSR, was perhaps best described by Christopher Browning as an instance of "racism gone berserk."[5] The question of the motives of many subordinates in the organizations that inflicted death on millions of people under the Nazi regime, however, remains unsettled, and Schmitz's and the judge's answers are not inconsistent with some respected academic opinions on these questions.

Heilbrunn is also critical of the film *Defiance* for relating the story of the Bielski Brothers, a gang of Jewish partisans who saved the lives of more than a thousand Jews in the part of the Soviet Union that is now the nation of Belarus. Heilbrunn does not claim that the film is inaccurate, but instead cites the distinguished Holocaust historian Raul Hilberg, as he makes the claim that in presenting Jewish resistance as typical, the Holocaust is depicted as a struggle between combatants, rather than as a slaughter of innocents. Neither the film nor either of the books on the Bielski Brothers argues that their organized armed resistance was typical of Jewish responses to Nazi oppression during the Holocaust.[6] Like some commentators on the Holocaust, Heilbrunn seems to be concerned that the average moviegoer might get a false impression from these "problematic films." The difficulty that Heilbrunn finds in each of these films and the fact that he seems to insist on a single interpretation of some events and issues in the Holocaust are striking, but not surprising, to anyone who has much engagement with academic or popular writing about the Holocaust or other genocides.

Heilbrunn's interesting review essay may not deserve a review of its own, but it is emblematic of the extreme sensitivity that writing and filmmaking in the field of Holocaust studies engenders. For reasons that are explored throughout this book, this vigilance on behalf of a desired, but not remotely realized, orthodoxy about certain questions related to the Holocaust extends to other genocides. It is perhaps instructive to begin with the author's own initial experience with the politics of writing and publishing about genocide.

A First Encounter with Analyzing the Study of Genocide

As I taught courses on the Holocaust and comparative genocide, I was struck by the intensity that surrounded debates about the uniqueness of the Holocaust and the widely disparate attention some genocides received relative to others. I noted that almost no one seemed to write about events that surrounded the mass killings in Bangladesh in 1971. I wrote an article comparing the vast amount of scholarly and journalistic attention paid to the genocide that occurred in Cambodia under the communist Khmer Rouge regime (1975–1979) and the relatively paltry amount of attention that was given to the mass killings of Bengalis in East Pakistan from March to December of 1971 even though it is likely that similar numbers of people were killed in each nation. Indeed, it is quite likely that more people were murdered in East Pakistan than in Cambodia under the Khmer Rouge. I was aware that there had been considerable coverage of the events in East Pakistan in 1971 in print and broadcast journalism in the United States. The tragedy in Bangladesh had also reached popular culture with a benefit concert for Bangladesh that had been held in Madison Square Garden in New York City on August 1, 1971. The concert featured such well-known musicians as Bob Dylan, Ringo Starr, George Harrison, Eric Clapton, and Ravi Shankar.[7] A film of the concert was made and released in 1972, and an album containing selections of songs played there was produced in late 1971. Since the early 1970s, however, the atrocities in Bangladesh have received almost no attention in Western media and have been generally neglected by genocide scholars.

I submitted my article on the disparate treatment of the two Asian genocides from the 1970s and 1980s to an academic journal that had an avowedly leftist or progressive bent. When the article was first reviewed by the journal's editorial board, I received an initial inquiry from the journal editor inquiring whether I would be willing to drop the Cambodia section and simply produce an article on why the Bangladesh genocide has been largely ignored. The ostensible reason was the journal had devoted many articles to Cambodia over the years. Given the ideological predilections of the journal and the unflattering depiction of left wing luminaries like Noam Chomsky and Samir Amin in the Cambodia section of the article, I was a bit discomfited by their suggestion. On the whole though, the request seemed reasonable as my own thesis stated that little had been published on the Bangladesh genocide of 1971.

The article was submitted to reviewers who were generally favorable, but did feel that it lacked a certain sensitivity in that it depicted Muslim violence against Hindus in what was then East Pakistan, while not also studying

Hindu violence against Muslims at other points in South Asian history. After my rejoinder that I was producing an analysis of a single event and not a comprehensive history of communal violence in India and Pakistan, the editor, who was clearly concerned by my lack of professional credentials in South Asian politics or history, placed me in direct contact with the reviewers. One reviewer invoked his South Asian heritage and thus his access to "collective memory" to indicate his certainty that there had been no singling out of Hindus for murder or ethnic cleansing in the course of the Pakistani army's brutal attempt to quell secessionist efforts in East Pakistan.[8] This reviewer also cautioned that such an article could be used to incite communal violence in South Asia. The reviewer did not respond to my inquiries about the many press accounts in 1971 of refugees reporting that Hindus were especially targeted for repression by the Pakistani army.

Despite some remaining reservations of the reviewers, after three rounds of revisions over several months, the journal's editor appeared satisfied with my efforts, produced a copyedited version of the text, and asked me to examine the article to "check over the attached version to see whether everything reads the way you intend."[9] I was also asked to do my best to bring the endnotes into conformity with the journal's style and to provide an abstract of about 200 words.[10] Normally, this would be regarded as the final stage in the production of a journal article. A month later, I received a call from the editor, who told me that the article was fundamentally flawed and so poorly constructed as to border on the incomprehensible. The article was so deficient in its argument, I was informed, that it essentially needed to be rewritten in its entirety. Furthermore, the editor insisted that I remove a paragraph about Edward Said, the late scholar and activist on behalf of the Palestinians. The objectionable passage referred to Said's insistence that Saddam Hussein had not used chemical weapons against the Kurds. When I insisted that the information on Said was correct and well sourced, the editor insisted that the information had to have been taken out of context. The call ended inconclusively, though I was extremely frustrated by what I regarded as frankly dishonest or at best disingenuous conduct by the journal editor. An author has little power in a situation such as the one that had arisen with regard to my article. The next day, despite all the work I had put into several revisions of the article and my initial satisfaction at having had my article accepted, I sent an e-mail to the editor withdrawing the manuscript from any further consideration for publication in his journal. The editor's terse two-sentence response was to express disappointment at my decision, and to say that he was only trying to improve the article.[11]

While I had no definitive proof, I was convinced that someone had raised an ideological objection to my article after it was accepted. Given the ideological tenor of the journal, the fact that the article was critical of the Left and the Right—but the material I was asked to remove was always information that placed leftist scholars, such as Said and Noam Chomsky, in a less-than-favorable light—and given the lack of any reasonable explanation by the editor for the dramatic change in his assessment of the article, I could only conclude that either the editor had been struck blind on the road to Damascus or some pressure had been brought to bear on the managing editor to not publish the article. My first venture into publishing about genocide politics was indeed a hard-learned lesson that in the politics of genocide scholarship, politics are very important. Politics play a role in much of academia as in most aspects of life, but when it comes to the topic of genocide, the stakes are higher. Genocide is the "ultimate crime," as Samantha Power memorably labeled it in her book, *A Problem from Hell: America and the Age of Genocide*. The charge of genocide places great opprobrium on the perpetrators or alleged perpetrators and, as will be argued in this book, endows the greatest moral and political capital on the victims.[12]

THE POLITICS OF GENOCIDE STUDIES

This book examines the study of genocide from a variety of perspectives. The chapter on Bangladesh was eventually published in another journal, and a revised version of that article inquires as to why a genocide widely covered at the time has slipped into relative obscurity since 1971.[13] This chapter explores the motives or more precisely the lack of incentives for scholars, politicians, and, to a degree, even the political elites in Bangladesh to pay little attention to the genocide in Bangladesh, especially the extent to which it was directed against the Hindu minority that resided in East Bengal in 1971 and continues to reside in the country to this day.[14] Such an analysis, like others in this book, cannot prove the motive of scholars and journalists who place certain genocides in a position of relative neglect. It can only explain why various actors have motives to behave in a certain manner and then examine the course of their actions and inaction in an effort to determine whether their actions are consistent with the postulated motives.

Chapter 3 on Cambodia explores the intense debate about the Khmer Rouge regime that has raged from the time the regime took power until the present. When the Khmer Rouge was in power, much of the controversy focused on the accuracy of the atrocity reports that emerged from a country that was largely isolated from the world. For the most part, those who had been opponents of U.S. military activities in Southeast Asia in the 1960s and 1970s were skeptical about reports of massive killing by the communists who had deposed the United States–backed Lon Nol regime. They regarded reports of a horrific communist regime in Cambodia as grist for the mills of those who wished to retrospectively justify their support for the long wars waged by the United States in Southeast Asia. Many Marxists were intrigued and even heartened by a government that sought an immediate transition to communism and was engaged, if to a radical extreme, in the delinking from the global capitalist economy that many on the left had long advocated. Conservatives who had supported efforts to defeat communism in Vietnam and Cambodia were quick to embrace the tales of massive human rights abuses in Democratic Kampuchea as vindication of the bloodbath that they believed followed communist ascendance to power anywhere in the world and that they had warned would occur in the event of communist victories in Indochina.

After the Khmer Rouge was driven from power in 1979 by a Vietnamese invasion, the reaction to events in Cambodia was more complex. Still, it will be argued that the imperatives of realpolitik best explain the decisions of many Western governments to condemn the Vietnamese invasion and permit the deposed Khmer Rouge to retain Cambodia's seat at the United Nations (UN) until the end of the Cold War. When the atrocities of Pol Pot and his cohorts could no longer plausibly be denied, the explanations for them often fit comfortably into the worldviews of authors who had larger ideological and political axes to grind. Thus, debates erupted about whether the Khmer Rouge was actually Marxist or whether it was in fact more accurately a racist regime.

Few topics in genocide studies have generated more intense and angry disputes over the years than the concept of Holocaust uniqueness.[15] Chapter 4 examines the sources of the argument that the Holocaust was unique and the claim, made either implicitly or explicitly, that the Jewish suffering at the hands of Nazi Germany was the worst atrocity in human history. A variety of writers advance this claim, some arguing for the thesis solely on the basis of their empirical analysis of various genocides, while others tie the uniqueness assertion to the need to mobilize support for the state of Israel. The Holocaust uniqueness assertion has been fiercely opposed by a number of writers, including spokespersons for the Armenian victims of the Ottomans and Gypsies who were murdered by the Nazis.[16] These authors claim that acceptance of the uniqueness perspective inevitably leads to academic and public neglect of other genocides. Few opponents of the uniqueness argument have been more vehement than those who claim that Holocaust uniqueness advocates deny or relegate to the margins of academic and public discourse the sufferings imposed on indigenous people in the Western Hemisphere. Both sides in this dispute are arguing indirectly and, in a few cases, directly, that the moral capital that can be earned by victim groups is finite and thus must be preserved for the group they seek to champion. The rhetoric on this issue is especially heated, because some scholars argue that Holocaust uniqueness claims amount to a form of genocide denial against victim groups that receive comparatively little attention in the United States. The charge of genocide denial is extremely provocative in the United States. Conversely, some Holocaust uniqueness advocates have lumped those who do not accept their argument on the incomparable nature of the Nazi attempt to exterminate the Jews with those writers who assert that the Holocaust never occurred. This controversy is analyzed in chapter 4, under the title "Who Suffered the Most?" This title for a chapter is likely to offend some readers, but it captures the vigorous, and at times vicious, nature of the debate about the relative significance of the Holocaust and the degree of attention that it receives.

Besides the Holocaust, the Armenian genocide in Anatolia during World War I has drawn the most attention from genocide scholars in the United States and Europe. Six of the eleven resolutions and statements listed on the web page of the International Association of Genocide Scholars (IAGS), an organization largely made up of academics and activists from the United States and Europe, concern the crimes of the Ottoman Committee for Union & Progress (CUP) or Young Turk government against the Armenians, and to a lesser extent other Christian minorities.[17] (These resolutions demand that the current government of Turkey acknowledge that the Ottoman government of 1915 committed genocide against the Armenians residing in Anatolia.) Much of the academic debate about the fate of the Armenians concerns the denial of the genocide by the Turkish government and some scholars of the Ottoman Empire in the United States. Chapter 5 does not focus on this debate, but rather proceeds on the basis of the fact that while there is room for much argument over the exact dimensions of the genocide and the role of Armenian nationalists in seeking to undermine the Ottoman regime, at this point there seems to be little doubt that the nationalist CUP regime committed a purposeful genocide against Armenians in Anatolia beginning in 1915.[18] The domestic and geopolitical reasons for the Turkish government's refusals to acknowledge the genocide are fairly well known and are given only cursory attention in this chapter.

Chapter 5 presents an analysis of the manner in which disputes over genocide recognition and denial often involve remarkable inconsistency, selective morality, unsustainable claims about the likely impact of genocide acknowledgment, and cultural biases. To a disturbing degree, political and academic groups single out one or two genocides and demand that nations apologize for them. One could be forgiven for thinking, based on resolutions that are passed by organizations such as the IAGS, that Turkey is the only nation to have committed genocide and not apologized to the victims or even acknowledged the event's occurrence. Those who have a different view of the events than that accepted by the IAGS are regarded as inherently immoral, perhaps suffering from mental pathologies or, at best, duplicitous by those who demand that the Turkish government adhere to their view of the events of 1915 and subsequent years. The actions and rhetoric of both scholars and politicians in the West, and especially the United States, are analyzed in the context of the themes described in this paragraph.

Exploring the concept of genocide provocation will inevitably land one in a political thicket. Because of the moral and political capital that often accrues to the victims of genocide, groups that claim to represent the interest of victims or those who are their descendants most often present the group subjected to genocide as among the most politically innocent peoples ever to inhabit the earth. The notion of genocide provocation is explored in two forms in chapter 6. First, the more common version is that a comparatively weak group may engage in actions designed to provoke atrocities by the state that has dominion over them in the hope that violent repression will induce outside intervention from stronger powers. The intrusion of external powers might give the insurgent group the means to defeat an opponent against whom it would otherwise have no realistic chance of victory. This concept of genocide provocation is explored in the context of the activities of Armenian nationalists in the Ottoman Empire in the late nineteenth and early twentieth centuries.

Genocide provocation might also occur when a political group engages in a course of action that it realizes will possibly, or even probably, lead to violent retaliation against civilians. In the case of Rwanda, some research indicates that the Tutsi-led Rwandan Patriotic Front (RPF) knew very well that its actions could lead to the murder of tens of thousands of Tutsi residing in Rwanda by the Hutu Power militants. The RPF did not anticipate that such actions would reach the level of genocide and regarded the loss of life likely to occur as a result of their attempt to seize state power as an acceptable cost of victory if such deaths were merely in the tens of thousands.

Both types of genocide provocation are often avoided in analyses of genocides because victim groups seem to feel that if they are presented as less than political innocents, some observers will conclude that the genocide was in some way justified. Human rights activists who advocate for humanitarian intervention in various parts of the world are reluctant to present political conflicts as anything less than pure struggles of good against evil. While it is difficult, if not impossible, to attribute motive with any great certainty, it would seem that those who advocate for outside interventions in situations such as Darfur believe that moral ambiguity or political complexity weakens the case for intervention. A civil war presents far more complex moral and political issues than unprovoked genocide.

IS STUDYING GENOCIDE DIFFERENT?

Reflecting upon the themes of this book, the natural question arises as to what, if anything at all, differentiates the study of genocide, as it is presented in this book, from the study of anything else. After all, scholars, journalists, and politicians are often motivated by political interests in choosing what issues to emphasize and what matters to ignore. It is perhaps human nature, or at least a common weakness, to be cognizant only of the facts or events that fit our preconceived worldview or promote our interests. All too often, few of us want to be bothered by information that may be inconsistent with our political or material interests. It is difficult to process information that contradicts our worldview. In the words of Tzvetan Todorov, "All or almost all of us prefer comfort to truth."[19] While Todorov was writing about genocide and other forms of mass political violence, his maxim would seem to apply to the human predisposition in many fields of endeavor.

Historian Donald Bloxham, writing about the effort of scholars to equate the Armenian genocide and the Holocaust, states, "The quest for a sort of total equivalence between historical episodes is something peculiar to genocide studies."[20] What seems to make genocide all the more contentious a topic is that it is often regarded as the ultimate crime. The word "genocide" was coined by Raphael Lemkin in response to the Nazi crimes against the Jews and others in the 1940s.[21] With the explosion of interest in the Holocaust in the last 30 to 40 years, there has been an increased interest in the study of genocide in many historical settings. To attribute genocide to a particular nation is to accuse it of the worst possible crime. To claim that a group has suffered from the crime of genocide is to elevate it to the first circle of victim groups and thus grant it a more substantial claim on the aforementioned moral capital that many people believe accrues to victimized groups.

Mahmood Mamdani, a Columbia University scholar of African politics, has argued that there is great inconsistency in the assessment, by many human rights activists in the West, of the humanitarian crisis in Darfur compared to equally devastating events elsewhere in Africa and in Iraq. Mamdani attributes this disparity to the political interests of the external powers and the alliances they have struck with various governments and political factions in Africa. The term "genocide" has become a weapon of political combat: "It seems that genocide has become a label to be stuck on your worst enemy, a perverse version of the Nobel Prize, part of a rhetorical arsenal that helps you vilify your adversaries while ensuring impunity for your allies."[22] Mamdani goes on to argue that the humanitarian intervention proposed by many Darfur campaigners in the United States and Europe is a new form of imperialism. In Mamdani's view, such actions are the "language of big powers" imposing their will on subaltern peoples.[23] One need not accept (or reject for that matter) Mamdani's view on imperialism and humanitarian intervention to recognize the truth in his claim that labeling a government as genocidal can be a weapon in the conduct of foreign policy.

The accusation of genocide can be a large rhetorical and moral club to be used against one's political opponents. As such, it is predictable that the legitimacy of deploying such a weapon would be fiercely contested. As this book demonstrates, the contest is indeed fierce, if not always morally or intellectually edifying.

CHAPTER 2

THE POLITICS OF GENOCIDE SCHOLARSHIP: THE CASE OF BANGLADESH

IN THE 1970s, two Asian genocides each resulted, according to most estimates, in the deaths of at least 1.5 million people. In March 1971, the Pakistani army launched a campaign to repress the independence movement of Bengalis in the eastern half of the geographically separated nation. The campaign of murder, rape, and pillage that continued until December 1971 caused 1 to 3 million deaths. By some accounts, 200,000 Bengali women were raped. The International Commission of Jurists concluded that a campaign of genocide involved

> ...the indiscriminate killing of civilians, including women and children and the poorest and weakest members of the community; the attempt to exterminate or drive out of the country a large part of the Hindu population; the arrest, torture and killing of Awami League activists and students, professionals, business men and other potential leaders among the Bengalis; the raping of women; the destruction of villages and towns.[1]

The Pakistani repression ended when India defeated Pakistan in a two-week war in December 1971. East Pakistan gained independence as the new nation of Bangladesh shortly thereafter.

In Cambodia, the Khmer Rouge seized power from the United States–backed Lon Nol regime in April 1975. The new communist regime attempted an immediate transition to communism, which included the forced evacuation of urban residents to the countryside. Ethnic minorities were especially targeted for persecution. By the time the Khmer Rouge was driven from power by an invading Vietnamese army in January 1979, at least 1.5 million Cambodians had died as a result of Khmer Rouge policies.[2]

Despite the similar death tolls, the two events have received very different levels of attention from scholars in the West.[3] Almost from the moment the Khmer Rouge took power, there were debates about whether or not genocide was being committed in Cambodia and, subsequently, about the nature of the genocide. While the events in what became the nation of Bangladesh received intense media coverage in 1971, there has been little scholarly interest in the question of genocide since that time. Those who write about the 1971 secession crisis in South Asia tend to ignore or pass briefly over the repressive measures imposed in East Pakistan, and little attention is paid to the Bengalis. In fact, the genocide in Bangladesh attracts so little interest that a portion of this chapter will be devoted to demonstrating that there is substantial evidence from a variety of sources to indicate that a genocide did indeed occur. When a seminar on the Bangladesh genocide (an unprecedented event in the United States) was held at Kean University in 2007, the website for the event described the purpose of the event: "...Through this introductory seminar, Kean University is revisiting the horrific genocide that Bangladesh suffered in 1971, an untold mass killing story to most of the western population."[4] Even as genocide became a much-studied topic in American colleges and universities, a seminar on the 1971 genocide was described as examining an "untold" episode in twentieth-century history.

I will examine this evidence and the reasons why the genocide has been widely ignored, beginning with an analysis of the selective interest that seems to afflict scholars of genocide, and politicians and activists of all political persuasions.[5] I will recount the background of the political conflict between East and West Pakistan, and apply the definition of "genocide" to the case of Bangladesh in 1971. The controversy surrounding the number of victims of the 1971 massacres will also be examined. A major section of the chapter will explore the evidence for genocide and its denial in Western scholarship. In conclusion, I will attempt to explain this neglect, and even denial, in much of the West.

SOME GENOCIDES ARE MORE COMPELLING THAN OTHERS: SELECTIVE COMPASSION & INTEREST

It is obvious that some killings of genocidal proportions generate considerably more attention and interest than others. A striking example of a neglected human catastrophe is the mass murder inflicted on the Congo by Belgian king Leopold II as he exploited the resources of the central African land during the decades surrounding the turn of the twentieth century. While Leopold's primary objective was not to eliminate the Congolese people, outright killings and the harsh conditions imposed on the indigenous people by the Belgians resulted in several million deaths. Despite the atrocities committed by the Belgians in the Congo, the first book-length study in English about this period was not published until nearly a century later in 1998.[6]

Among genocides, the Holocaust is today in a category by itself with regard to intensity of interest. There is not only a vast academic and popular library of work about the Holocaust, but also a sizable body of literature on why so much attention is paid to it and the ways in which that interest has developed over time. A striking example of the change in the status of the Holocaust in American academia is the career of eminent Holocaust historian Raul Hilberg. As a graduate student at Columbia University in the 1950s, Hilberg was told that writing a dissertation on the Holocaust was an academic death sentence.[7] Later, Hilberg struggled for years to find a publisher for his book, *The Destruction of the European Jews*, a work that is now widely regarded as an authoritative history of the Holocaust.[8] By the 1990s, interest in the Holocaust was such that Hilberg could publish a memoir that essentially detailed his career as a Holocaust scholar.[9] University of Chicago professor Peter Novick published a work that demonstrated how little interest there was in the Holocaust in the first few decades after World War II; it also attempted to explain the reasons for the very intense interest over the past 25 years in terms of the emergence of identity politics and Jewish fears of assimilation in American society.[10] Israeli historian Tom Segev explored the changing significance of the Holocaust in Israeli society.[11] In a fiercely polemical work, Norman Finkelstein argued that the study of the Holocaust has been promoted tirelessly since 1967 by some in the American Jewish community to justify Israeli aggression, award victim status to prosperous American Jews, and, essentially, extort money from Swiss banks.[12] Other recent work has investigated the ways in which the Holocaust has been presented in the media, museums, and historical sites.[13]

At times, genocide denial or indifference to genocide may be a function of partisan or nationalist motivations. George Orwell asserted in his essay "Notes on Nationalism" that the

> nationalist not only does not disapprove of atrocities committed by his own side, but he has a remarkable capacity for not even hearing about them. For quite six years the English admirers of Hitler contrived not to learn of the existence of Dachau or Buchenwald.... Huge events like the Ukraine famine

of 1933, involving the deaths of millions of people, have escaped the attention of the majority English Russophiles.[14]

In a study of genocide denial in Australia, Ben Kiernan notes the efforts of some in Australia to deny the genocide perpetrated against the Aborigines in the course of the white settlement of that continent and the genocide perpetrated by the government of Indonesia in East Timor from 1975 to 1999. Kiernan attributes these refusals in part to the reluctance of partisans of the Right to support causes associated with the political Left. The denial of these two genocides was also convenient for those who were supportive of the anticommunist Suharto regime in Indonesia as well as for those who opposed the movement to recognize Aboriginal land rights. Kiernan acknowledges that, in other instances, such as Stalinist Russia or Khmer Rouge Cambodia, leftists have been reluctant to recognize the genocidal actions of communist regimes.[15]

In some cases, ideological opponents may switch sides with regard to the degree to which they recognize claims of genocide as credible. In the 1980s, Iraq waged the Anfal campaign against the Kurds in the northern part of the country. Estimates of deaths in that campaign, which included the use of chemical and biological weapons, range from 50,000 to 182,000.[16] Because the United States was at least loosely allied with Iraq in its war against Iran at the time, U.S. government agencies produced reports casting doubt on the responsibility of the Saddam Hussein regime for using what were to be later labeled "weapons of mass destruction." After Iraq invaded Kuwait in 1991, the United States no longer cited these reports and claimed that Saddam had indeed committed terrible atrocities against the Kurds. In the wake of the 1991 Gulf War, critics of U.S. policies, such as Edward Said, took up Defense Department claims to cast doubt on the allegations against Iraq. Said cited an Army War College report that declared that Iran was responsible for at least one of the most atrocious poison gas attacks in the Kurdish village of Halabja.[17] In the case of the Iraqi Kurds, a willingness to believe that genocide occurred was time limited and also seems to have been a matter of political convenience.

EAST PAKISTAN, 1971: BACKGROUND OF THE CRISIS

The tensions between East and West Pakistan that led to the crisis in 1971 cannot be recounted in detail here. However, some aspects of the difficult relations between the geographically, ethnically, and linguistically distinct sections of Pakistan from its founding in 1947 to its breakup in 1971 are relevant to this chapter, as they demonstrate the ethnic and nationalist tensions that often precede genocide. Unlike most modern states, East and West Pakistan were not contiguous, but were separated by a thousand miles. East Pakistan was carved out of the Bengali-speaking region of India, and the predominantly Bengali East Pakistanis believed they were not fairly represented in political, economic, and cultural life. Although it was the most widely spoken language in Pakistan, Bengali was denied status as a national language until 1956. And, from the country's founding in 1947, Bengalis rioted against what they perceived to be the inferior status accorded to their language.[18] While East Pakistan contained a majority of the country's population, most high-ranking civil servants and military officers were from West Pakistan.[19] Furthermore, while a significant portion of the country's foreign exchange was derived from jute grown in East Pakistan, it received just 35 percent of the money spent on development projects.[20] Not surprisingly, the Bengalis believed that they were an economic colony of West Pakistan.

Two events in late 1970 sparked the political crisis of 1971. In November, a cyclone and subsequent floods devastated East Pakistan. The death toll from the natural disasters was difficult to determine, but it has been estimated at 250,000 to 500,000 people. Bengalis believed that the central government in West Pakistan was slow to react and that its response to the catastrophe was inadequate.[21]

In December 1970, Pakistan held elections to a New Constituent Assembly that was to write a new national constitution. The 1970 elections were the first in Pakistani history to be held on a one-person, one-vote basis and, therefore, a party that could sweep East Pakistan was in a position to dominate the national government. In these elections, the Bengali-based Awami League, led by Sheikh Mujibur Rahman, won a majority of the seats in the Assembly. The ethnic divisions in Pakistani politics were starkly illustrated by the election results. The Awami League captured 167 of the 169 constituencies in East Pakistan, giving the League an absolute majority in the new 313-seat Assembly. The Awami League advocated a six-point autonomy plan, first articulated in 1966, that would have granted the Bengalis a semi-independent status within Pakistan.[22] With its electoral victory, the Awami League was in a position to enact its program and to name Mujib, as he was popularly known, as prime minister. Neither of these outcomes was acceptable to the military elites who dominated Pakistan. On March 1, 1971, after Zulfiqar Ali Bhutto, head of the Pakistan Peoples' Party that had won 80 constituencies in the elections, announced that his party would boycott the Assembly, Pakistan's military dictator, Yahya Kahn, delayed the convening of the Assembly. In East Bengal, the postponement of the Assembly and, thus, the denial of the fruits of electoral victory to the Bangladeshis was met with mass outrage. Demonstrations were followed by widespread strikes that left East Pakistan paralyzed. At this point, the Pakistani military leadership decided to quell the uprising in Bangladesh with brute force. Military action began on March 25, 1971, with a mistaken belief on the part of the Pakistani generals that the Bengalis could be quickly subdued by violence.[23]

QUANTIFYING THE VICTIMS

Estimates of the number of those killed in Bangladesh in 1971 vary greatly. A low-end estimate by American political scientists Richard Sisson and Leo E. Rose, who denied that a genocide took place, was that about 300,000 were killed in the actions of the Pakistani army, the atrocities that Bengalis committed against the Bihari minority, and in warfare between the Pakistani army and the rebel Mukti Bahini forces that battled for Bangladeshi independence.[24] A. M. A. Muhith, a Bangladeshi writer, estimated that about 3 million Bangladeshis were killed by the Pakistani army between March and December 1971.[25] Rounaq Jahan also placed the number of dead in the range of about 3 million.[26] In a book on democide, R. J. Rummel estimated that about 1.5 million people were killed in Bangladesh in 1971.[27] Based on a survey that he acknowledged was incomplete, Kalyan Chaudhuri estimated the number of Bengalis killed as 1,247,000.[28] Visiting Bangladesh in January 1972, just over a month after India defeated Pakistan in a two-week war that began on December 2, 1971, journalist Sydney Schanberg reported that foreign diplomats and independent observers estimated a death toll ranging from at least several hundred thousand to more than a million people. Schanberg reported that these same observers indicated that, if one could calculate all deaths that could be attributed to the repression imposed by the Pakistani army, including deaths among both the roughly 10 million refugees who fled to India and those whose lives were disrupted inside East Pakistan, the total number of dead would very likely approach the 3 million total claimed by Bengali leader Sheikh Mujibur Rahman.[29] With the exception of Chaudhuri, who used Bangladeshi newspaper accounts and government reports, none of the authors provided detailed evidence for the number of deaths they projected.

EAST PAKISTAN, 1971: WAS THERE A GENOCIDE?

The very definition of "genocide" itself has given rise to considerable controversy, and there are various competing concepts of what constitutes a "genocide."[30] As Eric Weitz notes, "genocide" is a much over-used term.[31] The definition used in this chapter is the one adopted by the 1948 United Nations (UN) Convention on the Punishment and Prevention of the Crime of Genocide, to which 142 nations are signatories. Article II defines "genocide" as follows:

> In the present Convention, genocide means any of the following acts committed with intent to destroy, in whole or in part, a national, ethnical, racial or religious group as such:
>
> a) Killing members of the group;
> b) Causing serious bodily or mental harm to members of the group;
> c) Deliberately inflicting on the group conditions of life calculated to bring about its physical destruction in whole or in part;
> d) Imposing measures intended to prevent births within the group;
> e) Forcibly transferring children of the group to another group.[32]

To use an important distinction specified in the 1948 Convention, the Bangladeshi genocide was a "partial" genocide and not a "total" genocide. In a total genocide, there is an attempt to eliminate the entire class of victims. Robert Melson characterizes the Holocaust, the Armenian genocide, and the 1994 Rwandan genocides as total genocides.[33] Melson defines a partial genocide as "...mass murder in order to coerce and to alter the identity and politics of the group, not to destroy it."[34] There was no attempt to eliminate the entire population of East Pakistan. The Pakistani army wished to eliminate those elements of the Bengali Muslim population that it believed were vital to the autonomy movement, to spread terror among the general population, and also to decimate the Hindus, who, it believed, played a malevolent role in East Bengal. The army's ultimate objective was to crush the movement for autonomy.

While the numbers of dead cannot be calculated with precision, there is no doubt that the Pakistani army killed vast numbers of Bengalis. Villages were burned and crops destroyed. Several million people fled, under wretched circumstances, to India. The destruction of homes and creation of refugees by terror undoubtedly increased the death toll. Bengali women were raped in large numbers by the occupying military. The toll from death, violence, and destruction targeted at ethnic and religious groups would indicate that the Pakistani army and its indigenous collaborators indeed committed genocide in Bangladesh in 1971. In order to make this case, I will examine the ideological and geopolitical aspects of the 1971 secession crisis. First, the claims of journalists, diplomats, aid workers, and others will be introduced to demonstrate that there is credible evidence that mass killings, rapes, and expulsions took place across East Bengal and throughout the nine-month civil war. The time, scale, and geographical breadth of the killings and other atrocities point to the likelihood that genocide occurred.

THE EVIDENCE OF GENOCIDE

A variety of sources depict systematic killing, rape, and destruction by the Pakistani army consistent with genocide. These eyewitness and journalistic accounts are not absolute proof of genocide, but they do indicate that the atrocities continued throughout the nine months of military repression in East Pakistan and that they occurred in many regions of the country. These reports indicate that students, politicians known to favor independence, intellectuals, Awami League activists, and Hindus were special targets of the army.

The military launched its operations on the night of March 25–26 with Operation Searchlight. Dhaka University was among the targets of this first attack on Bengali nationalism. On April 29, 1971, Ohio Republican Senator William Saxbe placed a letter from a constituent, Dr. Jon E. Rohde, in the Senate record. Dr. Rohde had served in East Bengal for three years as a physician with the United States Agency for Independent Development (USAID). His letter contained the following account of what he witnessed before he was evacuated from Dhaka:

> My wife and I watched from our roof the night of March 25 as tanks rolled out of the Cantonment illuminated by the flares and the red glow of the fires as the city was shelled by artillery and mortars were fired into crowded slums and bazaars...On the 29th we stood at the Ramna Kali Bari, an ancient Hindu village of about 250 people in the center of Dacca Ramna Race Course, and witnessed the stacks of machine gunned burning remains of men, women, and children butchered in the early morning hours of March 29...At the university area we walked through...two of the student dormitories at Dacca University [were] shelled by the army tanks. All inmates were slaughtered....A man who was forced to drag the bodies outside, counted one hundred three Hindu students buried there...We also saw evidence of a tank attack at Iqbal Hall where bodies were still unburied.[35]

Dr. Rohde's assessment of the situation in East Bengal was as follows: "The law of the jungle prevails in East Pakistan where the mass killing of unarmed civilians, the systematic elimination of the intelligentsia, and the annihilation of the Hindu population is in progress."[36]

Another American evacuated from Dhaka, Pat Sammel, wrote a letter to the *Denver Post* that was placed in the House record by Representative Mike McKevitt of Colorado on May 11, 1971. Sammel wrote:

> We have been witness to what amounts to genocide. The West Pakistani army used tanks, heavy artillery and machine guns on unarmed civilians, killed 1,600 police while sleeping in their barracks...demolished the student

dormitories at Dacca University, and excavated a mass grave for the thousands of students; they've systematically eliminated the intelligentsia of the country, wiped out entire villages—I could go on and on. It's hard to believe it happened.[37]

Further reports of a massacre at Dhaka University can be found among James Michener's interviews in Teheran with Americans who were evacuated from the East Pakistani capital. Several evacuees reported that they had seen Pakistani leaders with specific lists containing the names of Bengali professors who were slated for execution. They also reported seeing mass graves of students who had been killed.[38]

Pakistani journalist Anthony Mascarenhas was permitted to tour East Bengal in April 1971. His reports indicate that government policy was to eliminate the Hindus by death or expulsion. The comments made by Pakistani military officials in Bengal are eerily reminiscent of Nazi notions of purification and the weeding out of bad elements from society. According to Mascarenhas, senior government and military officials in East Bengal stated: "We are determined to cleanse East Pakistan once and for all of the threat of secession, even if it means killing off two million people and ruling the province as a colony for 30 years."[39] Another officer claimed that it had reached the point where Bengali culture had in fact become Hindu culture: "We have to sort them out to restore the land to the people, and the people to their faith."[40] A major in the Pakistani army told Mascarenhas: "This is a war between the pure and the impure...The people here may have Muslim names and call themselves Muslims. But they are Hindu at heart. We are now sorting them out...Those who are left will be real Muslims. We will even teach them Urdu."[41] Mascarenhas identified the principal targets of the campaign in East Bengal who were singled out for murder and/or intimidation: Bengali militiamen in the East Bengal regiment and the East Pakistan Rifles; Hindus who, as has been noted, were viewed as the rulers of East Pakistan and the corrupters of Bengali Muslims; all Awami League officers and volunteers; students, especially college and university men and some women who were viewed as militants; and Bengali intellectuals and teachers who were regarded as militants.[42]

To instill terror, there was much random violence inflicted on Bengalis. Rounaq Jahan aptly summarized the pattern of the killings: "Though Hindus were especially targeted, the majority of the victims were Bengali Muslims—ordinary villagers and slum dwellers—who were caught unprepared during the Pakistani army's sweeping spree of wanton killing, rape, and destruction."[43] The genocidal campaign aimed to deprive the Bangladeshis of the capacity for physical, political, and intellectual resistance. One Pakistani officer spoke in defense of the actions by arguing that only men were being killed.[44] As R. J. Rummel remarked, it was as if killing unarmed men was somehow virtuous.[45]

Mascarenhas reported that officers at the Pakistani army's eastern command headquarters in Dhaka made clear the government's policy with regard to East Bengal. The Bengalis had shown themselves to be unreliable and would be ruled by West Pakistanis. The Bangladeshis were to be reeducated along Islamic lines, and the two regions of Pakistan were to be joined by a strong religious bond. Finally, when the Hindus had been eliminated by death or expulsion, their property was to be distributed among middle-class Muslims.[46] While at Comilla on East Pakistan's eastern border with India, Mascarenhas heard officers discussing their search for Hindus. Those Hindus apprehended were killed, while others abandoned their homes, and entire villages were burned for small acts of defiance.[47] Mascarenhas's reports of his ten-day tour of East Pakistan indicate that the genocidal rhetoric expressed by many officers of the Pakistani army were not idle boasts.

New York Times reporter Sydney Schanberg reported that many Hindu shopkeepers were killed in Dhaka. (It is well worth noting that, while Schanberg covered both the Cambodian and Bangladeshi genocides, he achieved much greater renown for his coverage of Cambodia, culminating in his portrayal as a heroic reporter in the film *The Killing Fields*.) The shops of those murdered were given to non-Bengali Muslims and others who collaborated with the occupation. In addition to the destruction of the merchant class, the Pakistani army also focused on Hindu religious sites and many Hindu temples were demolished. The campaign against Bengali culture was not confined to Hindus. Schanberg reported that automobile license plates with Bengali script were changed to English.[48] Pakistani soldiers informed Bengalis that Urdu was a more civilized tongue and they should abandon Bengali.[49]

Schanberg believed that by late June 1971, the killing had become less indiscriminate and more targeted. He wrote that missionaries in remote regions of Bangladesh were reporting that massacres occurred on an almost daily basis. One missionary told Schanberg that over a thousand Hindus were killed in one day in the southern district of Barisal. According to another missionary, a meeting to effect a reconciliation was called in the northeastern Sylhet district. When a crowd gathered, troops arrived, selected 300 Hindus from the crowd, and shot them.[50]

Further evidence of the genocidal intent of the Pakistani army is provided in A. M. A. Muhith's account of his conversations with West Pakistani officials in May and October 1971. According to Muhith, the West Pakistanis argued that killing 300,000 or even 3 million Bangladeshis was justified if it would preserve the nation of Pakistan as it was constituted in 1947. Muhith also claimed that West Pakistani soldiers frequently compared Bangladeshis to monkeys or chickens.[51] General Niazi, the West Pakistani commander in East Bengal, was reported to have referred to Bangladesh as "a low lying land, of low lying people."[52]

Interviews conducted in early April with foreign evacuees from Chittagong, East Pakistan's second largest city and principal port, provide further evidence that the army's killings were not confined to the capital city. As in Dhaka, the army sought to punish the poorest people who were thought to be strong supporters of independence. The flimsy homes in the most impoverished districts were burned. A Danish graduate student reported counting 400 bodies in the river, and an American evacuee reported that he saw dead bodies and witnessed looting and arson by the Pakistani army.[53] Over the course of 1971, nearly 100,000 young Bengali men received military training in East Pakistan or in India and took up arms against the Pakistani army. In retaliation for guerrilla activities, the Pakistani army destroyed entire areas where insurgent actions had occurred. Killing, burning, raping, and looting took place in the course of these raids.[54]

Part of the campaign to terrorize the Bengali population involved mass rape, with estimates of the number of women raped ranging from 200,000 to 400,000. Some of the victims were imprisoned in camps where they were subjected to several sexual assaults a day.[55] Some women claimed to have been assaulted by as many as eighty men in a single day.[56] The women who had been sexually assaulted found themselves in especially dire straits in a society in which female chastity was so highly prized. A postindependence campaign to find husbands for the women, who were dubbed national heroines, was largely unsuccessful.[57] The mass rape of Bengali women has received very little attention, and virtually all published accounts reference Susan Brownmiller's 1975 work *Against Our Will,* which contained eight pages on the rapes.[58] Bangladeshi scholar A. M. A. Muhith did note the mass rapes in his book on the 1971 crisis and claimed that there were 200,000 verifiable victims of rape in East Pakistan. Muhith also noted that this figure excluded those who died or refused to come forward out of fear and/or shame.[59]

The evidence available from journalists, refugees, and aid officials indicates that the killings and rapes committed by the Pakistani army were spread across East Bengal, and that the atrocities occurred during the entire nine-month period of the military occupation. Furthermore, about 10 million refugees eventually fled East Pakistan for India. While it is impossible to estimate the deaths caused by dislocation and deprivation, the horrible conditions under which the refugees fled and were housed undoubtedly led to significant loss of life. Observers estimated that between 65 and 90 percent of those fleeing to India were Hindus.[60]

The atrocities, the massive flow of refugees to India, and the geopolitical maneuvering were all reported extensively in the United States. A study of the coverage in the *New York Times* of various instances of mass killings in the 1970s and 1980s indicates that the events in Bangladesh were well reported in that paper. For example, the killings of the Khmer Rouge received 791 column inches in the paper in 1975, the year in which the U.S.–backed Lon Nol regime was displaced by the Khmer Rouge and the initial stages of the Cambodian genocide were launched. In 1971, the events in Bangladesh received 690 column inches.[61]

THE POLITICAL AND
IDEOLOGICAL CONTEXT OF GENOCIDE

The circumstances of the Bangladeshi genocide were similar to those of several other genocides. The Bengalis were ethnically and linguistically distinct from West Pakistanis. A minority—in this case, Hindus—was thought to be undermining national unity. This minority was identified with a foreign power, India, a nation that had fought two wars against Pakistan. The extent to which Pakistani political and military officers actually believed the ethnic and religious arguments directed at the Bengalis, and the degree to which such statements were cynical attempts to motivate soldiers, is impossible to determine. Either way, such sentiments have accompanied many genocides, and they were present in Bangladesh in 1971.

Muhammad Ali Jinnah, the leader of the Muslim League and the man regarded as Pakistan's founder, propagated the notion that there were two nations on the Indian subcontinent. Against the Congress Party, Jinnah argued that Hinduism and Islam were distinct social orders and that it was fantasy to think they could coexist in a single nation.[62] Islam was the essential element of Pakistani national identity and Muslim nationalism was, at least rhetorically, to be a factor in the 1971 genocide, despite the fact that both East and West Pakistan were predominantly Muslim. While there were massive population shifts between the newly emerging states in 1947, a substantial Hindu minority remained in East Pakistan. By 1970, that population was estimated to comprise 10–12 million of the approximately 75 million residents of East Pakistan. For the Punjabis who dominated the West Pakistani military and government, Hindus residing in the East would provide a convenient scapegoat for Bengali nationalist demands.

Religion, however, religion was not the only basis for classifying the Bengalis as a weaker people. The British had regarded the Punjabis as a martial race and recruited most of the military from among them. Ian Talbot has argued that, while British reliance on Punjabi recruits had a pragmatic basis, this policy was later buttressed by the myth of Punjabi superiority based on ethnic origin and racial characteristics. Talbot says of Punjabi recruits to the colonial Indian army: "They were designated as martial castes whose racial superiority made them natural warriors."[63] These stereotypical notions persisted in the military recruitment practices of the postcolonial state. Indeed, the Pakistani army acted with brutality against ethnic groups other than the Bengalis, such as the Baloch, whose autonomy movement was repressed.[64]

Language was also a source of conflict from the moment Pakistan was founded. Bengali was the language of the more populous East Pakistan and by far the most commonly spoken language in the new state. In West Pakistan, Punjabi, Sindi, Siraiki, and Pashto were the predominant languages. To many of Pakistan's founders, however, Urdu was an essential element of the Islamic nature of the new state,[65] although it was used by only a small minority in West Pakistan.[66] For the *muhajir* (refugee) elite that had left India, the new state was composed not just of East and West Pakistan, but also of those Muslims who remained in India. Urdu proponents argued that the language was part of Islamic culture in South Asia and that it was more closely related to Arabic than other South Asian languages.

From Pakistan's founding, demands for the inclusion of Bengali as a national language were regarded as a threat to the Muslim nature of the new state. Jinnah believed that Urdu should be the language of Pakistan and that demands for Bengali were Indian-inspired. Such assertions were made in 1948 in the wake of the terrible communal violence that resulted in at least 200,000 deaths in the Punjab in 1947 in the events that accompanied the partition of the subcontinent.[67] Hindus, Muslims, and Sikhs were all victims and perpetrators in the murder, rape, and torture that accompanied massive ethnic cleansing and population transfers at the end of British colonial rule.[68] Speaking in Dhaka on March 24, 1948, Jinnah clearly equated the demand for Bengali parity with Urdu as a threat to Pakistani and Muslim unity.

> Our enemies, among whom I regret to say, there are still some Muslims, have set about actively encouraging provincialism in the hope of weakening Pakistan, and thereby facilitating the re-absorption of this province into the Indian Dominion. A flood of false propaganda is being daily put forth with the object of undermining the solidarity of Muslims of this state...Is it not significant that the very persons who in the past have betrayed the Muslim or fought against Pakistan should now suddenly pose as the saviors of your rights and incite you to defy the government on the question of language?[69]

Genocide frequently involves efforts at purification or cleansing.[70] The ethnicity that is regarded as an impediment to national unity is also often identified with a foreign power that is viewed as a threat to national existence. By 1970, cleansing the Hindus from East Pakistan would come to be regarded as a means of unifying the Muslim state.[71] Bengali nationalism itself was said to be rooted in the Hindu corruption of Bengali Muslims. Former Pakistani Prime Minister Chaudri Muhammad Ali argued that the Awami League victory in the 1970 election was a triumph for Hindus.[72]

The notion of purging Hinduism and its alleged manifestations from East Bengal had begun to permeate the cultural sphere in the 1950s. At that time, the central government attempted to force the Bengalis to substitute Arabic and Urdu words for Bengali words. As part of the effort to cleanse Bengali culture of Hindu influence, the works of Rabindranath Tagore, the Nobel Prize-winning Bengali Hindu, were banned from mention on state-owned radio and television by the Pakistani government in the 1960s.[73]

Once the secession conflict began, the West Pakistani generals thought that the Bengalis would not be capable of sustained resistance. The belief that the Bengalis would quickly be vanquished was rooted in a perception that the people of East Pakistan were culturally and racially inferior to those in the West. Pakistani military ruler Ayub Kahn (1958–69) elucidated a common view of the East Bengalis when he said that they

> probably belong to the very original Indian races.... They have been in turn ruled by the caste Hindus, Moghuls, Pathans, or the British. In addition, they have been and still are under the considerable Hindu cultural and linguistic influence. As such, they have all the inhibitions of downtrodden races and they have not yet found it possible to adjust psychologically to the requirements of the new born freedom.[74]

The killing of so many Bengali Muslims by the army was a departure from the communal violence between religious nationalists that has continued in South Asia since independence and today includes violence against Muslims by Hindu nationalists in India, and Muslim nationalist attacks against Hindus in Bangladesh.[75] In the secession crisis of 1971, the Pakistani army killed many fellow Muslims in East Pakistan.[76] Wardatul Akmam attempts to synthesize the national, ethnic, and religious aspects of the 1971 genocide. He explains the intentions of the Pakistani government in the following manner:

> The ideology to destroy the Bengali nation was that they were descendants of aboriginal Indian tribes. They do not deserve to rule but only to be ruled. Therefore, they were to be crushed in such a way that they could never again demand the fruits of election victory. The Hindus as the victims had the double negative characteristics—they were Bengali and Hindus who

were considered enemies of Islam and agents of India. So, they had to be exterminated.[77]

In addition to internal national dynamics that may result in genocide, international conflict and war are also often precursors of genocide. Christopher Browning places the Nazi decision to solve the *Judenfrage* (Jewish Question) by extermination in the context of the murderous campaign that the Nazis planned to wage in the Soviet Union, which they believed to be ruled by a Judeo-Bolshevist regime.[78] The Ottoman genocide of the Armenians occurred during World War I as "Muslim Turkey" battled, among others, "Christian Russia." The Ottoman Empire and Russia had long been rivals for territory and influence in the Black Sea, Caucasus, and Balkan regions.[79] Pakistan and India were founded amid murderous violence. The issue of control of the northern region of Jammu and Kashmir has been a source of fierce controversy between the two nations since 1947. A three-week war in 1965 resulted in an Indian victory. The level of hostility between the two nations was exemplified by Indian Prime Minister Shastri's declaration to a crowd in Calcutta in 1965 that Pakistan lacked the culture of a civilized country.[80] Speaking in the capital of West Bengal, Shastri assured the crowd that India had no quarrel with the Bengali population in East Pakistan. On the other hand, some West Pakistani elites regarded Hindus as fifth columnists who were agents of an enemy state that posed a mortal threat to Pakistan. Conflict between the Pakistani regions was exacerbated by the discrimination encountered by the Bihari minority in East Pakistan. The Biharis, not all of whom were from the Indian state of Bihar, were Urdu-speaking Muslims who migrated to East Pakistan during the partition process. During the independence struggle, Bengalis killed thousands of Biharis.[81]

The ideological elements that have been conducive to genocide in other times and places were present in East Bengal in 1971.[82] A population regarded as racial inferiors wished to secede from a nation that it believed exploited its natural resources. The Hindu minority in East Pakistan was believed to be allied with a hostile foreign state and the source of secessionist impulses. Cleansing the population of Hindus by death and expulsion was to be the way to remove the corrupting influences and restore the Muslim unity of Pakistan.[83] Intellectuals, students, military officers, politicians, and supporters of Bengali nationalism were special targets of the genocide.

MEMOIRISTS AND SCHOLARS: THE DENIAL OF THE BANGLADESHI GENOCIDE

The U.S. diplomats who wrote about the nine-month occupation of East Pakistan showed very little concern with human rights violations and paid considerable heed to the geopolitical considerations that motivated U.S. foreign policy in the region. In his memoirs, Henry Kissinger, who was National Security Advisor during Richard Nixon's first term (1969–73), acknowledged that Pakistan's reaction to the crisis in East Pakistan was "brutal and short sighted."[84] At another point in his long chapter on events in the subcontinent, Kissinger stated that Pakistan "had unquestionably acted unwisely, brutally, and even immorally, though on a matter which under international law was clearly under its domestic jurisdiction."[85] Despite the acknowledgment of Pakistani wrongdoing in the East, Kissinger never discussed the number of civilians killed, nor did he mention the mass rape of Bengali women in a very detailed chapter.

Even Kissinger's brief expressions of disdain in his memoirs for Pakistani army repression in East Pakistan appear to have been made after the fact. In a study of the period, Christopher Van Hollen finds that Kissinger appeared to have had no moral qualms about the vengeance his allies were wreaking on the Bengalis in March and April 1971. In Van Hollen's words: "At no time during that period is Kissinger on record as voicing outrage or humanitarian concern as the Pakistani armed forces obeyed Yahya's crackdown orders with a vengeance."[86] In Kissinger's worldview, geopolitical strategy was primary and exclusive of any concern for human rights. Even if Pakistani actions were immoral, they were, in Kissinger's view, an internal Pakistani matter. Furthermore, Kissinger argued that the United States had few means to influence the actions of the Pakistani government. For the National Security Advisor and grand strategist, the real reason why the United States could not condemn the brutal repression occurring in East Pakistan was that there were strategic objectives that overrode humanitarian concerns. In Kissinger's words, "To some of our critics, our silence over Pakistan—the reason for which we could not explain—became another symptom of the general moral insensitivity of their government. They could not accept that it might be torn between conflicting imperatives."[87]

At the time of the genocide in the East, Pakistan was serving as an intermediary between China and the Nixon administration. Kissinger was engaged in secret negotiations with China, with whom Nixon wished to set up at least some form of diplomatic relations. China would play an important role in U.S. Cold War policy as a partner of the United States against the Soviet Union. Kissinger argued that he could do nothing that would jeopardize the vital role that Pakistan was playing in nurturing the nascent relationship between the United States and China. Some of Kissinger's strongest critics have argued that the National Security Advisor himself admitted that Romania offered another conduit to China.[88] Whether or not Nicolae Ceauşescu was a viable intermediary for Kissinger's China diplomacy, it is clear that any inclination to consider halting the genocide as more important than geopolitical concerns was quickly discarded.

The administration had early warning that American diplomatic officials regarded events in East Pakistan as genocidal. In early April 1971, a group of American diplomats in Dhaka, led by Consul General Archer Blood, sent a telegram to the State Department protesting the administration's refusal to condemn the mass killings of the Bengalis. The telegram stated in part:

> ...Our government has failed to denounce the suppression of democracy. Our government has failed to denounce atrocities...we have not chosen to intervene, even morally, on the grounds that the Awami conflict, in which unfortunately, the overworked term genocide is applicable, is purely an internal matter of a sovereign state...We, as professional public servants, express our dissent with current policy and fervently hope that our true and lasting interest here can be defined and our policies redirected.[89]

Nixon and Kissinger reacted with fury to the Dhaka telegram, and the President ordered that Blood be transferred from his post.[90] Indeed, a reader of the 78-page chapter on the South Asian crisis of 1971 in Kissinger's memoirs is led to the inescapable conclusion that the author was angered far more by the Foreign Service Officers' disagreement with the administration's policy in the region than he was by the genocide that he did not acknowledge.

American credibility was another consideration that trumped a concern for the human rights of Bangladeshis who were being slaughtered. The Nixon administration claimed to fear that the Chinese would be less interested in a relationship with the United States if the latter were perceived as not standing by an ally. As the events in Bangladesh widened into a war between India and Pakistan, the United States began to tilt toward Pakistan. Again, the major concern was with geopolitical considerations. As reported by U.S. diplomat Dennis Kux, Nixon confided to French President Pompidou that he was determined to preserve the balance of power in Asia. The American president believed a victory of India over Pakistan was the same as a victory of the Soviet Union over China.[91]

The absence of academic work in the United States on the genocide in East Pakistan/Bangladesh is striking. The most thorough academic study of the secession crisis of 1971, published by University of California political scientists Richard Sisson and Leo E. Rose in 1990, stated that there was in fact no genocide in Bangladesh.[92] The initial efforts by the Pakistani army to repress the surging activities of Bengali nationalists were labeled "Operation Searchlight," and numerous accounts published at the time asserted that Pakistani tanks fired on dormitories at Dhaka University. According to Sisson and Rose, the Pakistani army preferred that the detention of Awami

League leaders and student activists be conducted in a peaceful manner. Sisson and Rose presented puzzling evidence for this contrarian assertion. They cited the book *Witness to Surrender* by Siddiq Salik, published in Karachi in 1977,[93] as supporting their assertion, but they appear to have been truly convinced by their interviews with the military officers involved in Operation Searchlight. Their corroboration of Salik's book seemed to close the case for Sisson and Rose.[94] Either they were unaware of the evidence pointing to genocide in Bangladesh or they chose to disregard it without ever informing the reader of their reasons for doing so.

In their text, Sisson and Rose did not address the issue of the total number of victims or the actions of the Pakistani army against the Bengalis in 1971. In a footnote, they provided a much lower estimate of victims, 300,000 to 500,000, than others who had attempted the imprecise task of counting the victims of the genocide. Their sources for this low estimate were two Indian officials responsible for monitoring affairs in Bangladesh at the time. While the slimness of evidence accepted by Sisson and Rose is not, of course, proof of the accuracy of any counterclaims, their view of the issue of civilian murder was clearly that it was peripheral to the events in South Asia in 1971.[95] The marginality of human rights violations was further evidenced by the fact that, while Sisson and Rose discussed the geopolitical implications of the influx of millions of refugees from East Bengal into India, they gave no consideration to the cause of the mass migration. Nor did they discuss the rape of Bengali women in 1971.

SELECTIVE COMPASSION

Despite the evidence of genocide through murder and rape in East Pakistan in 1971, little attention has been paid to the human suffering in Bangladesh. No book-length study of the genocide in Bangladesh has been published in the United States; essays about it have appeared in some collections on genocide but not in others. Some recent books on the 1971 Pakistani war of secession even deny that there was genocide in East Pakistan. Other memoirs and accounts of the era make only passing references to the repression and atrocities. One article on the Bangladesh genocide was published in the *Journal of Genocide Research* in 2002; all of the sources in this interesting article, which applies different definitions of "genocide" to the Bangladeshi case, cite actual evidence of genocide from publications dating from the early 1970s.[96] In the past few decades, there has been little investigation of even the basic question of how many victims were killed by the Pakistani army in 1971.

Three factors go a long way toward explaining the extent to which a genocide will be studied in the United States: the degree to which political points can be scored by an ideological or partisan faction; the status of the perpetrator regime in the aftermath of the genocide; and the power of the American community of the ethnic group that was victimized. (There are, of course, other, more prosaic factors, such as changes in academic fashion that can explain why topics fall in and out of academic favor.) In the case of Bangladesh, the interests of the regimes that have governed the country since 1971 must also be examined.

A genocide will receive more attention when an intellectual or academic faction feels that it stands to gain politically or intellectually from promoting a certain perspective and from interpreting or researching the genocide. Conservatives will focus on the crimes of regimes that the United States has opposed or now opposes. The Left is more interested in atrocities committed by U.S. allies, especially if there is American complicity. As we shall see in chapter 3, when the first reports of Cambodian genocide emerged, conservatives—who for decades had warned of the calamities that communism would bring to Southeast Asia—felt vindicated. The academic and activist Left, which had so vigorously opposed U.S. policies in Southeast Asia, argued vehemently that these stories were atrocity propaganda and that the policies of the Khmer Rouge were rational attempts to address the disastrous conditions of the country they inherited.[97] Both the Left and the Right had a significant stake in interpreting the events in Cambodia.

After the fall of the Khmer Rouge, there were still ideological wars to be fought over the Cambodian genocide. For those who wished to continue to attack the Left, Cambodia represented the inevitable result of attempts to build a socialist utopia: proof of the evils of Marxism. The U.S. government, motivated by Cold War alliance politics, actually supported Pol Pot and the Khmer Rouge in diplomatic circles until the early 1990s.[98] It is ironic that the end of the Cold War facilitated further research on the horrors perpetrated by a communist regime. With diplomatic imperatives altered, the U.S. government could reassign to the Khmer Rouge the evil status it had before it seized power and acquired a grudging acceptance—despite mass murder—because of its alliance with the Chinese and opposition to the Vietnamese who were allied with the Soviet Union. Federal funding for the Yale Cambodian Genocide Project was available only after the fall of the Soviet Union. In this instance, the changed state of geopolitics facilitated the study of a particular genocide.[99]

The study of genocide in Cambodia has also been facilitated by the fact that, since 1979, the country has been governed by regimes intent on exposing the crimes committed by the Khmer Rouge. Western scholars had access to various archives soon after the Khmer Rouge was driven from power. The S-21 torture and extermination centre was opened in 1980 as the Tuol Sleng Museum of Genocidal Crimes.[100] Mai Lam, the Vietnamese colonel who set up the museum and who had also created the Museum of American War Crimes in Ho Chi Minh City, had no interest in hiding the savage barbarism that occurred at S-21 where 14,000 people were tortured and murdered. As an official of a communist government, Mai Lam wished to distance the Khmer Rouge regime from socialism. The museum made many comparisons between the policies of the Khmer Rouge and those of the Nazis.[101] In 1992, the Cornell University library microfilmed the entire S-21 archive. The establishment of Tuol Sleng and the Cornell microfilming were possible because the genocidal regime was conquered. Pakistan, on the other hand, has not had a government that wished to facilitate research on the genocide committed by the military in Bangladesh.

As previously mentioned, despite extensive media coverage of the events in Bangladesh in 1971, there has been relatively little scholarship on the genocide in the more than three decades that have elapsed since the breakup of Pakistan. In a 2001 comparative study of genocide that includes coverage of the Armenians, the Holocaust, Cambodia, Rwanda, and Bosnia, Alex Alvarez never mentions Bangladesh.[102] Bangladesh is likewise never mentioned in the edited collection, *Studies in Comparative Genocide*.[103] A book edited by Robert Gellately and Ben Kiernan, two eminent American genocide scholars, has chapters on many genocides, but Bangladesh is not among them.[104] The 1971 genocide in East Pakistan is included in the previously cited work by R. J. Rummel and in the volume on twentieth-century genocides edited by Samuel Totten, William S. Parsons, and Israel W. Charny.[105] Neither of these works, however, cites any new research on the genocide in Bangladesh.

Access to the records of perpetrators and survivors greatly facilitates the investigation of a particular genocide. Pakistan has little interest in promoting greater knowledge of a genocide inflicted by the nation's military regime. Documents that might shed greater light on the intentions and motivations of the Pakistani government in 1971 are simply not available to researchers. Pakistan is not alone in its resistance to admitting to its role in genocide. In fact, many governments are unwilling to admit past acts of genocide. As will be discussed in chapter 5, the Turkish government fiercely resists the notion that genocide was committed against the Armenians during the course of World War I.[106] The neglect, and even denial, of the genocide in Bangladesh is attributable to several other factors. Mainstream American policymakers, Henry Kissinger being of course a prime example, have little interest in focusing on a genocide that featured the United States "tilting" toward the perpetrators. American scholars whose works have dealt with events on the subcontinent in 1971 are far more interested in the various permutations of diplomatic strategy than the slaughter of a few million Bengalis.

As will be evident in the next chapter, the study of Cambodia, on the other hand, has served the political and ideological needs of several factions in American politics since the Khmer Rouge took power in April 1975. There is simply not much political mileage to be made of the genocide in East Pakistan. Some critics of Kissinger, such as Christopher Hitchens, author of *The Trial of Henry Kissinger,* included the Bengalis on the list of atrocities associated with Henry Kissinger.[107] (The film version of *The Trial of Henry Kissinger* does not mention Bangladesh.) But, because the United States was much less complicit in the human rights violations in Bangladesh than in other cases and because Sheikh Mujibur Rahman was not a compelling figure on the left, Bangladesh remains a relatively uninviting topic for the American Left. The subversion of the elected Marxist government of Salvador Allende in Chile and the establishment of a military dictatorship there resulted in far fewer deaths than the slaughter in East Bengal. For the U.S. Left, however, Allende represents a far more sympathetic political figure than Mujib, who had a much less coherent ideological program and ran a corrupt government before his assassination in 1975.[108] The American Right has little interest in promoting the study of a genocide that involved a Republican president siding with Pakistan, a Cold War ally, against India, which was viewed as the Soviet Union's proxy in South Asia.

The military regimes that ran Bangladesh from 1975 to 1990 also had little incentive to promote the study of the 1971 genocide. The Mujib government was overthrown in a military coup in 1975 and, for the majority of the next fifteen years, Bangladesh was dominated by military regimes led by Generals Ziaur Rahman and H. M. Ershad.[109] Since the Awami League that Mujib headed was closely associated with the independence movement of 1971, the military governments were not eager to emphasize the events that led to independence. Furthermore, both Ziaur and Ershad were responsible for the genocide committed against the Jumma tribes in the Chittagong Hill Tracts.[110] Their own complicity in genocide may have been a further factor in their reluctance to emphasize the genocide of 1971. In the case of Bangladesh, the nation created in the 1971 civil war, a museum devoted to the atrocities committed by the Pakistani army, in what is called a liberation war, was not established until 1996.[111] The liberation war remains a matter of intense debate within Bangladesh to this day. In 2004, there was even controversy over whether Mujib or Ziaur was the first to declare independence from Pakistan.[112]

The military governments were allied with those who wished to make Islam predominant in Bangladeshi politics. For example, in 1977, Ziaur amended the constitution to replace secularism with "absolute faith and trust in Almighty Allah."[113] In 1988, Ershad declared Islam to be the state religion.[114]Accordingly, the military regimes courted religious elements that had opposed independence and even collaborated in the genocide. In the years after Mujib was deposed, measures were taken to rehabilitate those who were accused of collaborating with the Pakistani army in the atrocities. The issue of the 1971 atrocities was a weapon in the struggle between Islamists and secularists in Bangladesh for decades after independence. In 1971, Golam Azam was the East Pakistan chief of the conservative religious party Jamaat-i-Islami, and in this role, he organized death squads that murdered Bengali intellectuals. In the 1990s, secularists wanted to try Azam for his part in these crimes, while Islamists defended him.[115] It has often been in the interest of governments and powerful political factions within Bangladesh to ignore or distort the genocide. The fact that local collaborators, or *razakars,* aided in the genocide makes the events of 1971 even more politically complex for any government in Bangladesh. The reluctance of Bangladeshi governments to explore the genocide fully is a further disincentive for Western journalists and scholars to take up the matter.

Political and judicial developments in Bangladesh in 2009 and 2010 may make the genocide a more significant issue within the country and, to a lesser degree, around the world. The Awami League, which returned to power as a result of its victory in the 2008 elections, has indicated its interest in prosecuting collaborators in the genocide. In July 2010, two prominent leaders of Jamaat were arrested and were scheduled to be tried for crimes committed in 1971.[116] The decision of one of the country's two major political parties to proceed with the prosecution of prominent Islamists will likely attract greater attention to the genocide.

Increased focus on and interest in a genocide is often driven by the victim group, or descendants or ethnic compatriots of the victims. American Jews have been key promoters of the study and remembrance of the Holocaust in the United States.[117] A study of the growing interest in the Ukrainian famine in the United States and Canada concluded that the establishment of Ukrainian émigré communities in North America was in part responsible for the increased attention garnered by that tragedy.[118] Armenians in the United States have been the motivating force behind the growth of the study of the Armenian genocide from the 1960s to the present.[119] There is not a sufficiently powerful Bengali ethnic presence in the United States to engender greater recognition of the events in Bangladesh in 1971. Great Britain has a substantial Bangladeshi community, but Bangladeshis in Britain are relatively poor and lack a significant university-educated elite who would be most likely to bring the genocide to the forefront of academic and political attention.

The genocide in Bangladesh is also neglected because some political and governmental officials in the United States, Pakistan, and Bangladesh have an interest in denying that genocide occurred there or at least in not emphasizing what happened in 1971.[120] There are few politicians and academics in the West who would gain political points by focusing on the genocide of 1971. The Bangladesh genocide is ignored because there is so little interest in Bangladesh among those who have the academic, financial, and political capital to draw attention to it.[121]

The case of Bangladesh is similar to that of other genocides. The extent to which attention is devoted to studying them is not related to the horror of the events that occurred, but to a variety of circumstances that have been explored in this chapter. Thomas Jefferson proclaimed that the proposition that all men were created equal was self-evident. It is also self-evident that, in some important ways, all genocide victims are not remotely equal. As the next chapter demonstrates, Cambodia under the Khmer Rouge was never neglected by academics or activists, but rather was the object of much disputation over virtually every aspect of the regime that attempted an immediate transition to communism.

CHAPTER 3

ARGUING ABOUT CAMBODIA: GENOCIDE AND POLITICAL INTEREST

THERE WAS MUCH TO ARGUE ABOUT

In her much discussed book, *A Problem from Hell: America in the Age of Genocide*, Samantha Power presented the apparent paradox of South Dakota Senator George McGovern, who had long been a leading opponent of U.S. military involvement in Southeast Asia, calling on the United States in 1978 to organize an international force to depose the regime of the Khmer Rouge (KR). McGovern's position was not shared by all former opponents of the war. Some believed that criticism of the human rights records of Vietnam and Cambodia under communist rule would simply legitimate the claims of American conservatives who had long held that there would be a bloodbath if the United States did not prevail in its struggle against communism in Southeast Asia.[1] Reports of atrocities and of the brutal suppression of human rights caused heated debate in the United States and Great Britain. The arguments over the proper way to interpret the Khmer Rouge regime and its attempted transformation of Cambodian society continued for another 30 years, albeit in various permutations. Much of the debate was intended to vindicate a particular political perspective, and it often appeared as though the Cambodian people were little more than props in the rhetorical, ideological, and policy strategies of academics, journalists, and governments.

The Khmer Rouge held power in Cambodia for three years and eight months (1975 to 1979). Ben Kiernan has concluded that between 1,671,000 and 1,871,000 people perished as a result of the KR's attempt to crush its perceived enemies.[2] The 1971 genocide in Bangladesh (lasting eight months) may have resulted in a similar number of deaths, but there was more time for scholars and activists to debate events in Cambodia as they were happening, and events in Bangladesh did not touch directly on the global war against communism.[3] As previously discussed in chapter 2, both genocides received considerable press attention, although—as indicated by coverage in the *New York Times*—journalistic interest in Cambodia declined after 1975. Despite the expulsion of Western journalists from Dhaka in late March 1971, there was considerably more access for journalists to cover events in East Pakistan than during the xenophobic dystopia of the Khmer Rouge. But during the past three decades, the killings in Bangladesh have received little attention from scholars and journalists in the West, while Cambodia has been the subject of intense academic and political debate. In no sense can Cambodia be regarded as a "neglected" or "forgotten" genocide.

In this chapter, I will argue that it appears that for many scholars, journalists, and politicians, the fate of the Cambodian people was of less consequence than the political interests to be advanced, by discussing events during the reign of the Khmer Rouge and during the years that followed. In the words of American scholar, Jamie Frederic Metzl, Cambodia became "something of a Rorschach test for those observing it."[4] It is not that every observer deliberately distorted events in Cambodia, but rather, many partisans viewed the developments in Democratic Kampuchea in a manner that confirmed their ideological convictions.

For some leftists, the autarkic economic policies of the Cambodian communists, though they appeared bizarre to many observers, represented a break with the global capitalist economy that would advance the liberation of poor people around the world. Many of those who had been opponents of U.S. military actions in Vietnam and Cambodia feared that the tales of murder and deprivation under the Khmer Rouge regime would validate the claims of those who had supported U.S. government actions aimed at halting the spread of communism. Conservatives pointed to the actions of the Khmer Rouge as proof of the inherent evils of communism and evidence that the United States had been right to fight its long war against communists in Southeast Asia over the objections of pusillanimous liberals and ideological leftists. And yet, when the Khmer Rouge was deposed by a Vietnamese invasion in January 1979, some of the same Cold War hawks and the U. S. government provided diplomatic support to the remnants of the regime despite its human rights record. In academic circles, scholars continued to argue fiercely over the question of whether the Khmer Rouge had really been Marxist. Even two decades after they took power, the Khmer Rouge stirred controversy.

WAS THERE A GENOCIDE?

Because the majority of the victims of the Khmer Rouge were not killed because of their ethnicity, Cambodia presents a very complex case for genocide scholars.[5] Had the United Nations (UN) definition of genocide included economic classes, or the killing of people who did not fit a particular government's version of the good society, Cambodia's experience would likely be accepted as genocide.[6] In his multivolume study of genocide, Mark Levene focused on the 1978 murders of people who were from the eastern zone of Cambodia adjacent to Vietnam. Levene notes that the Khmer Rouge especially targeted those it labeled "Khmer with Vietnamese minds."[7] Levene also provides a good synthesis of the utopian and nationalist elements in the KR agenda:

> The new regime's agenda for the creation of [an] entirely classless Khmer society of atomized individuals working solely for the country on its unquestionable command, implicitly carried with it a warning that any individual or group that could not meet these specifications would be eliminated. This forecast was vastly amplified by the Centre's reading of Khmer history as a mythic saga of classical greatness in which the Cambodian race-nation had been pure and authentic, juxtaposed with a more recent decay due to foreign encroachment and influence. As such, the Khmer Rouge recipe for a return to greatness was predicated on the liquidation of all elements...tainted by such foreign, colonial or imperial legacies. Sealing off the country...and evacuating all the towns in order to put everyone to work in the countryside, thus became the touchstone of the regime's visioning of revolutionary reawakening and, at the same time, the route by which its dystopian experiment began to disintegrate under the weight of the impossible rice harvest techniques it set itself....[8]

Eric Weitz included Cambodia in his comparative study of four twentieth-century genocides. In the chapter "Racial Communism: Cambodia under the Khmer Rouge," Weitz argued that Democratic Kampuchea synthesized racism and communism.[9] Because so many of its victims were eliminated for political rather than racial reasons, rational-choice scholar Manus Midlarsky calls the Cambodian atrocities a "politicide" rather than a genocide.[10]

Ben Kiernan has demonstrated that although the Khmer Rouge were Marxist-Leninists, strong nationalist elements colored their ideology and practice long before they defeated the Lon Nol regime. Vietnam and the Vietnamese minority in Cambodia were perceived by the Khmer Rouge as particularly dangerous enemies. Even before assuming power, KR leaders had worked to eliminate Vietnamese "influence" in the country, asserting that "the Vietnamese" were just as dangerous to the Khmer people as the hated Lon Nol regime.[11]

Kiernan estimates that no more than 2,000 of the 70,000 Buddhist monks in Cambodia in 1975 were still alive in 1979. About 10,000 to 20,000 indigenous Vietnamese and over 200,000 Chinese perished under the Khmer Rouge. Kiernan further estimates that approximately 90,000 of the quarter million Chams (Cambodian Muslims) were killed by early 1979. The majority of the victims were Khmers, with a somewhat higher death rate among "New Citizens," namely, those who had lived in the cities. About 25 percent of these perished, in contrast to a 15 percent death rate among "base citizens," that is, Khmers who had lived in rural areas before 1975. Kiernan estimates that 1,671,000 people were killed in Cambodia—about 21 percent of the 1975 population[12]—if we include not only executions but also the starvation and disease resulting from the economic disruption caused by the attempt at an immediate transition to communism.

During the period of Khmer Rouge rule, a fierce debate raged over the extent to which the accounts of mass murder inside Cambodia were actually true. In the years after the ouster of the Khmer Rouge, the murderous nature of the regime was not much contested; nearly all who write about Democratic Kampuchea acknowledge that at least several hundred thousand people perished as a result of the regime's policies. Subsequent debate has focused on the motivating factors behind the policies of the Khmer Rouge. Both periods of debate are analyzed in subsequent sections of this chapter.

AN "ENLIGHTENED" POLITY?

When the Khmer Rouge drove out the American-backed Lon Nol government in 1975, many longtime opponents of U.S. policy in Southeast Asia displayed considerable sympathy for the new government. Some were optimistic about the prospects for Cambodia under the Khmer Rouge.[13] U.S. Senator George McGovern, the 1972 Democratic presidential nominee, expressed admiration for the abilities of the incoming government.[14]

Early evidence of the atrocities taking place in Cambodia after the fall of the Lon Nol regime derived primarily from refugees who soon began arriving in Thailand. Perhaps inevitably, many observers treated their accounts with some skepticism: refugees are by definition people dissatisfied with conditions in the country from which they fled. And if the consistency of their stories may be regarded as corroboration of their accuracy, some, conversely, perceive it as evidence of coordination or even manipulation.[15] In the case of Cambodia, some outsiders were skeptical because the refugees could be regarded as "class enemies" of the new communist regime.

Many on the U.S. Left in particular discredited the first reports of the atrocities attending the Khmer Rouge's "evacuation" of Phnom Penh, arguing that the peasant-based regime's policies accorded with the construction of a better society for the majority. In their book, *Cambodia: Starvation and Revolution*, Gareth Porter and George C. Hildebrand, fierce opponents of U.S. government actions during the Vietnam War, argued that emptying the capital was a justified response to the food and health crises afflicting a city swollen with refugees from American bombing and the fierce combat occurring in the countryside: the only way to unite food and population was to bring the latter to the countryside. Ieng Sary, foreign minister and deputy prime minister of the revolutionary government, asserted in a news conference at the UN that the government did not have the means to transport food to the city. Porter and Hildebrand granted considerable credibility to a political movement that had defeated what they regarded as an extended and bloody imperialist effort on the part of the United States.

The mandatory evacuation of hospital patients from Phnom Penh created quite a stir in the Western press. Porter and Hildebrand, however, remained untroubled even by the much-criticized forcible removal of sick people from urban hospitals.[16] They argued that the purpose of the abandonment of the latter was to move patients from substandard conditions to the better care available in the countryside. Summing up the entire policy of moving the population to the countryside, Hildebrand and Porter claimed that "what was portrayed as a destructive backward-looking policy motivated by doctrinaire hatred was actually a rationally conceived strategy for dealing with the problems that faced postwar Cambodia."[17] According to Porter and Hildebrand, press accounts about Khmer Rouge atrocities were propaganda: "Cambodia is only the latest victim of the enforcement of an ideology that demands that social revolutions be portrayed as negatively as possible, rather than as a response to real human needs which the existing social and economic structure was incapable of meeting. In Cambodia—as in Vietnam and Laos—the systematic...mythmaking must be seen as an attempt to justify the massive death machine which was turned against a defenseless population...to crush their revolution."[18]

Porter and Hildebrand's enthusiasm appears in photos in their book that depict peasants cheering the completion of a water conservation project. Another photo shows a seemingly contented woman working in a textile plant in Phnom Penh (the KR did maintain a few essential operations in the city). The chronology in their reference section notes that all citizens were permitted to vote in the elections of March 20, 1976, regardless of their positions during the war. The reader learns that the resignation of Prince Sihanouk and the elevation of Khieu Samphan to president took place "in accord with constitutional procedures."[19] One could come away from the book with the impression of Cambodia as a fledgling liberal democracy. George Kahin, an eminent scholar of Southeast Asia at Cornell University and longtime critic of U.S. involvement in Indochina, lent credence to the tome in a short introduction stating, inter alia, that "anyone...interested in understanding the situation obtaining in Phnom Penh before and after the Lon Nol government's collapse and the character and nature of the programs that replaced it will, I am sure, be grateful to the authors of this valuable study."[20] In testimony before a Congressional committee in 1977, Porter cast doubt on atrocity reports based on interviews with those fleeing Democratic Kampuchea, and reiterated the argument that refugees were people who are dissatisfied with a government. As attractive as his stance may have appeared to the Left, Porter's testimony met with criticism in the Congress. The most notable critic was Stephen Solarz of New York, who expressed outrage that anyone could make such claims on behalf of the Khmer Rouge government, terming their mass murders "one of the most monstrous crimes in the history of the human race."[21]

SAMIR AMIN, MALCOLM CALDWELL, AND THE "NEW WAY FOR THE OPPRESSED"

Many leftist theorists of the "capitalist world economy" have long argued that "Third World" nations are exploited due to their structurally disadvantaged position, a position that has (in some cases) been perpetuated for centuries by the states of the "First World."[22] Marxist theorist Samir Amin has argued that states on the periphery must resist the depredations of First World capitalism by finding a way to cut themselves off from the world economy.[23] Amin appeared to be quite taken with the Khmer Rouge, regarding them as innovators in "the struggle against imperialism." Writing in 1977, Amin found much to admire in their policies of economic autarchy and "deurbanization."[24] In classic Maoist style, Amin praised the KR for identifying a "correct hierarchy of contradictions."[25] In a paper he presented in Tokyo in 1981, Amin adopted a more qualified stance, but still maintained that the Khmer Rouge had "defined a strategy of anti-imperialist struggle" and that the "revolution had been carried out by the peasants themselves."[26] Amin now admitted that there had been excesses, but stressed that these had been consistent with past peasant revolts. (Amin argued in the same paper that Stalin had been a better Marxist than his successors.) Like some other Marxist analysts of the Cambodian events, Amin could deny the "Marxist" character of the revolution because it occurred in a country virtually devoid of an industrial proletariat. Whatever Amin's motivations, his peasant-revolt analysis removed the revolution from the category to which many conservatives desired to assign it.

Malcolm Caldwell, a lecturer in Southeast Asian studies at the London School of Oriental and African Studies, was one of the most dogged academic supporters of the Khmer Rouge. As chair of the Campaign for Nuclear Disarmament, Caldwell was well known in British political circles. He was also a Labour Party candidate in local elections in the London borough of Bexley in 1977.[27] One fellow activist in the campaign for nuclear disarmament regarded Caldwell as a mainstream figure on the left wing of British politics on most issues. As early as summer 1975, Caldwell published an article discrediting the atrocity stories appearing in the West. The author noted that revolutionary struggles inspired by Mao Zedong advocated the social and political extermination of a class, but not in its physical annihilation.[28] In contrast, the imperialist nations engaged in the wholesale slaughter of innocents.[29] Viewing the nations of the West as instruments of their capitalist classes, Caldwell argued that "unable to envisage any alternative to ... naked force, they impute to the victors the actions which they themselves would have had no hesitation in taking were circumstances reversed.... Their dominance successfully challenged, they bluster and accuse.... As the revolution proceeds, so too does mankind slowly but steadily toward a world where 'bloodbaths' themselves will be, like the class which has launched so many a horrible nightmare of the past."[30] For the urban residents who had been deported to the countryside, Caldwell seemed to offer little but contempt: "No doubt it will be hard for some urban dwellers accustomed to pushing pens or turning ledgers to adjust to the labour in rice-fields, but such hardship as may arise cannot be construed as a bloodbath, unless many commit suicide rather than submit to it."[31]

For Caldwell as for Amin, the primary virtue of the Khmer Rouge government was its innovative program of economic development; the Cambodian communists' autarkic polices were consonant with the objectives of many critics of global capitalism. The regime sought self-sufficiency in agriculture while radically dissociating Cambodia from the world economy, indeed from most of the world in general. The creation of rural communes in particular was perceived as a step toward a classless society. But Caldwell pursues a line of argument somewhat different from others by blaming the Soviet Union and Vietnam for the allegations of mass murder and the suppression of human rights. Cambodia was allied with the People's Republic of China and, thus (in Caldwell's view), inevitably subject to malicious slander by Moscow and its client states.

> Faced with determined attempts on the part of both the Western and the Soviet media to portray it as a crazed pariah, Kampuchea has—without abandoning its policy of "first things first" (i.e., irrigation and rice)—succeeded in convincing many of its Asian neighbours and other Third World countries that the calumny is unwarranted. Two things are of note here: first, much of the Moscow/Hanoi propaganda is drawn from the notorious *Reader's Digest* book by Barron and Paul, *Murder of a Gentle Land*, which has long since been ... discredited in the West (it was serialized on Hanoi radio); second, the wilder allegations against Kampuchea current in the West never gained much

popular credence or currency in neighbouring countries (in Thailand because it is common knowledge how refugee stories are selected and magnified).[32]

According to Caldwell, Democratic Kampuchea was forced to fight against the slander of both superpowers.

In his essay "Cambodia: Rationale for a Rural Policy," Caldwell argued that the policies of the KR were based on sound principles:

> To most of the outside world, events in Cambodia (Democratic Kampuchea) appear totally outlandish and incomprehensible. Most commentators conclude that the charitable explanation for them lies in bungled and inept improvisation by ignorant and ill-organised cadres floundering in disastrous circumstances and sustained only by opportune callousness and a monopoly of firearms. This study argues that, on the contrary, the leaders of the Cambodian Revolution had evolved both short-term tactics and a long-term socio-economic strategy, based upon a sound analysis of the realities of the country's society and economy in the years before liberation; that in the face of great difficulties they have attempted to implement these in the last three years; and the chosen course is a sound one whether one judges it in terms of its domestic appositeness or in terms of its reading of the future international economy.[33]

According to Caldwell, their policies were appropriate to both domestic needs and the future world economy. The leaders resembled Chairman Mao in their willingness to join the peasants in manual labor while disdaining abstract intellectual endeavors. The KR chiefs were, in Caldwell's view, organic leaders who learned directly from the peasants:

> . . . radicals like Khieu Samphan and the others were not "theoretical leftists." On the contrary, they always not only stressed the importance of cadres throwing themselves into manual labour alongside peasants, but set a personal example. They scorned material rewards and comforts, fully sharing the lives of the poor. Phnom Penh had no attractions for them, and since liberation they have continued to retain their working offices deep in the rural areas and to take a turn at field work. They thus understood and understand peasant problems infinitely better than those western scholars who now appoint themselves to pass judgment on them.[34]

For Caldwell, residents of Phnom Penh, who had had no real exposure to the Khmer Rouge, had been incapable of immediately understanding the good sense of the new government's policies. He argued that the peasants, many of whom had lived under Khmer Rouge sway before April 1975, already grasped the wisdom of the "new way." The deficiencies of those who had lived in the comparative comfort of the city justified a measure of authoritarianism on the part of the nation's liberators: "Urban dwellers re-settled from Phnom Penh in 1975 could not possibly have at once shared that outlook and it need occasion us no surprise that to begin with they required close supervision when put to work shifting earth and collecting boulders; we should bear this in mind when evaluating refugee stories, particularly those referring to the immediate post-liberation period."[35]

Caldwell claimed that he and his allies were getting out the truth about a regime vilified by commentators answering to the capitalists who profited from their control of the global agricultural system:

> The forethought, ingenuity, dedication and eventual triumph of the liberation forces in the face of extreme adversity and almost universal foreign skepticism, detachment, hostility and even outright sabotage ought to have been cause for worldwide relief and congratulation.... But we have to understand that what the Cambodian people accomplished struck fear in the hearts of all those who at present control the "free" world's food production business to their own immense profit, and it is they to whom our "free" media respond rather than to the call of truth.[36]

The policies of the Khmer Rouge represented the wave of the future, according to Caldwell. "Others ought to and may well seek to emulate the policies that emanated from Democratic Kampuchea," he wrote. "I do not think there can be much doubt that when time has lent perspective to our view, the Kampuchean Revolution will appear more and more clearly as one of the significant and early indications of the greatest and necessary change beginning to convulse the world in the later 20th century and to shift it from a disaster-bound course to one holding out promise of a better future for all." Indeed, the rising standard of living that Caldwell saw in Cambodia would soon inspire the rest of the Third World: "We can surely rejoice that the people of Kampuchea are assured now of steadily rising living standards while those of their still 'free world' neighbors continue to deteriorate. That deterioration is not in itself a cause for rejoicing, but may infer from the juxtaposition that the lesson [of the Khmer revolution] will not long be lost upon the as yet un-liberated peasants."[37]

Caldwell toured Cambodia with American journalists Richard Dudman and Elizabeth Becker in December 1978 just before the Vietnamese invasion sent the Khmer Rouge regime packing. Granted a personal meeting with Pol Pot, Caldwell was impressed by the KR leader's "intellect," and remained sanguine about his government's prospects. Despite his public stand, Caldwell was murdered under mysterious circumstances during the group's last night in Phnom Penh.[38]

Malcolm Caldwell believed he had found a regime that had defeated imperialism and was committed to constructing an egalitarian society. The

Khmer Rouge was committed to dissociating Cambodia from global capitalism and abolishing the internal market as well. For Caldwell, only the North Korean government had achievements similar to those likely to occur under the Khmer Rouge. Caldwell was determined to defend the regime against those capitalists who profited from exploiting peasants across the Third World. His enthusiasm for Democratic Kampuchea may have been exceptional, but he expressed the sentiments of many Western leftists at a time when state socialism still seemed, at the very least, a possible alternative to capitalism.

NOAM CHOMSKY AND "ATROCITY PROPAGANDA"

MIT linguistics professor Noam Chomsky was one of the most prominent American intellectuals opposed to U.S. military involvement in Indochina.[39] Though his anarchist ideology differentiated him from many radical critics of U.S. foreign policy, his books against the war made him a highly regarded figure for many on the American Left. Conversely, Chomsky was much loathed by anticommunists who supported the American effort to contain communism in Vietnam, Cambodia, and Laos. More than three decades later, Chomsky remains a figure of immense controversy for his dozens of books depicting the United States as an imperialist power bent on world domination.[40]

Following the communist victories in Indochina, Chomsky joined the debate over what was actually happening in these countries and what lessons should be drawn from these events. Chomsky would make his case most explicitly in a book review he published with Wharton School finance professor Edward S. Herman in the *Nation* in 1977.[41] American conservatives and much of the media had been highlighting reports that depicted severe human rights abuse in Cambodia, Vietnam, and Laos, but the stories from Cambodia were the most horrific and widely reported. An influential compilation was *Murder of a Gentle Land: The Untold Story of a Communist Genocide*, published in 1977 by John Barron and Anthony Paul.[42] This book gained a very wide circulation when an abridgement appeared in *Reader's Digest,* the right-leaning periodical with an estimated monthly circulation of 18 million, and of which Barron and Paul were both editors. In the preface, Barron indicated that he had received briefings from the State Department, the Defense Department, and the National Security Council as well as three unnamed foreign embassies. But the authors' main sources were refugee accounts collected in camps along the Thai-Cambodian border between October 1975 and October 1976. Refugees were interviewed elsewhere as well. Barron and Paul argued that "the documentation conclusively shows that cataclysmic events have occurred in Cambodia and that their occurrence is not subject to rational dispute."[43]

The Cambodian atrocity stories gained further attention with the publication of Francois Ponchaud's *Cambodge: Annee Zéro*, also in 1977. Ponchaud had greater credibility in some circles than Barron and Paul because he had lived in Cambodia from 1965 to 1975 and spoke Khmer, though the influence of his book in the United States was limited by the fact that it did not appear in the English translation until August 1978.[44] Both books came under attack by Chomsky and Herman. As elsewhere, in this review, Chomsky and Herman couched the case as an analysis of inconsistencies in mainstream coverage of human rights violations, arguing that the media systematically treated as credible accounts of atrocities from nations the U.S. government opposed, while largely ignoring them in "American client states."

In an article in the *New York Times Magazine*, Robert Moss, citing Barron and Paul, also claimed that by 1977 at least one million Cambodians had died as a result of Khmer Rouge policies.[45] Chomsky and Herman suggested that if such deaths occurred, they were a result of the lag effects of the war that ended in 1975, in particular the massive aerial bombardments by the United States.[46] They argued that "the 'slaughter' by the Khmer Rouge is a Moss-*New York Times* creation": "While [newspaper] editors prate about morality, people are dying in Cambodia as a direct result of the policies that they supported, and indeed concealed."[47] Much of the U.S. media was guilty of ahistoricism, according to them: any consumer of American newspapers and television news might get the impression that the first killings of noncombatants had been committed by communists after 1975. Extremely critical of reports about Khmer Rouge atrocities, Chomsky and Herman accused journalists such as Fox Butterfield of the *New York Times* of ignoring U.S. destruction in Indochina while finding only negative things to write about the postrevolutionary regimes.[48] Their logic seemed to be that because the United States inflicted massive damage on Southeast Asia, and because the American media downplayed atrocities by the United States, reports of crimes by the Khmer Rouge should be treated with skepticism. Yet Chomsky and Herman also made clear that they believed the positive reports about the Khmer Rouge, characterizing Hildebrand and Porter's work as a "carefully documented study of the destructive American impact on Cambodia and the success of the Cambodian revolutionaries in overcoming it...based on a wide range of sources."[49]

Chomsky and Herman were still arguing in 1979 that reports of Khmer Rouge genocide were largely unreliable, rooted too heavily in refugee testimony.[50] They approvingly quoted independent scholar Michael Vickery's report that many refugees had fled Cambodia because they "disliked the rigorous working life" imposed by the Khmer Rouge.[51] Apparently, Chomsky and Herman did not consider mass murder a possible impetus driving Cambodians to flee, and that instead an aversion to rigorous work might have impelled them to leave their homeland.

Noam Chomsky's efforts to counter reporting on atrocities in Democratic Kampuchea apparently went beyond publication of his own essays. Examining materials in the Documentation Center of Cambodia archives, American commentator Peter Maguire found that Chomsky wrote to publishers such as Robert Silver of the *New York Review of Books* to urge discounting atrocity stories. Maguire reports that some of these letters were as long as twenty pages, and that they were even sharper in tone than Chomsky's published words.[52]

Chomsky and Herman argued that atrocity reports from Cambodia served to obscure the prior U.S. role in the region, could be used as propaganda against all liberation movements by oppressed people, and, that such reports of massacres were often disseminated by those who had been selective in their concern for human rights. It is, of course possible, and indeed likely, that all of these assertions are true and that genocide had, in fact, occurred in Cambodia under the Khmer Rouge. In international relations, political opponents are often quick to point to the hypocrisies in the arguments of their foes while turning a blind eye to the inconsistencies in their own.

ENTER THE CONSERVATIVES

The position that conservatives took with regard to the Khmer Rouge from 1975 through early 1979 hardly requires explication, their long-held positions seemingly vindicated. Those who had supported U.S. military intervention in Indochina had warned of a bloodbath if the communists came to power in the region; *Reader's Digest* now took the lead in disseminating the flood of refugee reports validating the anticommunists' dire predictions. For the Right, the atrocities of the Khmer Rouge offered an opportunity to lambast the Left for opposing the containment of communism. The genocide in Cambodia presented further evidence of the evils of Marxism and a rallying point for reinvigorating the fight against "communist expansionism" in Southeast Asia.

The atrocities of the Khmer Rouge presented a welcome opportunity to attack the Left's hypocrisy in not condemning them. In his highly publicized commencement speech at Harvard in 1978, exiled Russian nationalist Aleksandr Solzhenitsyn asked of those who had criticized U.S. involvement in Southeast Asia, "Do these convinced pacifists now hear the moans coming from there?...Or do they prefer not to hear?"[53] In the 1990s, European scholars compiled the *Black Book of Communism*, an 800-page indictment of all things communist. The author of this volume's chapter on Cambodia, Jean-Louis Margolin, argued that the Cambodian revolution is best understood as an innovative and horrific, but logical, extension of Mao's Great Leap Forward and Great Proletarian Cultural Revolution, and indeed the ultimate culmination of Marxism-Leninism.[54]

The Vietnamese occupation of Cambodia in January 1979 brought new permutations to the debates about the Khmer Rouge. Scholars, politicians, and activists on both the left and the right would now have new tasks regarding the deposed Khmer Rouge. At the same time, U.S. policy in Central America became a major source of political controversy. During the 1980s, the government headed by Ronald Reagan determinedly sought to prevent Marxist or socialist parties from gaining power in a region so close to the United States, providing military assistance to governments in El Salvador and Guatemala that were threatened by armed leftist insurgents. These governments were accused of murdering dissidents and slaughtering thousands of peasants who sympathized with movements fighting for the redistribution of wealth in impoverished nations. The U.S. government also sought the overthrow of the revolutionary Sandinista government of Nicaragua by arming counterrevolutionary exiles based in neighboring Honduras. Critics of Reagan's polices argued that he was aligning the United States with murderous thugs; Reaganites saw stopping left-wing movements in Central America as essential to limiting Soviet influence in the region.[55] Anticommunists who supported Reagan's policies made the argument that their leftist opponents had been wrong on Southeast Asia, and that their judgment could not be trusted on Central America.

Cold War politics motivated two additional conservative arguments. First, those who opposed U.S. support for military regimes in El Salvador and Guatemala and who castigated American efforts to overthrow the Sandinista regime in Nicaragua should remember the catastrophe that their opposition had enabled in Southeast Asia. And second (if sometimes implicitly), human rights considerations should be subordinated to the global struggle against communism. A corollary to the second argument was that the subordination of human rights considerations might extend to countenancing a quasi-alliance with the deposed Khmer Rouge. The byline to an op-ed piece in the *Wall Street Journal* by conservative scholar Stephen J. Morris implied as much: "Mr. Morris is a researcher associated with the Institute of East Asian Studies, University of California/Berkeley. He recently visited areas of Cambodia controlled by the resistance that is fighting Vietnamese military occupation."[56] This "resistance" was dominated at that time by none other than the deposed Khmer Rouge.

While advocating the overthrow of the Sandinistas and the repression of left-wing insurgencies in El Salvador and Guatemala, conservatives such as Morris advocated a political alliance that included the Khmer Rouge along with the noncommunist resistance in Cambodia because it would restrain the expansion of Soviet influence—to them the more threatening form of communism. Serge Thion describes the complex political posturing that took place in the years after the Khmer Rouge was replaced by the Vietnamese-sponsored People's Republic of Kampuchea.[57] Though the new government in Phnom Penh included many officials who had held positions under the Khmer Rouge, it eagerly labeled its predecessor genocidal. On the other hand, Thion explains, the reason the 1991 Paris Peace Accords on Cambodia eschewed reference to genocide is that the American and Chinese governments didn't want it. Thion accuses U.S. officials of hypocrisy for claiming they had sought to prevent the return of the Khmer Rouge when they had in fact blocked a proposal at a 1981 Geneva conference that would have sought a political solution involving the disarmament of the Khmer Rouge.[58]

As with other events in Asia, response to the genocide in Cambodia and its aftermath became entangled in Cold War realpolitik. Though the Vietnamese drove the Khmer Rouge from power and brought to an end the mass killings, the invasion was condemned by the Carter administration.[59] The Khmer Rouge was sponsored by China, and the Carter administration was committed to improving U.S.-Sino relations as a counter to Soviet influence. As the deposed Khmer Rouge regrouped along the Cambodian border, the United States encouraged the Chinese and Thai governments to provide aid to these remnants of the genocidal regime.[60] Carter's National Security Advisor, Zbigniew Brzezinski, acknowledged that because of Pol Pot's odious record, the United States could not support him, but Brzezinski later told Elizabeth Becker, "I encouraged the Chinese to support Pol Pot...Pol Pot was an abomination. We could never support him, but China could."[61]

The Carter administration's tacit support for the Khmer Rouge was all the more striking because Jimmy Carter made a commitment to promoting human rights such a prominent feature of his foreign policy aspirations. Despite Carter's description of the KR as the world's worst human rights violator, historian Kenton Clymer has argued that human rights considerations did not seem to influence U.S. policy toward Cambodia.[62] (Clymer notes that Carter barely mentions Cambodia in his memoirs.) According to Clymer, Carter often yielded to national security imperatives as they were formulated by Brzezinski and in these cases human rights concerns faded from view. Clymer concludes, "Nowhere was this more clearly the case than in Cambodia."[63]

The United States and its allies opposed unseating the Khmer Rouge's designee as Cambodia's representative in the United Nations until the

Cold War was winding down in the early 1990s. Only then did the United States, having participated in a decade-long proxy struggle in which the consequences of the genocide had been far from the primary concern, end its economic and diplomatic sanctions against Cambodia's existing government.[64]

In the 1980s, the United States did not restrict its hostility to Cambodia's post-Khmer Rouge government to the diplomatic arena. American humanitarian organizations were prevented from sending any aid that could be regarded as promoting economic development. Beginning in 1980, only basic relief supplies could be sent. For example, the American Friends Service Committee was denied a permit to ship a small sawmill and power tools.[65] American charitable organizations did not argue that Vietnam had invaded Cambodia out of altruism, but they did call for recognition that Heng Samrin's government was, at the very least, not genocidal.

Official support for the study of the Cambodian genocide expanded with the end of the Cold War. The collapse of the Soviet Union rendered Cambodia a matter of academic rather than geopolitical concern. The establishment of the Cambodia Genocide Program (CGP) at Yale University facilitated new scholarly research. In April 1994, Congress passed the Cambodian Genocide Justice Act, committing the American government to pursuing justice for victims of the genocide. In December 1994, the State Department awarded $499,000 to the Yale project. During the next two years, the governments of Australia and the Netherlands as well as the Luce Foundation provided additional funding. In 1997, the State Department provided CGP with 1 million dollars and allocated an additional $150,000 in 1999.[66] With no pressing political interests at stake, the U.S. and other governments were now willing to fund research into a genocide that was, after all, committed by communists against whom the United States had struggled for 45 years.

The web page of the genocide project at Yale provides a description of the comprehensive project. The CGP has set out to gather and preserve all existing information about the Pol Pot era in Cambodia. It is also willing to make this information available to any court that prosecutes surviving perpetrators of the genocide.[67] But soon after its establishment, the CGP found itself embroiled in political controversy when conservatives attacked the selection of Ben Kiernan as its director. Kiernan had, as a young man (he was born in 1953), written sympathetically of the Khmer Rouge during its first years in power.[68] Kiernan changed his views in 1979, and since then had documented and analyzed the barbarous nature of the Pol Pot government.[69] Still, Kiernan was attacked in *Time*, *Commentary*, and the *Wall Street Journal* as unfit to lead a program devoted to the study of genocide in Cambodia. Leading Republican

Senators Trent Lott, John McCain, Jesse Helms, and Bob Dole called for Kiernan's removal as director.

The attack on Kiernan was launched by a *Wall Street Journal* guest column by Stephen J. Morris, an Australian, who was then a research associate at Harvard's Department of Government. Morris was part of the Right that had for decades propagated the as-yet unsubstantiated claim that the Vietnamese still held hundreds of American prisoners of war (POWs) after the end of the Vietnam War. Morris had, moreover, been among those who argued for aid to the noncommunist Cambodian rebels who were in alliance with the Khmer Rouge in the 1980s.[70] Morris documented Kiernan's early enthusiasm for the Khmer Rouge and dismissed his subsequent condemnations of its atrocities as simply an effort to distinguish between good and bad communists. Morris called on the government to rescind the grant to Yale, calling on Secretary of State Warren Christopher and Assistant Secretary Winston Lord to reopen the award process. "If they refuse to reverse a terrible decision that disgraces American honor and spits upon the graves of more than a million Cambodians," he urged, "then Congress should take this matter into its own hands."[71]

In rebuttal, Kiernan offered numerous examples of his criticisms of the KR, cited misquotations by Morris, and noted that in the 1980s Morris had himself consistently supported the Khmer Rouge in Cold War maneuverings that had found a place in academic politics.[72] The bitter nature of this debate appears starkly in Kiernan's closing sentences: "The question is why... people with no credibility are taken seriously by anyone. Morris, for instance, has no scholarly publications, and an impressive track record of seeing his accusations exposed as groundless (*WSJ*, 5 June 1990 and 28 April 1995). It is not surprising that despite his trumpeted Harvard affiliation, he has never held a faculty position."[73]

In another twist in the journalistic and academic wars over Cambodia, a 1996 article in the *Wall Street Journal* accused Kiernan of withholding sensitive documents concerning Americans classified as Missing in Action (MIAs) in Southeast Asia.[74] This placed Kiernan at the center of the argument over whether American POWs and MIAs had been left behind when the United States withdrew its military from the region. Some in the United States claim that the Vietnamese retained U.S. POWs after most were returned in 1973. To date, no credible empirical evidence has ever been produced to support this charge. (Other critics have argued that the Vietnamese government has been less than cooperative in assisting efforts to determine the fate of American MIAs.) Kiernan has argued that the files, properly organized, had been available to Pentagon researchers by early 1997.[75]

It would appear that some scholars were guilty in the eyes of certain conservatives of being "premature" critics of the Khmer Rouge, ergo pro-Hanoi.[76]

For the latter, it seems, it had been appropriate to oppose the Khmer Rouge from 1975 to 1979 and then again after the collapse of the Soviet Union in 1991. Despite certain disagreements, Cambodia scholar Stephen Heder defended Kiernan's qualifications to head the CGP, and noted that any appointee could have been criticized from some political platform or other.[77]

In Kiernan's view, the desire to obscure the Cambodian genocide was rooted in Cold War politics. In an essay written in 2000, he argued that

> both the creation of historical memory and its erasure depend upon contemporary politics as much as history itself. . . . Stephen Morris, Congressional Republicans and the *Wall Street Journal* editorial page all considered their own political agenda more important than documenting the crimes of the Khmer Rouge and bringing the criminals to trial for genocide. This agenda reflected the anti-Soviet alliance between the United States and China during the later stages of the Cold War, an alliance which often brought together conservative anti-communists and Maoist radicals.[78]

Kiernan's opponents' general theme was that he was engaged in distinguishing between good communists (the Vietnamese) and bad communists (Khmer Rouge), that is, that he was pro-Vietnamese. Some argued that individuals sympathetic to the Vietnamese-imposed government ignored severe human rights abuses on its part, and obscured the fact that many former Khmer Rouge cadres now found themselves in its employ. Journalist William Shawcross maintained that "former Khmer Rouge officers were often deemed to be more reliable than former officials or soldiers of the Thieu or Lon Nol regime. For the Khmer Rouge, re-education might consist of a short course in Hanoi's interpretation of Marxism-Leninism. For non-communists it could mean indefinite incarceration."[79]

The Vietnamese, subject to international condemnation for the invasion, had a powerful incentive to highlight the atrocities of the Khmer Rouge. They were eager to develop a museum and to make available to Western scholars the archives of the horrific torture and murder center S-21, where more than 14,000 victims perished.[80] Mai Lam, the Vietnamese colonel who had earlier created the Museum of American War Crimes in Ho Chi Minh City, had every interest in highlighting the savage barbarism of S-21. But as an official of a communist government, he needed to distance the previous regime from socialism, and so the museum drew many comparisons between the practices of the Khmer Rouge and those of the Nazis.[81] In 1992, Cornell University Library microfilmed the entire S-21 archive. Both the establishment of the archive and the granting of permission to a foreign institution to microfilm it, reflected Vietnam's desire to shed light on the Khmer Rouge's murderous activities.

Steve Heder has demonstrated that the Vietnamese planned trials of officials of the deposed regime, at least those who had not acknowledged the new government. Those who cooperated would not be prosecuted. Heder further noted that the court system established by the Vietnamese "promoted not careful examination of individual guilt, but arbitrary judgments based on the political positions of the accused."[82] But, according to him, the Vietnamese communists blame the crimes of the Khmer Rouge on "fascism," not communism.

The first opportunity to make documentary films about the crimes of the regime fell to a producer from the German Democratic Republic (GDR). As an ally of the Soviet Union, the GDR was also an ally of Vietnam. Gerhard Scheumann made three films about Indochina, including *Pilots in Pajamas*, a propagandistic documentary featuring captured American pilots.[83] Interviewed in the 1990s, Scheumann stated that he had been horrified that the crimes of the KR had been carried out under the hammer and sickle, and argued that the policies of Democratic Kampuchea were a distorted version of communism. For Scheumann, the source of the Khmer Rouge's deviationism was Maoism, and in particular the Cultural Revolution, which the KR apparently considered insufficiently radical. Despite all this, Scheumann had been prevented from emphasizing any communist influence, even Chinese. Originally, the first narration line of the script for *Kampuchea: Death and Rebirth* was to have been "Our thinking about Kampuchea has to start here, at the former Chinese embassy in Phnom Penh." As Scheumann soon found out, however, such an approach was "not in line with current political thinking."[84] Scheumann was no less repelled by what he perceived as the hypocrisy of the West: "As long as Pol Pot and Ieng Sary ruled in Cambodia, it was in the eyes of the West the most wayward form of communism. When the Vietnamese came and chased the Khmer Rouge out, the Vietnamese were suddenly the aggressors.... That is why the mass murderers were represented in the UN."[85]

THE SCHOLARLY DEBATE

After Vietnam replaced the Khmer Rouge, expressions of intellectual admiration for their government grew scarce.[86] A few writers continued to minimize their atrocities. Though not an apologist, Cambodian scholar Sorpong Peou distanced himself from the use of the word genocide when writing of their crimes.[87] Peou also argued that the widely documented repression of the Cham was not based on their Muslim faith, but in the general violence inflicted on Cambodian society. A certain dubious relativizing of the violence of the Khmer Rouge may appear in Peou's rhetorical question to Kiernan in a review essay published in this journal: "What constituted the difference between the Vietnamese leadership and the Khmer Rouge group?"[88] Kiernan was in fact widely identified with the position that, whatever the flaws of the Vietnamese, they had ended a genocide in Cambodia. If, as Peou seemed to imply, the Vietnamese communists were just as bad, then the invasion of January 1979 was unjustified. Perhaps Peou's position emerged most clearly in his concluding paragraph: "The lesson that can be learned from Cambodia is that any attempts at state-building through revolutionary change in Third World countries are bound to bring about enormous destruction and perpetuate the cycle of violence."[89] In short, for Peou, all revolutionary movements were bad.[90]

Michael Vickery argued that the killing resulted from peasant outrage, especially directed against the former city dwellers, and that it was this outrage that dictated events.[91] Vickery, who provides a low-end estimate of 750,000 deaths in Cambodia from 1975 to 1979, claims that the mass violence should not be associated with Marxism because that violence had destroyed the comparatively small urban proletariat. Furthermore, Vickery argues that nationalism, populism, and peasantism were more important than communism as influences on Khmer Rouge practice.[92] Like Vickery, Ben Kiernan has not located the source of the Cambodian genocide in Marxism. While not denying the Marxist influence on the Khmer Rouge, Kiernan nonetheless argues that racial and religious notions overrode ideas about class in the worldview of Pol Pot and other KR leaders. Kiernan points to the persecution of ethnic minorities, Buddhist monks, and the Muslim Chams to support his thesis, the essentials of which appear early in his book on the subject: "The two most important themes in the history of the Pol Pot regime are the race question and the struggle for central control."[93] Kiernan does, however, note that Maoism provided a model for Khmer Rouge ideology because it altered Marxism by maintaining the "capacity of human willpower to triumph over material conditions and so reverse historical trends."[94]

For his part, Stephen Heder has argued that Kiernan misreads the evidence and that Marxism and communism were indeed sources of Cambodia's genocide.[95] In a lengthy review of Kiernan, Heder claims that "the dichotomy between Marxism and racism [is] untenable and that both Marxism and communism were at the core of racism and genocide in Democratic Kampuchea."[96] Heder's argument is that Kiernan's Marxist sympathies prevent him from seeing the real origins of ethnic persecution in Democratic Kampuchea: "Since for Kiernan, Democratic Kampuchea's genocide cannot be related to a dangerous tendency intrinsic to Marxist and communist orthodoxy, it must have been a result of an intentional racist plan."[97] Heder has claimed that Marxism in practice tends to engender "class and racial genocide."[98] Addressing Khmer Rouge policies specifically, Heder's analysis of Communist Party of Kampuchea (CPK) policy vis-à-vis the Cham and Chinese "resonated" with Weitz's argument that Stalinist practice could be racist "without the overt concept and ideology of race." For Heder, "Stalinism's harsh extremes were embedded in its state socialist project, with its particularly systematic and virulent form of social engineering and its premium on uniformity and adhesion to communism."[99] Heder claimed that Marxist revolutionaries will exterminate or at least brutally repress any group whose tendencies or identities make it seem less than amenable to the construction of the envisioned communist society.

David Chandler, too, regards the Khmer Rouge's crimes as outgrowths of Marxist-Leninist theories and practices. Chandler has criticized Kiernan for his reluctance to acknowledge the role of Marxist ideology in the horrors that befell Cambodia from 1975 to 1979.[100] Vickery, Kiernan, Heder, and Chandler are perhaps the four most prominent scholars of the Khmer Rouge era who write in English, but they remain fundamentally divided on the basic nature of the Khmer Rouge government.

Scholars also differed over the Vietnamese-installed government, the People's Republic of Kampuchea (PRK), some emphasizing that it halted the genocide and others discounting that fact. Some focused on the PRK's own human rights violations and undemocratic character. The disputes have at times been heated. In his review of David Chandler's biography of Pol Pot, Kiernan criticized his former teacher for, among other things, making "unjustified concessions to Khmer Rouge propaganda" and for citing in evidence confessions that the KR had obtained under torture. Kiernan suggested that Chandler's work reflects a certain anti-Vietnamese bias, for example, blaming Vietnam for the war between the two countries. Kiernan also faults Chandler for seeing Marxist, but not Nazi, parallels with the Khmer Rouge. Kiernan claimed that Chandler's anti-Vietnamese bias, like that of many Cambodia scholars, is in part attributable to their present or former employment by the U.S. government, other Western nations, or the UN.[101]

In a review of Kiernan's book on the Pol Pot era, Chandler refrains from questioning the author's motives and acknowledges the fine contributions it makes. Chandler does criticize Kiernan's unwillingness to see a strong Marxist bent to the KR regime. Chandler stresses that the latter considered itself Marxist-Leninist, and that it was cheered along by several Marxist-Leninist regimes. Chandler takes Kieran to task for ignoring much of the literature produced by other scholars and for questioning some of their motivations.[102]

The apex of the dispute was reached in Stephen Heder's review of a volume edited by Kiernan, *Genocide and Democracy in Cambodia: The Khmer Rouge, the United Nations and the International Community*. Heder disagreed with

Kiernan's interpretation of the nature of the Khmer Rouge and Vietnamese-installed governments. Indeed, Heder argued that Kiernan was unwilling to engage in discussion of issues of human rights and democratic transitions and implied that this reluctance was attributable to his commitment to the regimes that succeeded the Khmer Rouge. Addressing Kiernan's role in the book, Heder says of the editor:

> Kiernan also pursues [a] crusade...against those who disagree with him. His ill manners in this regard are reminiscent of the Pol Potism which at other levels he...despises. He suggests that those with contrasting views are subjectively or objectively in league with...the forces responsible for Pol Pot's genocide....The deus ex machina here is the alleged super influence of that certain superpower, the U.S. Kiernan would have readers believe that, to paraphrase the notorious Khmer Rouge adage, this influence has created a raft of people with the bodies of journalists, human rights activists and scholars but U.S. government minds, all of whom disagree with him for that reason. This nonsense must be recognized and criticized for what it is, a smear tactic pursued in lieu of genuine debate about facts and analysis.[103]

Even in the heated rhetoric permeating the growing field of genocide studies, the charge of Pol Potism stands out.

POLITICAL INTEREST AND THE TRUTH

The availability of evidence has rendered it impossible to deny the crimes—whatever one terms them—of the Khmer Rouge. A major American university maintains a project to study the Cambodian genocide and to assist in bringing its perpetrators to justice. The Pol Pot regime's atrocities remain on the radar screen of American academics, if not so much any longer of journalists and politicians. It is obviously impossible to determine the political motives behind academic debates, especially concerning an emotionally charged topic such as genocide. Sophal Ear, the author of an undergraduate honors thesis whose mother fled Cambodia with him and his siblings, suggests that those who were sympathetic to the Khmer Rouge were not interested in the truth, though this cannot be proven; one can understand why an observer might draw that conclusion.[104] Any cynic (realist?) might have predicted that conservatives would maintain that the Khmer Rouge's genocide was simply standard communist policy, and that left intellectuals would attribute the misdeeds of the revolution (when they could not be denied credibly) to ethnic chauvinism or peasant rage, rather than adherence to any Marxist doctrines. Metzl noted that many leftists ended their support for the Khmer Rouge only after the split between Cambodia and Vietnam became overt in 1978;[105] it was possible then to acknowledge the misdeeds of one communist regime and remain on the side of another.

No writer is more unsparing in his treatment of those who sought to defend the Khmer Rouge or at least cast doubt on the veracity of atrocity stories emerging from Cambodia, than Sophal Ear, who escaped from Cambodia as a one-year-old with his mother and siblings following the death of his father from disease and malnutrition. Ear wrote a long undergraduate thesis at the University of California at Berkeley on what he regards as the leftist academic view of Khmer Rouge-controlled Cambodia. Ear labels this perspective the "Standard Total Academic View" (STAV). Ear's angry views can best be captured in his own words:

> [Malcolm Caldwell's] *Kampuchea: Rationale for a Rural Policy*, was my first glimpse into a community of academics, I had no idea existed....This...was not some extreme "fringe" faction of Cambodian scholars, but virtually all of them....Their view of the Khmer revolution...became the Standard Total Academic View...or the STAV. These scholars...became the Khmer Rouge's most effective apologists in the West. While they expressed unreserved support for the Khmer revolution, fully twenty percent of the Cambodian population may have perished....an unequivocal record of complicity existed between a generation of academics who studied Cambodia and the Khmer Rouge.
>
> To the STAV scholars, Democratic Kampuchea symbolized their wildest hopes and dreams. From the classroom to the politburo, the new Kampuchea was, to these scholars, theory becoming reality....
>
> It would be facile to dismiss the authors...as outliers or exceptions, but for one problem: they were not the exception. In fact, these scholars were the norm, hence the title of STAV scholars. Their stance was not the result of some freak accident of nature, but an institutionalized revolutionary conditioning. Indoctrination, whether through academia or by other means, seems to be the only plausible explanation. In Australia, England, and America, Ben Kiernan, Malcolm Caldwell, and Noam Chomsky reached similar conclusions on Cambodian refugees. The only common denominator: a proclivity for revolutions in an academic backdrop. Seeking "truth wherever it may lead," in the words of Thomas Jefferson, had no place when it came to revolutions. For that purpose, the empirical process was turned upside down, first came theory, followed by evidence.[106]

In an article published in *Khmer Conscience* in 1995, Ear writes with the greatest personal bitterness toward those who advocated the STAV: "As all those individuals who proudly signed off on the pro-Khmer Rouge articles and books they published, while the author and his family were enslaved in the name of Socialism, so too will this author accept responsibility for his published material."[107] Obviously Ear does not believe these writers are willing to acknowledge their statements that supported the Khmer Rouge or at least minimized the suffering of the Cambodian people. His strong and biting words imply that these writers and activists are guilty of hypocrisy and deceit.

It is obviously impossible to attribute with certainty political motives to academic debates even about a politically laden topic such as genocide. Ear's belief that those who were sympathetic to the Khmer Rouge were not interested in the truth cannot be proven despite his outrage at their willingness to dismiss the evidence of atrocities that emerged in the years the Khmer Rouge was in power. It is clear that great energy has been devoted to the question of the Khmer Rouge's Marxist roots. A cynic might predict that many of the conclusions are based in the conservative conviction that genocide was a predictable outcome of communist rule in Cambodia. Those academics, journalists, and activists sympathetic to left or Marxist perspectives were more likely to attribute the misdeeds of the revolution (when they could not credibly be denied) to racism, ethnic chauvinism, or peasant radicalism rather than the particular ideology to which they subscribed. In a similar vein, Metzl has noted that many leftists only ended their support for the Khmer Rouge after the split between Cambodia and Vietnam became overt in 1978.[108] It was then possible to remain on the side of a Marxist regime while acknowledging the misdeeds of another communist state.

But one cannot say with certainty whether or not the reactions of specific academics, journalists, or politicians to reports of the atrocities were cynical. It is obvious that many of those who had opposed the U.S. war efforts in Indochina had their reasons to be skeptical of horror stories emerging from Thailand. The same conservatives who embraced the reports of the horrors of Cambodia would just a few years later downplay news of massacres in Guatemala and El Salvador—perhaps with no more and no less cynicism or naiveté. Whatever the case may have been in Central America, many of the same anticommunists were later willing to indirectly associate the United States with the Khmer Rouge. Politics makes strange bedfellows, and the odiousness of a particular regime does not change that basic axiom. The alignments of the major world powers in regard to the Khmer Rouge after January 1979 were based on self-interest and displayed neither consistency nor any special concern for the well-being of the Cambodian people.

Orwell's comments about the blindness of the nationalist and the partisan, quoted in chapter 2, are worth repeating here: "...the Nationalist not only does not disapprove of atrocities committed by his own side, but he has a remarkable capacity for not even hearing about them."[109] This book demonstrates repeatedly that reluctance to acknowledge the obvious was hardly unique to Cambodia or to the era of Orwell.

If there is one lesson that can be drawn from the controversies over the Khmer Rouge and its reign of terror, it is that victims of genocide and other acts of horrific political violence are of interest to most people and most governments only when political capital can be gained from lamenting their suffering. At other times, genocide is ignored, rationalized, or excused, as people—whether consciously or unconsciously—see only what conforms to their ideological predispositions. The history of the Holocaust is replete with examples of indifference to the victims of Nazism due to political interest.[110] One might have hoped after that experience and the voluminous writing on the subject for a new, universal moral standard that would make genocide intolerable irrespective of strategic and political interests.[111] Unfortunately, such a standard was not seen in the case of Cambodia.

CHAPTER 4

WHO SUFFERED THE MOST? GENOCIDE STUDIES AND THE POLITICS OF VICTIMIZATION

THE PURSUIT OF UNIQUENESS

Some of the most heated debates in the field of genocide studies have occurred over the issue of Holocaust uniqueness. The uniqueness controversy revolves around the claims of some scholars that the Nazi genocide against the Jews is an act unprecedented in human history and that therefore—either explicitly or implicitly—the Holocaust is entitled to a special place in academic and public discourse. Uniqueness advocates claim that the Nazis were the only genocide perpetrators who deliberately intended to exterminate an entire people. Other groups that suffered massive population decimation as a result of state-sponsored violence are said to have suffered many such losses as a result of neglect and/or ill-treatment that was not necessarily intended to result in death. (Some make this argument in the case of the Native Americans in North and South America as well as Ukrainians who perished under Stalin). Holocaust uniqueness advocates further argue that many other perpetrators intended to kill only a part of the victim group. This argument is often made about the Ottoman Armenian victims of the Committee for Union and Progress (CUP) regime in the World War I era. For example, Holocaust uniqueness advocates note that some Armenians survived by converting to Islam and some women were spared death by being forcibly married to Muslim men.[1]

Those arguing for a broader inclusion of groups in the study and recognition of genocide frequently argue that the exclusion of other victims is rooted in racism or other forms of bigotry. Ian Hancock, an advocate for greater recognition of the *Porrajamos,* the Romani (Gypsy) Holocaust, recalls speaking about the persecution of Gypsies at a Hillel center: "I was interrupted by a woman who leapt to her feet and angrily demanded why I was even comparing the Gypsy case to the Jewish case when the Jews had given so much to the world and Gypsies were merely parasites and thieves. On another occasion a gentleman in the audience stood up and declared that he would never buy a book on the Holocaust written by a Gypsy."[2] While Hancock's examples may represent extreme reactions to his perspective, they exemplify the intense passions engendered by controversies over the degree of suffering by various ethnic groups.

Holocaust uniqueness claims are often coupled with the contention that the existence of the state of Israel is justified by the Holocaust. The Holocaust, it is argued, coveys moral capital on Israel and grants it substantial freedom of action in dealing with the Palestinian populations over whom it exercises control. This moral capital must be guarded because, like any commodity, an increase in the supply will decrease the value of the commodity. Those who denounce Holocaust uniqueness arguments do so in terms every bit as strident as those employed by some of the Holocaust exclusivists. Moral capital is apparently a finite good and thus requires defending with the tenacity that might be expected when guarding any other valuable and scarce resource.

This chapter will examine the work of writers who are, in varying degrees, well known for some of their writings about Holocaust uniqueness and the relationship of the Holocaust to other genocides. One of those writers included in this chapter, Ward Churchill, has been discredited by a university report that found him guilty of misrepresenting some sources and not substantiating many of his claims. Still, whatever their degrees of fame and infamy, all those writers herein analyzed have been important players in the acrimonious debate over the attention, importance, and political implications accorded to genocides and other instances of mass murder and large-scale suffering. It will be argued that many of these writers regard the study of comparative genocide as a zero sum game in which the material and moral gains that come from victim status depend on making that status unique or at least rare.

DEBORAH LIPSTADT AND THE PURSUIT
OF THE EXCLUSIVITY OF JEWISH SUFFERING

Deborah Lipstadt achieved considerable public renown when she was sued by British writer David Irving, a prolific author of books on Nazi Germany, who argued that he had been libeled in Lipstadt's 1994 book, *Denying the Holocaust: The Growing Assault on Truth and Memory.*[3] Lipstadt labeled

Irving a Nazi sympathizer and Holocaust denier who distorted evidence to produce conclusions designed to induce a favorable opinion of Hitler and his regime. Hoping to take advantage of British libel laws that are much more favorable to the plaintiff than those in the United States, Irving sued Lipstadt and Penguin Books, her publisher. In a lengthy trial, Irving lost a case in which the judge's verdict was sweeping and damning, as it judged the plaintiff to be guilty of academic fraud. Not only did the judge find Lipstadt's characterization of Irving to be correct, but the evidence presented at the trial destroyed whatever remained of Irving's credibility as a scholar of the Third Reich.[4] The trial also revealed Irving, despite his protestations to the contrary, to be a white supremacist and anti-Semite.[5] The verdict in the Irving trial was a great public triumph for Deborah Lipstadt and for those who combat Holocaust deniers. Despite this, much of the controversy Lipstadt generated with her claims about the Holocaust and its uniqueness predated her adventure in a London court.

In *Denying the Holocaust*, Lipstadt claimed that there was a growing movement by some to deny that the Nazi regime exterminated millions of Jews, and by others to minimize the Holocaust by arguing that there had been many similar such actions around the globe over the course of history. Lipstadt makes no real distinction between these very different claims and argues that those who regard other events as similar to the Holocaust are guilty of constructing "immoral equivalencies."[6] On the first count of outright Holocaust denial, Lipstadt chronicles the writings of authors so obscure that very few academics, let alone even the most informed sectors of the general public, would have ever even heard their names. Authors such as Austin App and Arthur Butz are largely unknown except to readers of Lipstadt's book and the insular world of Holocaust deniers. These authors take positions on the Holocaust that are backed by so little evidence and reason that no serious historian of the Nazi era takes them seriously. There is no question that those described by Lipstadt are Holocaust deniers, but given the obscurity and academic irrelevance of those chronicled in Lipstadt's book, a reader might question the use of the adjective "growing" in the subtitle of her book. There is scant evidence that Holocaust denial was growing in 1994 or that it has an increasing number of adherents in 2010.

For Lipstadt, those who argue that the Holocaust was not unique by equating other atrocities or genocides with the Holocaust are engaged in creating "immoral equivalencies."[7] Lipstadt explained her view in depth in a review of the high school curriculum, *Facing History and Ourselves*:

> So why am I left uneasy? My discomfort has less to do with the way the Holocaust is approached and more with the context into which it is placed. Facing History addresses a broad array of injustices including the Armenian

genocide and American racism. It attempts to bring the Holocaust into the orbit of the students' experiences by providing a section at the end of each chapter called "Connections," which includes subjects such as racism and violence in America—though not contemporary anti-Semitism. It presents the Holocaust as an occasion for teaching lessons in moral reasoning and good (American) citizenship; as an object lesson, a generic inoculation against prejudice.

The problem with this approach is that it elides the differences between the Holocaust and all manner of inhumanities and injustices. To say that the Holocaust is not the same as other more local and less bureaucratized and single-minded examples of mass killing is not to rule out all points of comparison. Ultimately, the only way we learn is through comparison. But the Holocaust remains unique for two primary reasons. It was the only time in recorded history that a state tried to destroy an entire people, regardless of an individual's age, sex, location, profession or belief. And it is the only instance in which the perpetrators conducted this genocide for no ostensible material, territorial or political gain.

Teachers of the Holocaust and writers of curricula on the topic must be scrupulously careful of imparting the message that at its heart the Holocaust is just one in a long string of inhumanities and that every ethnic slur has in it the seeds of a Holocaust.[8]

In this review, Lipstadt makes the case for Holocaust uniqueness and also criticizes those who would not grant the Holocaust status as a singular evil. In another section of her review of the high school curriculum, she attacks the content of the program as being anti-Semitic because its authors speak favorably of Nation of Islam leader Louis Farrakhan. There is no doubt that Farrakhan has issued many anti-Semitic utterances, but his appeal to some African Americans is hardly rooted in his intemperate remarks about Jews.[9] Lipstadt seems to invoke Farrakhan's anti-Semitism to disparage those who equate others' suffering with that of the Jews.

In *Denying the Holocaust*, Lipstadt argues that there is a moral stature given to the victims of genocide: "The general public tends to accord victims of genocide a certain moral authority. If you de-victimize a people you strip them of their moral authority, and if you can in turn claim to be a victim as the Poles and the Austrians, often try to do, the moral authority is conferred on or restored to you."[10] Lipstadt clearly believes that Austrians (who often claimed to be the first victims of National Socialism as a result of the 1938 *Anschluss* that incorporated them into the Third Reich) and Poles had no right to victim status. In the case of Austria, there is, of course, much evidence of widespread popular approval of Hitler's decision to incorporate Austria into the Third Reich, and many Austrians played prominent roles in the Final Solution.[11] The notion that Austrians were the first victims, while still bruited about by some in that country today, is at best a dubious assertion. Unlike Poles and other Slavs, Austrians were not singled out for brutal repression based on an imputed racial identity that made them enemies of the German *Volk* (people or race), but rather were incorporated into the Third Reich because the Nazis regarded German Austrians as their racial comrades (*Volksgenossen*) who should unite with their fellow members of the master race to further the formation of the racial community (*Volksgemeinschaft*).

If the Austrian claim to be victims of the Nazis strains credulity, there is credible evidence that Poles and others Slavs were the intended and, in many cases, actual victims of Nazi genocide. (It is important here to recall the definition of genocide in part as well as genocide in whole.) Whether in the annexed regions of western Poland such as the Warthegau, Danzig-West Prussia, or Silesia, or the colonized region of the General Government, the Nazis intended to decapitate Polish society by executing many members of the educated classes and subjecting much of the rest of the population to a brutal life as barely literate slave laborers.[12] While it is true that the Nazis did not intend to eliminate every Pole, their policy toward Poles is best described as one of murder and enslavement, combined with racial harvesting of those segments of the population that were judged to possess significant Aryan traits. The Nazi treatment of the Polish population is clearly an example of genocide (genocide in part), as adopted by the United Nations (UN) convention on genocide. Speaking of German occupation policies, particularly in Eastern Europe, Christopher Browning states, "The Nazi regime stood ready to impose on conquered populations in Europe, especially Slavs in the east, methods of rule and policies of population decimation that Europeans had hitherto inflicted only on conquered populations overseas."[13] Just days before launching the invasion of Poland on September 1, 1939, Hitler's remarks to his generals, as recorded by an anonymous note taker, included, "destruction of Poland in the foreground. The aim is the elimination of the living forces… Have no pity. Brutal attitude. The strongest has the right. Greatest severity."[14]

Lipstadt is correct that the Nazis clearly had no intention of exterminating all the Poles, but there seems to be little evidence for placing the Poles in the same category as the Austrians. The Nazis, after all, regarded the German residents of Hitler's native land as their Volksgenossen who were fit for incorporation into the Reich, much as the Sudeten Germans were included in the Reich later in 1938. The Poles were, by contrast, Slavic "*untermenschen*" (subhumans). The Nazis shot tens of thousands of Polish professionals they regarded as members of the leadership class. Polish universities were closed, as the Nazis believed there was no need to educate those they regarded as their racial inferiors.[15] About 3 million non-Jewish Poles died during the long Nazi occupation of Poland.[16] Lipstadt's pairing of Austria and Poland as nations with equally unviable claims to victim status is not validated by reliable historical evidence. In making her case for the uniqueness of the Holocaust, she neglects the broad suffering, including widespread murder, inflicted on Polish Gentiles. The fact that about 90 percent of Polish Jews perished under the Nazis compared to 10 percent of non-Jewish Poles indicates different German objectives with regard to the two groups, but it does not indicate that Poles were not victims of the Nazis to a degree that a claim of genocide (in part) is implausible.[17]

The Nazi desire to murder and enslave Slavs was not confined to the Poles. It should be recalled that in launching Operation Barbarossa, their attack on the Soviet Union on June 22, 1941, the Nazis intended to kill directly or by food deprivation, tens of millions of Slavs. In the words of Holocaust scholars Deborah Dwork and Robert van Pelt, "It was in the Soviet Union, not Greece, that the Nazis used famine as an instrument of genocide."[18] The Nazis anticipated that up to 30 million citizens of the Soviet Union might perish in the first year of Barbarossa.[19] Millions of Soviet POWs perished as a result of inhumane treatment by their German captors, especially in the first year of the war on the Soviet Union when German labor shortages were not as acute as they would become as the war progressed.[20] Writing about the general disposition toward Soviet POWs and civilians among the German invaders, Christopher Browning states, "Criminal orders from above and violent impulses from below created a climate of unmitigated violence."[21] Again, the Nazi aims toward the non-Jewish peoples of the Soviet Union were not the complete extermination that they eventually decided upon for Jews, but they did reach the level of genocide. There is little doubt that Lipstadt errs when she does not acknowledge that Slavs were victims of Nazi genocide.

In the course of explaining her immoral equivalencies quote, Lipstadt briefly considers three cases of mass violence and explains why they are not valid comparisons with the Holocaust. She considers the genocide of the Ottoman Armenians that began in 1915. On the Armenians, she writes, "The brutal Armenian tragedy, which the perpetrators still refuse to acknowledge adequately, was conducted within the context of a ruthless Turkish policy of expulsion and resettlement. It was terrible and caused horrendous suffering but it was not part of a process of total annihilation of an entire people."[22] Here, Lipstadt is in consonance with most literature on the Armenian genocide.[23] Some Armenians were not killed and indeed those in Constantinople (Istanbul) and Smyrna (Izmir) were generally left unmolested, at least at the beginning of the genocide. There was, however, a government-sanctioned policy that entailed a murderous effort to cleanse eastern Anatolia of Armenians.[24]

Lipstadt also claims that the violence that Stalin and his cohorts committed during their long reign in the Soviet Union should not be equated with Hitler's war against the Jews. She differentiates between the terror of

Nazism and that of Stalinism by arguing that, while the Nazis targeted a particular group, Stalin's terror was arbitrary. Lipstadt is indisputably correct when she claims that "the fate of every Jew who came under German rule was essentially sealed,"[25] but Stalinist terror can hardly be characterized as arbitrary. During agricultural collectivization, those classified as wealthy peasants, or *kulaks*, were singled out for repression.[26] Stalin also deported various ethnic nationalities that he perceived as threats to Soviet power.[27] There is vigorous debate about the motives of Stalin's regime in the events that led to the Ukrainian famine in the 1930s. Some scholars claim that there was an ethnic motivation to the deprivation of food to Ukraine that caused millions of deaths, while others argue it was a result of Soviet agricultural policies aimed at sequestering food supplies for urban areas.[28] Stalin also killed substantial numbers of Poles as he sought to repress the anticommunist nationalist sentiment so prevalent among the Polish people. As with her Poland-Austria comparison, Lipstadt, in pursuing a unique status for the Holocaust, goes far beyond what historical evidence permits us to conclude about the victims of Stalin.

Writing about another twentieth-century genocide, Lipstadt has no doubts about the savagery of the Khmer Rouge regime, which she says was "barbaric" in its treatment of the Cambodian people.[29] Her view that the Cambodian communists focused on killing those who they believed had collaborated with the Americans is overly narrow and not supported by the scholarly literature on the topic. The Khmer Rouge targeted not only perceived American collaborators but also those Cambodians it characterized as class enemies, a category that was very broadly defined in the People's Republic of Kampuchea. As was noted in chapter 3, other victims of the Khmer Rouge were Muslim Chams, Buddhist monks, those of Vietnamese origin residing in Cambodia, and Chinese Cambodians. All of these groups were singled out for persecution by a government that combined dystopian Marxism with xenophobia.[30] Indeed all of the 12,500 Vietnamese who remained in Cambodia after 1975 were murdered.[31] Thus, it would seem that Pol Pot was determined to murder all the Vietnamese under his control. Of course, unlike Hitler and the Jews, Pol Pot could not possibly gain control over the large majority of Vietnamese, who of course did not reside in Cambodia. Still, Lipstadt does not present an accurate depiction of the crimes of the Khmer Rouge. As with the Soviet Union, wittingly or not, Lipstadt misrepresents the scope of the Cambodian genocide in an effort to strengthen her argument for the uniqueness of the Holocaust.

In addition to rejecting all equivalence between the Holocaust and other genocides, Lipstadt offers stinging criticism of what she calls the "yes, but" syndrome. For example, she examines the claim that there was a Holocaust, but the Nazis were only trying to defend themselves from communism. There are few historians outside of those involved in the *Historkerstreit* or Historians Conflict in Germany in the 1980s who would defend such a view. While the battles in Germany in the 1980s over the interpretation of the Holocaust cannot be chronicled here, it is worth noting that the notion of the Holocaust as self-defense is particularly associated with conservative German historian Ernst Nolte, who argued that Hitler believed the Jews were responsible for the horrors that Bolshevism had brought to the Soviet Union. Nolte claims Hitler attacked the Jews to save Europe, and especially Germany, from a fate similar to the terror inflicted by the Bolsheviks. If such a claim about Hitler's worldview were true, it would only confirm what we already know: that Hitler was a rabid and murderous anti-Semite who attributed all the world's evils to the Jews. The possibility that he deluded himself into holding the Jews responsible for Bolshevism does not detract from the horror that was the Holocaust. Another controversy of the Historikerstreit concerned the claim of some German historians that the Holocaust was only one of many terrible atrocities in world history. Of course, this assertion has been made by many scholars and activists who are not right-wing German nationalists. Lipstadt's concern here is to discredit anyone who might consider another evil to have been similar to the Holocaust.[32]

Lipstadt further argues that there are those who believe that the Jews brought the genocide upon themselves through their subversive actions in various countries. This argument is the product of the lunatic fringe of political and academic debate. Lipstadt also mentions the fallacious claims that most Jews who perished under Nazi rule died of starvation and disease or were killed as partisans and spies. Few serious historians have made such claims. Oddly, one who did make such an assertion is not included in Lipstadt's book. Princeton University historian Arno Mayer, in *Why Did the Heavens Not Darken,* argued that from 1942 to 1945, "certainly at Auschwitz, but probably overall, more Jews were killed by so called natural causes than by unnatural ones."[33] In his book, which contains a number of claims much contested by many historians, Mayer presents no footnotes, endnotes, or references to substantiate specific claims.[34] His work contains only a bibliography at the end. Holocaust historian Christopher Browning accuses Mayer of "specious scholasticism" and says that Mayer's claim about natural and unnatural deaths "finds no support whatsoever in any documents or historical studies that I have seen."[35] In the afterward to the paperback edition of his book, Mayer does refer to "the monstrous nature and equally monstrous general magnitude of the Judeocide, for which the evidence is simply overwhelming and incontestable."[36] Mayer is not a Holocaust denier in the manner that David Irving is; however, some of his fundamental assertions are unsubstantiated and others are patently false.

In Lipstadt's view, the final "yes, but" fallacy is that others have suffered a fate similar to that of the European Jews. To refute this "fallacy," she returns to a defense of Holocaust uniqueness. Here it is worth quoting Lipstadt at length: "The question that logically follows from this is, why do we 'only' hear about the Holocaust? For the deniers and many others who are 'not yet' deniers, the answer to this final question is obvious: because of the power of the Jews. 'Yes, but' is a response that falls into the gray area between outright denial and relativism. In certain respects it is more insidious than outright denial because it nurtures a form of pseudo-history whose motives are difficult to identify. It is the equivalent of David Duke without his robes."[37] Likening those who argue that the Holocaust is not an event without parallel in history to a neo-Nazi like David Duke is to employ strong and incendiary language to rebut an assertion that can be subjected to empirical investigation. The notion that American Jews were prominent in promoting interest in the Holocaust after the 1960s is a key argument in Peter Novick's provocative book, *The Holocaust in American Life*.[38] While Novick's views on the emergence of the Holocaust as a moral symbol in the United States are by no means universally accepted, it is hard to imagine that a reasonable person would compare Novick, a respected retired University of Chicago historian, to David Duke.

In her blog, Lipstadt also presses the bounds of historical credulity when she implies that every Jew in the world was threatened by Hitler, while Armenians outside Turkey were in no danger from the genocidal Ottoman regime and, thus, had nothing to fear from it:

> According to today's *New York Times*, the Swiss have convicted a Turkish politician of denying the Armenian genocide. I am pretty sure that, given that the guy was a Turkish politician, he was a traditional Armenian genocide denier. These folks are not much different than Holocaust deniers. However, what if the person had been an historian who, while not denying the barbarity of the Turks towards their Armenian victims, questioned whether it should be termed a genocide? [I, by the way, believe it should be.] The person might take this position because Armenians in other places in the world were safe from the Turks. Would that person be sentenced as well? What kind of chill does this put on academic discourse? This is a dangerous Pandora's Box.
>
> Posted by Deborah Lipstadt at 3/10/2007 11:11:00 PM

It is worth recalling that the United Nations definition of genocide includes genocide in part. Thus, a claim that the Ottoman CUP government did not intend to kill Armenians all over the world would not be a refutation of the claim of genocide. It is also not entirely clear that Hitler had any designs on Jews who lived in New York or Chicago or others outside the European sphere that he intended to rule. Lipstadt is arguing again for an exclusivist position on Jewish suffering, thus enhancing Jewish moral capital.

By 2005, Lipstadt was arguing that the study of comparative genocide involved no imputation of a hierarchy of suffering:

> ...But on a more serious plane, when you focus on the Holocaust and argue that in many respects it is unlike the other terrible genocides, that doesn't mean that you are saying, "Oh the other sufferings are inconsequential." If a Cambodian person says, "My parents died in the Cambodian genocide," and I say, "The Cambodian genocide was not a holocaust," not only is that insensitive, it is comparative pain and comparative pain is stupid. If I were sitting here and you said to me, "I just had a root canal." And I said, "Oh, I had two of them." Does that make you feel better? Comparative pain is a completely useless exercise. So to argue that Holocaust has unique elements is not to diminish the suffering of others.[39]

Lipstadt seeks to avoid being crass in her uniqueness claims, but to reuse her dental work analogy, it is clear that she believes her people had two root canals.

In a 2005 interview, Lipstadt explains what she believes is another fear Jews have of Holocaust comparisons, while also expressing concern about events in Sudan:

> What happens is that some Jews fear that if they make these comparisons it takes attention away from Jewish pain and suffering. Jews fear that because they have a profile of being successful today, people don't think they really suffered. I say to my students when we discuss why the United States did so little, I say there was the Depression and there was isolationism—I sound like such an apologist. I sound like the person who disgusted me when I was a college student and heard this. And I said, "Some day people are going to say, 'What were you doing during the genocide in Sudan?'" I try as often as I can, [though] I don't always succeed, to mention the Sudan. Rwanda happened 10 years ago. Bosnia happened six years ago. But the Sudan is happening right now. [emphatically] A genocide. And we should be going nuts. We're not.[40]

While conceding that many groups had suffered genocide and that the world has not paid sufficient heed to the victims, Lipstadt continued to argue that the Holocaust confers considerable political entitlements on Jews and especially the state of Israel. In a 2007 editorial in the *Washington Post*, Lipstadt condemns Jimmy Carter's controversial and provocatively titled book on the Israeli-Palestinian conflict, *Palestine: Peace Not Apartheid*, by charging Carter with neglecting the Holocaust and indulging anti-Semitic stereotypes.[41] Lipstadt's title for her op-ed piece is quite revealing: "Jimmy Carter's Jewish Problem." In her column, Lipstadt accused Carter not just of taking wrong positions on the security fence that the Israeli government constructed in the West Bank, but of insensitivity to Jewish suffering, especially during the Holocaust. Some excerpts illustrate Lipstadt's arguments:

> One cannot ignore the Holocaust's impact on Jewish identity and the history of the Middle East conflict. When an Ahmadinejad or Hamas threatens to destroy Israel, Jews have historical precedent to believe them. Jimmy Carter either does not understand this or considers it irrelevant.
>
> Nitpickers might say that the Holocaust did not happen in the region. However, this event sealed in the minds of almost all the world's people then the need for the Jewish people to have a Jewish state in their ancestral homeland. Carter never discusses the Jewish refugees who were prevented from entering Palestine before and after the war. One of Israel's first acts upon declaring statehood was to send ships to take those people "home."
>
> Carter has repeatedly fallen back—possibly unconsciously—on traditional anti-Semitic canards. In the *Los Angeles Times* last month, he declared it "political suicide" for a politician to advocate a "balanced position" on the crisis. Perhaps unused to being criticized, Carter reflexively fell back on this kind of innuendo about Jewish control of the media and government. Even if unconscious, such stereotyping from a man of his stature is noteworthy. When David Duke spouts it, I yawn. When Jimmy Carter does, I shudder.[42]

Lipstadt apparently finds no significant differences in the views of Jimmy Carter and David Duke when it comes to issues regarding the power of the Israel lobby in the United States and on Holocaust sensitivity. This is a strained comparison, especially for someone who wrote about immoral equivalencies. Lipstadt apparently sees, or at least professes to see, no difference between a view that the Israel lobby is among the most powerful interest groups in the United States and a Nazi perspective that claims Jews plot world domination through various cabals.

Lipstadt's primary criticism of Carter is that he does not mention the Holocaust in his discussion of Israeli policy in the West Bank. She assumes the relevance of the Holocaust to the Israeli-Palestinian conflict in 2007, but ignores significant differences between Hitler and either Hamas or Iranian president Mahmoud Ahmadinejad. Militarily and economically, Nazi Germany was one of the world's most powerful states. Hamas has no state and governs only the Gaza Strip, a small, impoverished, and very densely populated area. Iran is hardly a world power, and the status of its nuclear arms program is a matter of some dispute. Unlike the period of the Holocaust, when the Jews of Europe were defenseless against a genocidal totalitarian regime, there is a Jewish state and it possesses nuclear weapons that would deter all but those bent upon their own suicidal destruction. Israel is also tightly allied with the United States, which in the first decade of the twenty-first century remains, by far, the dominant military power on the planet.

To accuse Carter of falling back on "traditional anti-Semitic" canards is to wave the banner of the Holocaust again. Those who argue that the pro-Israel lobby in the United States, most notably the American-Israeli Public Affairs Committee (AIPAC), is extremely successful at promoting Israeli interests with policymakers in the U.S. government are accused by those supporting the status quo in U.S.-Israeli relations of propagating conspiracy theories of a Jewish intent to rule the world.[43] The Nazis also believed in such fantastic theories of Jewish aspirations to global power. A reader can hardly escape the conclusion that there is an attempt to discredit critics of Israel by tarring them not only with the allegation of anti-Semitism, but also quasi-Nazism. It is hard to imagine what analysis of the success of pro-Israel lobbies or Jewish advocacy groups in the United States might pass Lipstadt's anti-Semitism filter whether one is explaining U.S. support for Israel or the attention paid to the Holocaust in the United States.

Lipstadt does not explain the degree to which she believes the genocide inflicted upon the Jews in the Holocaust grants the Israelis license to treat a subject population as they desire. Clearly, she believes there is a degree of latitude granted to Israel by the Holocaust or she would not criticize Carter for omitting a discussion of the Final Solution. However, she fails to ponder the question of the degree to which a group's past suffering grants it moral capital, and how this moral standing should manifest itself in public policy. Likewise, one wonders about the relevance of the traumas and tragedies of pre- and post-Holocaust Jewish refugees from Europe to an argument about Israeli occupation policy in the West Bank and its tight control of the Gaza Strip, other than the claim that past suffering permits an unspecified immunity from criticism. Specifying the grounds for, and degree of, this immunity would be a difficult and perhaps impossible task.

Lipstadt further argues that in the aftermath of World War II, and in response to the Holocaust, Jews were granted the nation of Israel by a major-ity of the world's people. One must ask what methodology determines that a large majority of the world's people decided that there should be a Jewish homeland in Palestine. In the 1940s, most of the population of the globe lived under colonialism or domestic dictatorship, and so world opinion would seem impossibly difficult to judge on this matter. Nor does Lipstadt consider whether the inhabitants of Palestine were consulted on the idea of a Jewish state, or the degree to which the desire of the world to compensate victims of the Nazis was to be borne by a population that had nothing to do with Hitler's attempted Final Solution of the Jewish question in Europe.[44] If the Holocaust, as a unique event, is the source of so much moral and political capital for Israel, it only makes good sense to preserve that capital by defending Holocaust uniqueness and discrediting all who challenge the exclusive status of the Holocaust.

ROBERT SATLOFF AND JEWISH MORAL CAPITAL

Lipstadt is not alone in arguing that Holocaust uniqueness conveys moral capital on Israel. Historian Robert Satloff is Executive Director of the Washington Institute for Near East Policy, an organization regarded as strongly pro-Israel. In a 2006 article in the *New York Review of Books*, Michael Massing described Satloff as a hawkish neoconservative.[45] In 2006, Satloff published *Among the Righteous*, a book that is a valuable contribution to our understanding of Jews in North Africa at the time of the Holocaust. Satloff concludes by making a moral capital argument by asserting that it is dangerous to compare Jewish suffering to that of others such as Cambodians, Rwandans, or Bosnians.[46] In Satloff's view, comparative claims that equate the misfortunes of other national or ethnic groups to those of the Jews reduce the moral claim of Jews to the state of Israel. "If the Holocaust were something unique, in which the world's most advanced society nearly succeeded in wiping out one of the world's oldest peoples, then it stands to reason that the victims deserve special remedy.... Providing special protection for these victims by helping them to realize their goal of creating a state of their own, where the eternally homeless would never again live at the whim of the local despot, is a reasonable solution. And Palestine, site of their ancient homeland, is a reasonable place to do this. But, if Jewish suffering were just another in a long list of unfortunate events in which the weak suffered at the hands of the strong, then it loses its specialness. And the world cannot indulge every people with a claim on its conscience."[47] Satloff employs a Holocaust uniqueness claim to assert that Jews deserve compensation for their suffering, while some victims of brutal regimes must be ignored or at least go without recompense for their suffering. It would be interesting to know how Satloff believes that the world, once it gets beyond according Jews the most consideration for their suffering in the 1940s, should determine which people with moral claims should be heeded and whose moral claims should be rejected or at least accorded low priority.

Satloff goes on to make a most dramatic claim about the possible moral value of Holocaust education. He believes that greater knowledge of the Holocaust and particularly the fact that some Arabs saved Jews during the Holocaust would make Arabs more moral people. "If as I suggested, Arabs learned more about the Final Solution—the event that gave birth to the word 'genocide'—then perhaps the Arabs would have responded more effectively to the gassing at Halabja or the slaughter in Darfur, which were both mass killings of non-Arabs in Arab lands"[48] Satloff neglects to mention that the United States, a country in which the Holocaust has received an enormous amount of attention, did not condemn Saddam Hussein's gassing of the Kurds at Halabja (the Iraqi dictator was viewed by U.S. policymakers as a useful check on the revolutionary Shia regime in Iran) or anywhere else until it was politically convenient to do so, following Saddam's 1990 invasion of Kuwait, a U.S. ally in the Persian Gulf.[49] Moreover, the United States did not respond forcefully to alleged genocide in Darfur, as Sudan was courted as an ally in the war with Al-Qaeda. Why Arabs should need this moral education more than Americans is never explained in Satloff's book. One can only speculate that perhaps Satloff is of the view that Arabs suffer from some deficiency of culture or religion that renders them in special need of the moral education that he claims comes from the study of the Holocaust. Perhaps, however, Satloff believes that a more thorough understanding of the Holocaust would lead Arabs to more pro-Israel positions on the future of Palestine and other disputes between Israel and the Arab states.

The views of Lipstadt and Satloff on the moral and political stature of the Holocaust are widely accepted in American culture. Still, these perspectives are not uncontested. No one has been more critical of the manner in which writers such as Lipstadt and Satloff employ the Holocaust than Norman Finkelstein.

NORMAN FINKELSTEIN AND THE HOLOCAUST INDUSTRY

Norman Finkelstein has long been one of the most vociferous critics of those who argue that the Holocaust conveys any special moral stature on Jews or the state of Israel. Finkelstein has used biting and derisive language to attack the uses of the Holocaust in American and Israeli politics as well as to condemn what he regards as the unjust treatment of the Palestinians in the West Bank and Gaza Strip by the Israeli government. Despite his record of numerous, albeit highly controversial, publications, Finkelstein was denied tenure in 2007 by DePaul University in Chicago after a contentious process that attracted national media attention.[50] After his dismissal from DePaul, Finkelstein was unable to find employment as a professor in the United States.[51]

In his book, *The Holocaust Industry: Reflections on the Exploitation of Jewish Suffering,* Finkelstein argued that there is a Holocaust industry in the United States that functions to legitimize Israeli repression of the Palestinians and to bolster the fortunes of Jewish advocacy organizations.[52] The groups and persons constituting the industry use the Holocaust, and the alleged power of Holocaust deniers, to portray Jews as victims and attain the moral stature granted to victims in contemporary culture. For Finkelstein, Jews in America in the 2000s are simply not credible victims compared to many other groups who claim that status in contemporary American society: "...among the groups decrying their victimization, including Blacks, Latinos, Native Americans, women, gays and lesbians, Jews alone are not disadvantaged in American society. In fact, identity politics and the Holocaust have taken hold among American Jews not because of victim status, but because they are *not* victims *(emphasis in original)*."[53] Furthermore, Finkelstein argues that the Holocaust could be used to deter criticism of Jewish groups and to immunize Jews with the status of victims: "Jews could even gesture to the quota system from which they had suffered in the past as a pretext for opposing affirmative action. Beyond this, however, the Holocaust framework apprehended anti-Semitism as a strictly irrational Gentile loathing of Jews. It precluded the possibility that animus towards Jews might be grounded in a real conflict of interests (more on this later). Invoking the Holocaust was therefore a ploy to delegitimize all criticism of Jews; such criticism could only spring from pathological hatred."[54]

While the Holocaust, like all present and past suffering, can be used as a moral weapon in political and academic conflict, it is quite another thing to imply that there might be a reasonable basis for anti-Semitism. One might object to the political views and actions of the majority of American Jews on a range of issues from affirmative action to Israel (although as Novick notes, American Jews have a wide variety of views on Israel and its various policies; however, pro-Israel groups in the United States often label opposition to Israeli policy or criticism of U.S. support of Israel as anti-Semitism). Regardless of political disagreement, it is impossible to imagine what actions by Jews might legitimate anti-Semitism or to use Finkelstein's precise phrase "animus towards Jews." It is also inconceivable that Finkelstein would ever argue that any policies that African-African organizations might pursue would justify a racist ideology or, to paraphrase Finkelstein's language, "animus towards African-Americans." Finkelstein implies that there is a reasonable basis for anti-Semitism and that disagreement with the policies of some Jewish organizations is a morally permissible basis for ethnic or religious bigotry. It is certainly true that Finkelstein believes the Holocaust is used to discredit all criticism of Jews, but he seems to claim that there might be reasons to disdain Jews in general.

Finkelstein's rhetoric matches, and sometimes exceeds, the vitriolic levels reached by many of the authors examined in this chapter. Regarding his assertion that fraudulent survivor claims for financial compensation were filed against Swiss banks, Finkelstein tactlessly states, "By the Holocaust industry's reckoning, concentration camp conditions could not have been harsh at all. In fact, one must suppose a remarkably high fertility and remarkably low mortality rate."[55] Whatever the merits of Finkelstein's belief that the Claims Conference that pressed the case against Swiss banks vastly inflated the number of Jewish Holocaust survivors, his language regarding concentration camp fertility is strikingly harsh. After all, his claim in this regard is rather unexceptional; when a designated status has the potential for financial rewards, many more people will attempt to gain this status in order to be eligible for monetary gain.

Finkelstein has been among Deborah Lipstadt's most prolific and vehement critics. He belittles Lipstadt's assertion that Holocaust deniers have any real place in the mainstream of American academic or political life. In the caustic style that typifies his writing, Finkelstein disputes the notion that Holocaust deniers have any real influence in the United States: "There is no evidence that Holocaust deniers exert any more influence in the United States than the flat earth society does."[56] According to Finkelstein, the writers that Lipstadt studies, such as Arthur Butz, are wholly obscure, and "to document widespread denial Lipstadt cites a handful of crank publications."[57] It is difficult to dispute Finkelstein's basic assertion that people such as Austin App, an obscure professor of medieval literature at the University of Scranton who died in 1984, or Northwestern University engineering professor Arthur Butz lack any significant influence on the discussion and debate about the Holocaust in the United States. Among historians and other Holocaust scholars in the United States, there are no credible academics who deny the Holocaust.

In his passion for rebutting Lipstadt, Finkelstein—like so many who write about the importance and relevance of the Holocaust—makes extreme and dubious assertions even as he contributes a cogent analysis of the use of victimization as a political weapon. In his contempt for Lipstadt, Finkelstein praises Holocaust denier David Irving without acknowledging that much of Irving's scholarship was exposed as tainted by shoddiness and blatant fraud in his libel trial against Lipstadt.[58] Contradicting his earlier claims about the irrelevance of Holocaust skeptics, Finkelstein argues that Holocaust deniers may be credible sources of information. He claims that Arno Mayer—in his book on the Holocaust, *Why Did the Heavens Not Darken?*—cites Holocaust deniers. Given his status as a noted academic at Princeton University, the remarkable aspect of Mayer's book, as noted earlier, is that he provides absolutely no citations at all, but only a list of books in a bibliography at the end. It is true that the bibliography of Mayer's book includes Arthur Butz's *The Hoax of the Twentieth Century*, but given the absence of references, it is impossible to discern what information or insight Mayer thinks he gains from the discredited work of Butz. As a prolific writer on the Holocaust, Finkelstein should be well aware of Mayer's propensity for making unsupported assertions that are discredited by empirical evidence.[59] According to Finkelstein, the distinguished Holocaust scholar, the late Raul Hilberg, also cited Holocaust deniers, but Finkelstein, a prolific footnoter, provides no references to Hilberg's work to substantiate his claim. Finkelstein is so intent on discrediting any position that he perceives as buttressing Israel that he follows the dubious path of granting some credence to Holocaust deniers.

Despite his extreme rhetorical excesses, Finkelstein poses one of the key questions around the issue of Holocaust commemoration when he asks why the United States has a government-mandated museum about a genocide in which the United States was neither perpetrator nor victim. Finkelstein argues that there is no similar museum devoted to crimes in American history. He poses a hypothetical scenario "Imagine the wailing accusations of hypocrisy here were Germany to build a national museum in Berlin to commemorate not the Nazi genocide but American slavery or the extermination of the Native Americans."[60] The difficulty in imagining Germany or any European country even contemplating such an action lends considerable credence to Finkelstein's argument. Finkelstein's contribution to the debate about the use of the Holocaust as a moral weapon in contemporary politics resides in his willingness to ask provocative questions that are often insightful.

Despite the merits of some of his arguments, Finkelstein's attacks on his opponents have strayed well beyond the substantive and reached the gratuitously insulting. In a memorial tribute on his website to Raul Hilberg, who died in early August 2007, Finkelstein made the following comments about Deborah Lipstadt:

> Her lawyers imposed a gag rule on Deborah Lipstadt during her trial with David Irving—she was banned not only from testifying in court but also from speaking to the press—because they knew full well that a single word from this know-nothing's mouth would sink the ship. In her account of the trial Lipstadt can barely conceal the lawyers' contempt for her, yet she is too thick-headed to notice the absurdity of her smug two thumbs-up after the jury announced its verdict. She had as much to do with the victory as I did with last night's performance of the Bolshoi.[61]

The reader's initial reaction might be to question the appropriateness of such nasty insults in an article that is, in essence, an obituary of a scholar who tended to prosaic language rather than rhetorical excess. On a substantive level, one must wonder why it would have been in Lipstadt's interest to testify in a trial whose outcome essentially depended on whether Irving could be fairly labeled a Holocaust denier. Lipstadt never retracted her claims that Irving was a Holocaust denier and thus, the case was really about Irving and his writings and his political views, especially the extent to which they revealed a racist or anti-Semitic disposition. Finkelstein's attacks and insults on Lipstadt are more revealing of the heated animosity that the debates about the Holocaust have generated than any real analysis of the trial or Lipstadt's claims about the Holocaust. As D. D. Guttenplan explained, under British libel law, Lipstadt had to prove that what she said was true. Because Irving sought to defend himself by arguing that, at the very least, there was reasonable doubt that large numbers of Jews were killed in the gas chambers at Auschwitz, the salient issue was whether there was any reasonable basis for his heretical assertions. Lipstadt never claimed to be an expert on matters such as the workings of the Auschwitz camp and left her defense to scholars who specialized in such matters.[62] The gratuitous insults of Lipstadt add nothing to academic or political debate.

Because he opposes the agenda of the Israel lobby in the United States and the actions of the Israeli government with regard to the Palestinians, Finkelstein feels the need to devalue the moral currency of his political enemies. While he is in no sense a Holocaust denier, Finkelstein pours vitriolic scorn on those who use the Holocaust to justify their political actions. His case is weakened by the extreme rhetoric that he employs on behalf of his arguments. While the scornful language might be attributed solely to Finkelstein's acerbic personality, it does seem to symbolize the passion in debates about the Holocaust and other genocides.

THE HOLOCAUST MUSEUM AND POLITICS

Finkelstein has posed the provocative question as to why the United States has constructed a museum devoted to the study of a genocide in which the Americans were neither the victims nor the perpetrators. The answer to this question appears to be rooted in the political problems of the Carter administration. During his campaign and early in his tenure as President, Jimmy Carter was believed by some Jewish leaders to be guilty, in the words of Peter Novick, of "excessive evenhandedness" with respect to the Israeli-Palestinian issue.[63] Edward Linenthal also lists Carter's unabashed evangelical Christianity as a factor in his distance from many Jews.[64] Rabbi Alexander M. Schindler, president of the American Union of Hebrew Congregations, recalled that "historically, anti-Semitism had its roots in fundamentalist religion." Schindler went on to say that it "... is unjust and paradoxical for religious Jews to look askance at a man because he is deeply religious."[65] While Carter did win 64 percent of the Jewish vote in 1976,[66] that total vote was closer to landslide loser George McGovern's 60 percent in 1972, than the 80 to 90 percent of the Jewish vote won by Democratic presidential candidates John F. Kennedy in 1960, Lyndon Johnson in 1964, and Hubert Humphrey in 1968.[67]

The Carter administration angered some Jewish groups with aspects of his Middle East policy. Its arm sales to Arab countries were attacked by pro-Israel groups and the administration angered these same groups when it announced that it considered the Palestine Liberation Organization (PLO) to be a legitimate partner in future peace talks over the status of the West Bank and Gaza Strip. Later in 1977, the United States and the USSR issued a joint statement that mentioned the "legitimate rights of the Palestinian people."[68] Andrew Young, Carter's ambassador to the UN, was forced to resign after unauthorized meetings with representatives of the PLO, at a time when the PLO was regarded as a pariah organization by pro-Israeli lobbying groups and parts of the American foreign policy establishment.

Carter clearly felt a need to repair political relations with Jews. One way he sought to achieve this objective was to support the creation of the United States Holocaust Memorial Museum (USHMM). Even on the issue of the museum, Carter found himself engulfed in controversy as he stepped into an early incarnation of the uniqueness debate by referring to "11 million innocent victims exterminated—6 million of them Jews."[69] The inclusion of other victims of the Nazis such as Gypsies, homosexuals, Poles, and Soviet prisoners of war (POWs) was seen by champions of uniqueness as an assault on the distinctively Jewish nature of the Holocaust. Despite his efforts to repair relations with Jewish voters, Carter won only 49 percent of the Jewish vote in 1980, by far the lowest percentage of any Democratic presidential candidate since 1960.[70] Clearly, the Holocaust Museum did not solve Jimmy Carter's political problems with the Jewish vote in 1980, although it is important to note that his percentage of the vote declined from its 1976 levels among many other segments of the population in his landslide loss to Ronald Reagan.

The very nature of the Holocaust Museum was, of course, political. Nothing is more illustrative of this fact than the distortion of the famous and often quoted words by dissident German pastor Martin Niemoller about indifference and the serial persecution of various groups in Nazi Germany. Pastor Niemoller's well-known quote states that when various groups were persecuted by the Nazis, he did not protest because he did not belong to any of these groups.[71] When the Nazis came for him, the famous poem concludes, there was no one left to speak up for him. While there is some controversy over the exact number of groups mentioned in Niemoller's disputed quotation, it is virtually certain that the communists were mentioned first (the communists were indeed the first victims of Nazi persecution and violence in the early months after Hitler achieved power on January 30, 1933).[72] Despite this, the museum, devoted to historical accuracy, omitted reference to the communists when it included the Niemoller quotation in the exhibition.[73] German communists were victims of the Nazis, but because communists were the Cold War enemy, a slight historical adjustment was in order. The communist victims of the Nazis simply disappeared from a major American historical museum.

The issue of whether to include information about other victims of the Nazis and what to include about them was a matter of intense contestation in the discussions around the founding of the USHMM. Many of those involved in the planning of the exhibits feared a diminution of the Jewish nature of the Holocaust if other victim groups were included.[74] Gypsies or Romani were undoubtedly victimized in a murderous manner by the Nazis, but the exact degree of that persecution remains a matter of considerable controversy.[75] Christopher Browning has perhaps the best synthesis on the question of Romani victimization and its place in the Holocaust. "If the criterion is the place of various groups in Hitler's worldview, then Gypsies and everyone else are at the periphery. Hitler was after all a phobic anti-Semite not a phobic anti-Gypsite. If, however, the question is the effect of the Nazis' machinery of destruction, it is certainly legitimate for Gypsies to claim 'we should be with you at the center of the story.'" In the end, numerous references of the Gypsies' persecution by the Nazis were included in the museum, though some spokespersons for the Gypsies argued for an enhanced emphasis of the suffering inflicted on their people, and they further claimed that racism against Romani peoples was the source of what they regarded as unjust resistance to a full recounting of Nazi oppression of Gypsies in the museum.[76]

Armenian American groups wished to have the 1915 Turkish genocide of the Ottoman Armenians included in the museum. The Armenian representatives argued that the Armenian genocide was a precursor to the Holocaust perpetrated against the European Jews in the 1930s and 1940s. Again, uniqueness advocates were eager to exclude extensive reference to other genocides. Stephen Solarz, the New York Congressman who had expressed such contempt for those who had a positive view of the Khmer Rouge in the 1970s, was more sympathetic to the denial of the Armenian genocide. He argued that the murders and deportations that are often labeled the Armenian genocide were "a hotly disputed series of events."[77] The Turkish government was also vehemently opposed to the inclusion of any reference to the Armenians in the museum and threatened that U.S.-Turkish relations could deteriorate as a result of the inclusion of the Armenians in the exhibits at the museum. Monroe Freedman, the first chairman of the USHMM Council, later stated that the Turkish government was as committed to keeping the Armenians from being included in the museum as any groups were to being included.[78] In the end, only a single reference to a disputed quote by Hitler about the world's amnesia regarding the Armenians was included in the permanent exhibit at the museum. (It is likely, but of course impossible to prove, that many Jewish supporters of Israel in the United States were eager not to antagonize Turkey, a nation with close ties to Israel.)

The USHMM was another venue for victims' groups to battle over recognition of the oppression inflicted upon them or their ancestors. The battles over the inclusion and exclusion of various historical events closely parallel the disputes that occur in academic circles.

NATIVE AMERICANS AND THE HOLOCAUST

Among the most vehement critics of Holocaust uniqueness claims are scholars and activists who champion the cause of Native Americans in the face of what they see as ongoing persecution and genocide denial. David Stannard, a scholar of Native American Studies at the University of Hawaii and proponent of the view that indigenous peoples in the Western Hemisphere were the victims of a massive genocide, levels a very strong charge against Lipstadt and others who argue for Holocaust uniqueness. Noting her claim that genocide victims are often accorded considerable moral stature, he argues that Lipstadt "sees discussion of genocide as a competitive endeavour and devotes much of her work to devictimizing and thus stripping of their possible moral authority any group other than Jews."[79] Stannard also accuses Lipstadt of "intellectual thuggery" for comparing those who doubt the Holocaust uniqueness thesis to David Duke.[80] Stannard argues that the notion of Holocaust uniqueness, and especially the claim that there was no suffering on a similar scale by the indigenous peoples of the Western Hemisphere, is a result of much hard work by certain Jewish scholars: "It is the hegemonic product of many years of strenuous intellectual labor by a handful of Jewish scholars and writers who have dedicated much if not all their professional lives to the advancement of this exclusivist idea... not only is the essence of their argument demonstrably erroneous, the larger thesis that it fraudulently advances is fundamentally racist and violence provoking. At the same time, moreover, it willingly provides a screen behind which opportunistic governments today attempt to conceal their own past and ongoing genocidal actions."[81]

Champions of the Native Americans are among the angriest critics of the attention paid to the Holocaust. They argue that the Holocaust, with the active support of American Jewish organizations, absorbs so much attention that other genocides are neglected and that uniqueness advocates seek to keep the oppression of Native Americans off the political and historical agenda. David Stannard and Ward Churchill have been the most tireless and strident advocates for this perspective.[82] Several claims need to be separated here. There is no doubt that the U.S. government and much of the public have not been willing to pay a great deal of attention to the fate of Native Americans and the murder and other forms of violence that Europeans inflicted on indigenous peoples while taking possession of the Western Hemisphere. Before turning to this issue, however, it is worth noting Gavriel Rosenfeld's telling observation that Jews cannot be blamed for the neglect of what he calls the darker aspects of American history, because these topics were also not given much attention before the Holocaust was a significant topic in American academic and popular culture.[83] While Rosenfeld is undoubtedly correct about the long neglect of the dispossession of Native Americans, it is also true that the issue of genocide in general has received increased attention in the past few decades, and that Native Americans have received relatively little of this attention. Obviously, uniqueness advocates also have not called for increased attention to the fate of Native Americans. Stannard seems to be correct that as genocide studies have gained a growing share of academic attention, the Holocaust attracts more consideration in the United States than all other genocides combined and that the case of the Native Americans holds little interest from those who benefit directly from the ethnic cleansing that occurred in North America.

Just as some Holocaust uniqueness advocates have, at times, downplayed the fate of other victim groups in an effort to strengthen their analysis and Jewish moral capital, so also does Stannard engage in what Gavriel Rosenfeld has rightly depicted as flawed reasoning about the Nazis' intent to exterminate all the European Jews.[84] For example, Stannard points to the Nazi decision not to kill Crimean Karaites (a people who denied they were Jews) and ultimately to spare most of the *Mischlinge*, or Jews of mixed ancestry, as evidence that Nazis did not intend to kill all European Jews.[85] Rosenfeld notes that in the cases of the Karaites and the *Mischlinge*, the Nazis opted not to kill those they did not define as Jews.[86] Stannard also makes much of the machinations of SS chief Reichsfuhrer Heinrich Himmler in the waning months of the war. Himmler, who, along with Hitler, was as responsible as anyone for the deaths of the millions of Jews who perished in the Holocaust, sought to save himself as German military defeat became inevitable. Himmler attempted to start negotiations with the Western powers that would have involved Germany offering to halt the killing of Jews and entering a military alliance of the United States, Britain, and Germany against the Soviet Union.

Himmler's desperate moves at the end of the war should not be seen as representative of Nazi policy toward the Jews at any point in their war of extermination against those they regarded as mortal enemies of the Aryan race. Stannard further argues that the offer by Himmler to call off the killing of Jews occurred at a time when one-third of European Jews were still alive. He neglects to mention, however, that by late 1944 the majority of surviving European Jews were beyond the reach of the Germans. Most Jews in the East were in the Soviet Union, Romania, and Bulgaria where they were behind the lines of the Red Army, which by this time had vast military superiority over the battered Wehrmacht. In the West, the largest numbers of surviving Jews were in France and Great Britain, again behind the lines of the military of the Western allied forces that the Germans could not challenge by this point in the war. It makes little sense to cite either the late war machinations of Himmler or the inability of the Nazis to reach most of the remaining Jews of Europe as evidence that the Nazis did not intend to exterminate all European Jews. Stannard would be well advised to consult the protocol of the January 20, 1942 Wannsee Conference, which clearly indicates the Nazi intention to kill all of Europe's Jews.[87]

The fact that the Nazis intended to kill all European Jews does nothing to diminish Stannard's claims about genocide in the Americas. Stannard makes valid points about the double standard between the scholarly and popular culture treatment of the indigenous peoples of the Western Hemisphere and the Jewish victims of the Nazis. Even valid criticisms of his arguments, which focus on the many differences between the Holocaust and the decimation of the Native Americans, do not really detract from his central assertion that it is easier to be interested in, and indignant about, a genocide that occurred far away from one's own country. Still, like many of those who are fierce advocates in the field of comparative genocide, Stannard yields to the temptation to engage in exaggeration, extremely selective use of information, and distortion to vindicate political views to which he has a passionate commitment. He does so unnecessarily from an academic or intellectual perspective, but like those writers he critiques, Stannard apparently regards genocide recognition and remembrance as a zero sum game. In an apparent effort to increase the moral capital of Native Americans, Stannard misrepresents elements of the Holocaust in an effort to reduce the moral capital of Jews.

WARD CHURCHILL: HOLOCAUST EXCLUSIVITY & CONTEMPORARY GENOCIDE

Ward Churchill has long been a prolific and very controversial writer on genocide and Native American history. He has argued that the neglect of the fate of Native Americans is genocide denial on a grand scale.[88] Churchill received the most notoriety when mainstream media attention was called to his essay about the World Trade Center (WTC) attacks of September 11, 2001. Churchill argued that corporate employees killed in the WTC were part of an American financial system that spread devastation and death to the peoples of the third world. In an essay written just after the September 11 attacks, Churchill dubbed these employees "Little Eichmanns." Specifically Churchill said of them:

> As to those in the World Trade Center...Well, really. Let's get a grip here, shall we? True enough, they were civilians of a sort. But innocent? Gimme a break. They formed a technocratic corps at the very heart of America's global financial empire. The "mighty engine of profit" to which the military dimension of U.S. policy has always been enslaved, and they did so both willingly and knowingly. Recourse to "ignorance" a derivative, after all, of the word "ignore" counts as less than an excuse among this relatively well-educated elite. To the extent that any of them were unaware of the costs and consequences to others of what they were involved in and in many cases excelling at it was because of their absolute refusal to see. More likely, it was because they were too busy braying, incessantly and self-importantly, into their cell phones, arranging power lunches and stock transactions, each of which translated, conveniently out of sight, mind and smelling distance, into the starved and rotting flesh of infants. If there was a better, more effective, or in fact any other way of visiting some penalty befitting their participation upon the little Eichmanns inhabiting the sterile sanctuary of the twin towers, I'd really be interested in hearing about it.[89]

Initially Churchill's views provoked little outcry. However, in 2005, a proposed Churchill speech at Hamilton College in Clinton, New York, was canceled after a student called attention to his remarks.[90] Shortly thereafter an investigation into Churchill was opened by the University of Colorado on charges of research misconduct and plagiarism. The long investigation led to the revocation of Churchill's tenure and his eventual dismissal from the university.[91] The committee that found Churchill guilty of most of these allegations acknowledged the political nature of the investigation when it stated, "Thus the committee is troubled by the origins of, and skeptical concerning the motives for, the present investigation."[92] In short, by the committee's own admission, Churchill was investigated because he wrote and said things that were very unpopular.

In an article in the online journal *Other Voices*, Ward Churchill argues that Holocaust exclusivists contribute to the ongoing genocides against native peoples by denying them the moral status that Lipstadt says accrues to genocide victims. By denying the genocide of indigenous peoples as it occurs, Churchill claims that exclusivists are aiding and abetting in contemporary genocide:

> In their more extreme formulations, proponents of Jewish exclusivism hold not only that the Holocaust was a uniquely Jewish experience, but that it is

history's sole instance of "true" genocide. Exclusivists have gone on record, explicitly and repeatedly, denying that everything from the extermination of the Pequots in 1637, to the Turkish slaughter of more than a million Armenians between 1915 and 1918, to the more recent genocides in Cambodia, East Timor, Bosnia, Rwanda and Kosovo aren't really examples of genocide at all. Hence, while neo-Nazis deny a single genocide, exclusivists deny *many*.[93] [Emphasis in original.]

Here, Churchill misrepresents most genocide scholarship. The only source cited in his footnote is the most adamant of the Holocaust uniqueness advocates, Steven Katz. On her blogs in recent years, Lipstadt has posts that indicate she does not take the position that the Holocaust was the only genocide, even while she steadfastly argues for the uniqueness of the Holocaust. Still, Churchill presses on:

As prominent exclusivist Deborah Lipstadt has noted, the "general public tends to accord victims of genocide a certain moral authority. If you devictimize a people, you strip them of their moral authority," and thus a substantial measure of their ability to attract public support. Lipstadt was writing from an explicitly Jewish perspective, of course, and of her own people's natural desire to be compensated in various ways for the horrors of the Nazi Judeocide. Her point, however, is equally valid with respect to *any* genocidally victimized group. Moreover, where genocide is an ongoing process—as with the Lubicons—the need for public support goes not to securing compensation, but survival itself.[94]

Denial of genocide, insofar as it plainly facilitates continuation of the crime, amounts to complicity in it. This is true whether the deniers are neo-Nazis, Jewish exclusivists, renowned international jurists or provincial Canadian judges... There is no difference in this sense between a J. C. MacPherson, a Deborah Lipstadt and an Adolf Eichmann.[95]

(J. C. MacPherson was the Canadian jurist who ruled that the supporters of the small band of Cree in the Lubicon Lake region of Alberta could not label as genocide the actions of the Daishowa Corporation that deforested their traditional lands.)
Churchill goes on:

And what of the victims?... To paraphrase Martin Luther King, Jr., those who endeavor to make the success of peaceful resistance to genocide impossible only make violent resistance inevitable. They can have no complaint, morally, ethically or otherwise, when the chickens come home to roost.[96]

In his inflammatory conclusion, Churchill likens Lipstadt and MacPherson to Eichmann, the same comparison that he made about corporate employees working in the WTC on September 11. The degree, if any, to which those who claim Jewish suffering was unique promotes a worldview that enhances contemporary genocide is difficult to gauge. It must be said that there is little attention paid to the suffering of indigenous people. However, it may attribute too much power to academics in general, and Jews in particular, to say that the comparative neglect of Native Americans is primarily the result of Jewish "exclusivists." We should recall Gavriel Rosenfeld's previously mentioned point that little attention was paid to the decimation of indigenous populations in the Western Hemisphere before the Holocaust uniqueness advocates emerged. It is also important to consider that for the most part, countries do not acknowledge genocides that they have perpetrated. (The Germans are something of an exception to this last point.[97])

For her part, Lipstadt is dismissive and contemptuous of Churchill's attacks on her. The following is an excerpt from her blog in 2005:

> Tuesday, February 15, 2005: Ward Churchill says Deborah Lipstadt is the same as Adolf Eichmann
>
> See http://www.thejewishweek.com/news/newscontent.php3?artid=10532
>
> Long before he called the people in the World Trade Center "little Eichmanns," Ward Churchill had written that there was "no difference...between a Deborah Lipstadt and an Adolf Eichmann." His comments were prompted by the fact that I do not equate the treatment of the Native Americans with the Holocaust. For his rather incomprehensible ramblings on this point, see www.othervoices.org/2.1/churchill/denial.html.[98]

For all the vitriol that characterizes his remarks and the deplorable inattention to accuracy of details large and small that characterizes his work at times, Churchill does indeed raise the important question of why the fate of indigenous peoples historically and currently receives so little attention from the academic and media communities. Churchill notes that the Holocaust deniers who Lipstadt decries are rightly regarded as fringe characters that should not be taken seriously. It is also true, however, that those who advocate for attention to Native American genocides are similarly relegated to the fringes. The paucity of attention to the fate of indigenous peoples in the Americas is undoubtedly a reflection of their political weakness in the United States. When he asks us to examine the fate of Native Americans and the ongoing consequences of the long subjugation of indigenous groups, Ward Churchill raises valid questions, and the value of the questions he poses cannot be dismissed because of his attachment to intemperate rhetoric and detachment from careful adherence to fact.

Churchill is explicit in his demand that Native Americans are entitled to the most moral capital. "I believe that American Indians, demonstrably one of the most victimized groups in the history of humanity, are entitled to every ounce of moral authority we can get. My first purpose is, and always has been, to meet my responsibilities of helping deliver that to which my people are due."[99] Despite his dubious assertion of American Indian heritage, Churchill could not be clearer in his claim that the people he champions deserve to be accorded more moral capital in academic and political circles. In the end, Churchill is best viewed as one more advocate trying to claim more moral capital for the aggrieved group he wishes to champion, in this case, Native Americans. Unlike many academics and activists who participate in comparative genocide debates, Churchill does not seek to deny or diminish genocides that have been perpetrated against other ethnicities. Whatever his flaws, the ousted professor may be worth emulating in this important regard.

VICTIMIZATION AND THE POLITICS OF GENOCIDE RECOGNITION

This chapter has focused on the material and strategic interests that are behind many claims to genocide uniqueness or genocidal suffering. It is important to recognize that there are psychological benefits to victim status as well. In the wake of the Nazi atrocities against the Jews, Slavs, Gypsies, and others in Europe, many Germans did not dwell on the horrific acts of a regime to which a large majority had granted either passive or active consent. Rather, they tended to feel sorry for the fate that befell them as a result of their weakened military position and ultimate defeat. The bombing of German cities that resulted in the deaths of about 600,000 German civilians, the mass rape of German women by the Soviet Red Army as it advanced into Germany, and the postwar expulsion of German civilians from many regions of Eastern Europe with the high number of deaths that accompanied this ethnic cleansing were the grievances embraced by many Germans during and after the war.[100] Though Germany has been remarkably open in acknowledging the nation's guilt with regard to the Holocaust, the fate of the many German expellees and their descendants has remained an issue for some Germans and Austrians for decades after the war.[101] It is hardly surprising that it is easier to focus on the suffering inflicted on that group in which one claims membership.

In the United States, a group asserting that it has been the most victimized people may hope to achieve monetary, policy, and moral status gains. The claims of many Jewish groups about the Holocaust and the nation of Israel have been explored. For Native Americans, the desire for the recognition that comes from victim status and the possible material interests in land claims, casino licenses, and the much more remote possibility of general reparations are the most obvious benefits that would result from greater recognition of Native Americans as genocide victims. There are also the psychological and emotional benefits that redound to those who can plausibly claim that their ancestors were genocide victims and that, in some cases, the present plight of one's group resulted from this genocide.

Peter Novick has noted the importance of the Holocaust as a source of Jewish identity. The long struggle by Armenians around the world to gain recognition for the genocide of the Ottoman Armenians, and especially for the Turkish government to acknowledge the role of the Ottoman state in the perpetration of the genocide, seems largely rooted in a need for recognition rather than any realistic hope for material gains. While some have postulated that Turkey might fear territorial claims such as the large concessions imposed at the 1920 Treaty of Sevres (these concessions were negated in 1923 by the Treaty of Lausanne), it is unimaginable that tiny Armenia would have the power to impose any material reparations, of land or money, on Turkey. It is also hard to imagine what interest powerful international actors would have to appease the demand of the Armenians against a comparatively large and strategically situated nation such as Turkey. It is difficult to conclude that many Armenians are so deluded as to think that a Turkish admission of fault for the fate of the Armenians would result in material gain.

The most disturbing aspect of the comparative suffering debates is the extent to which the arguments about one's own group must lead to the denigration of the suffering of others. It is as if suffering is a limited commodity, and genocide—as the most precious brand of the commodity—must be especially guarded, lest its attribution to other groups lead to a diminution of its value. Jewish proponents of Holocaust uniqueness have been quite explicit in arguing for the special deference due to Israel because of Jewish suffering at the hands of Nazi Germany. What is unclear is the extent of the burden the Palestinians, who have actually paid the price for the establishment of the state of Israel, should be asked to bear. To date, a disproportionate share of that burden has been shouldered by the Palestinians.[102] The notion that the Holocaust precludes any criticism of Israeli policies in the West Bank, Gaza Strip, Golan Heights, Jerusalem, or Lebanon is often asserted or at least implied, but the actual logic of this argument is never fully delineated. The assumption appears to be that because Jews were murdered by the millions and threatened with complete extermination in Europe, the state of Israel is entitled to a very wide latitude as it pursues its security interests with regard to its Arab neighbors and Palestinian subjects. The political and moral consequences of the Holocaust are often assumed to be self-evident.

The critics of Holocaust uniqueness or Jewish exclusivity raise valid questions and present challenging issues about power and recognition of victimization, but they often do their cause significant damage by distorting historical events. The claim that the indigenous peoples of the Western Hemisphere were subjected to genocidal measures by the ancestors of those who hold dominant positions in most countries in North and South America is not validated by the assertion that the Nazis did not kill the Karaites or the Mischlinge. It is not necessary to make claims that present the Nazis as less murderous and less racist than they were in order to argue that the Holocaust does not convey special privileges to Israel. To claim that other groups, which were victims of genocide at other times in history, deserve full recognition of the injustice inflicted upon them does not diminish Jewish suffering at the hands of the Nazis. Snide remarks about the "remarkable fertility" at concentration camps do nothing to enhance academic or public debate about the entitlements of genocide.[103]

Defenders of Israel also damage the cause of accurate and reasoned discourse when they seek to diminish recognition of the suffering of non-Jews. Likewise, little purpose is served by arguing, as Deborah Lipstadt does, that obscure cranks who deny the existence of the Holocaust are serious scholars whose work is taken seriously in any forum, or that such fantasists as Holocaust deniers are growing in influence. The world's most prominent Holocaust denier as of 2010 was Iranian president Ahmadinejad, a man who also denied that there are any homosexuals in Iran and who claims to have been covered in a divine halo when speaking at the United Nations.[104] While no one considers Ahmadinejad an authority on the Holocaust, his position as president of a regional power makes his Holocaust denial more significant than that of obscure American professors who hold a similar view. Still, it is likely that Ahmadinejad is a Holocaust skeptic because of his disdain for Israel. If the Holocaust is the stated moral justification for the existence of Israel, then it serves the purposes of the Iranian president to label the Holocaust a fictional event.

In an age of identity politics and the celebration of victimization status (especially in colleges and universities), it is hardly surprising that there should be such fierce rhetoric about comparative suffering and the entitlements that flow from such suffering. Still, the debate, if it need be cast in these competitive terms, might be better conducted with far less invective and hyperbole. Most of all, a respect for fact and reason, however much a hindrance they might prove to be for the polemicists of certain perspectives, would enhance the quality of discourse on hotly debated topics such as comparative genocide or whether a particular historical event was genocide at all. Reasoned discourse might seem an unattainable objective, but it can at least serve as an aspiration.

So long as victim status is regarded as a commodity that can be bartered in the political and academic marketplace, there would seem to be little hope that there will not be vigorous efforts to gain more of the commodity and to lessen or eliminate entirely the victim status held by others. A plea for rational discourse and respect for evidence might seem entirely reasonable, but it is not likely to be heeded when the stakes are perceived to be high.

CHAPTER 5

THE DISPUTED FATE
OF THE OTTOMAN
ARMENIANS

A FIERCELY CONTESTED GENOCIDE

In the past several decades, there has been more heated controversy about what actually happened to the Ottoman Armenians during World War I than about most other genocides. The basic facts are hotly disputed, and those who disagree accuse each other of base motives. Scholars who argue that what some call "genocide" was instead communal conflict between Turks and Armenians that resulted in hundreds of thousands of deaths on both sides are accused of being tools of the Turkish government, which has steadfastly denied the occurrence of an Armenian genocide. Those who assert that there was a coordinated and centrally directed genocide of the Ottoman Armenians are often accused of bias against Muslims and Turks, and of focusing solely on the suffering of the Armenians while ignoring the atrocities committed against Muslims in the Balkans, the Crimea, and the Caucasus in the waning decades of the Ottoman Empire.

In recent years, some historians who were previously skeptical of claims about an Armenian genocide have altered their views to accept the proposition that there was indeed mass killing of Armenians in the Ottoman Empire that can be classified as genocide. For example, Donald Quataert, a distinguished Ottoman historian at SUNY-Binghamton, notes that while he has reservations about the passions engendered by the use of the term "genocide," he felt that there was greater evidence available of the systematic killing of Armenians at the behest of the central government when he published the second edition of his book on the history of the Ottoman Empire from 1700 to 1922 in 2005 than when the first edition appeared in 2000.[1] In a

2006 article, Quataert states that "what happened to the Armenians readily satisfies the U.N. definition of genocide."[2] Quataert also laments that many Ottomanists, himself included, have been reluctant to delve into the fate of the Armenians. He attributes this reticence to a desire to resist the negative depictions of Turks in particular, and Muslims more generally, propagated by many political and academic critics of Turkey.

The Turkish government has, on many occasions, prosecuted its own citizens for speaking about the genocide of the Armenians (or for that matter, the persecution of the Kurds, which has occurred on an ongoing basis since the 1920s). In August 2005, the most prominent Turkish novelist, Orhan Pamuk, who would win the Nobel Prize for Literature in 2006, was charged with the crime of denigrating "Turkishness." Pamuk faced three years in prison because he made references to both the Armenians and the Kurds in an interview with a Swiss newspaper in February 2005. Pamuk said: "Thirty thousand Kurds and one million Armenians were killed in these lands and nobody but me dares to talk about it."[3] The prosecution of Pamuk was enmeshed in Turkish domestic and international politics, and the charges against him were eventually dismissed.[4] Turkish-Armenian journalist and editor, Hrant Dink, who was assassinated by a seventeen-year-old Turkish nationalist in 2007, had been prosecuted three times for insulting Turkishness. He was acquitted once and convicted twice and given a six-month suspended sentence. His son Arat Dink was also convicted of insulting Turkishness for republishing his father's remarks and penalized with a one-year suspended prison sentence.[5]

The fierce passions aroused by the Armenian genocide have not been confined to Turkey. When Leo Kuper wrote the first academic book that surveyed genocide, he called the Armenian case "the forgotten genocide of the twentieth century."[6] Today, Kuper's appellation would seem much less fitting. The large majority of genocide scholars are firm supporters of the proposition that there was a genocide of the Ottoman Armenians in the period 1915–1923, and books that survey genocide or ethnic massacres inevitably include a case study of the Armenians. The International Association of Genocide Scholars (IAGS) has stated that there was a state-sponsored genocide of the Armenians and has called on the Turkish government to acknowledge that its predecessor regime, the nationalist Committee for Union and Progress (CUP), was responsible for the genocide. Turkey has fought back vigorously against these allegations and has used economic intimidation and threats to U.S. national security interests in its many efforts to suppress consideration of the Armenian question.

The Armenian genocide has not been neglected in the recent scholarship on genocide in the United States. The journal *Holocaust and Genocide Studies* is published by Oxford University Press in association with the United

States Holocaust Memorial Museum (USHMM), and most of the articles in the journal are devoted to some aspect of the Holocaust. However, articles on other genocides are also considered for publication. Since its founding in 1986, *Holocaust and Genocide Studies* has published nine articles on the Armenian genocide, but not more than two articles on any other genocide other than the Holocaust, which is the subject of over 90 percent of the scholarship that has appeared in the journal. This counting of articles by particular genocide is not meant to cast aspersions on the motives or conduct of the editors of *Holocaust and Genocide Studies*, but only to note that the Armenian genocide has received comparatively extensive coverage in the premier genocide journal in the United States.

If the Armenian case is no longer the twentieth century's forgotten genocide, it might now carry the title of the most contested. Every small aspect of the Armenian genocide is the subject of heated disputation. For example, it is widely asserted that Adolf Hitler told his generals in the summer of 1939 about impending atrocities that the SS would commit against Polish civilians and reminded them, among other things, that no one remembered the Armenians. Other researchers have disputed this quote, which is included in the main exhibition at the USHMM.[7]

In fact, the inclusion of any reference to the Armenians in the Holocaust Museum, however small, sparked controversy. As was noted in chapter 4, Armenian American groups lobbied for the representation of the Armenian genocide as a precursor of the Holocaust. Some academics opposed any inclusion of the Armenians in the museum's exhibition. In 1983, Richard Chambers, professor of Near Eastern Languages and Civilization at the University of Chicago, wrote that any mention of the Armenians in the museum would be a "grave injustice to the Turkish people."[8] As the permanent exhibition of the USHMM was being designed, the Turkish government was of course adamantly opposed to including the Armenian genocide in the exhibit. Monroe Freeman, who served on the USHMM Council, said of the Turkish government: "As much as anyone wanted to be represented that's how much the Turkish government wanted the Armenians out. There was pressure on us and pressure on the White House staff."[9] Consistent with concerns about Holocaust uniqueness discussed in chapter 4, Miles Lerman of the USHMM Council was concerned about extending recognition to genocide victims from a broad range of groups: "If you are introducing the Armenian tragedy to the Holocaust, why not the tragedy . . . of the Cambodians? Why not the tragedy of the American Indians?"[10] In the end, after much contention, reference to the Armenian genocide was limited to the single disputed Hitler quote.[11]

The controversy surrounding the inclusion of references to the Armenians in the Holocaust Museum is just one instance of the many ways in which the politics of Armenian genocide remembrance are manifested in the United States and elsewhere. This chapter will examine the treatment of the Armenian genocide in American politics and in academic circles in the United States. The political aspects of the Armenian genocide are not nearly as complicated as the academic controversies. Politicians who wish to court Armenian American support resolutions calling for Turkey to acknowledge the responsibility of the Young Turk regime that came to power in 1908, for the genocide of the Armenians. The executive branch of the U.S. government, irrespective of the president's party, is primarily concerned with protecting U.S. strategic influence in a region of the world that was of vital importance during the Cold War and, in the twenty-first century, is courted as an ally in the battle with Islamist opponents of the United States. For many decades, American presidents and diplomats have been extremely reluctant to antagonize Turkey over a distant historical event.

It is not the purpose of this chapter to resolve the many controversies regarding the Armenian genocide. Some of these issues cannot even be discussed in a single chapter. This chapter provides an analysis of the academic, electoral, and geopolitical considerations that influence the very heated controversies that surround the Armenian genocide.

U.S. POLITICS: CONGRESS AND THE ARMENIAN GENOCIDE

In the political realm, resolutions regarding the Armenian genocide tend to be highly polemical in their approach to the issue and designed to please the very small segment of the American electorate—namely, Armenian Americans—that is attentive to this issue. For many years, members of Congress have introduced resolutions calling on the Turkish government to admit that the Young Turk government of 1915 committed genocide against the Armenians. Congressional resolutions on the Armenian genocide are most often introduced by Representatives from southern and central California where there are large Armenian American populations. To explore the nature of these resolutions, two such measures introduced in 2005 are considered.

One of the 2005 resolutions was introduced by California Democratic Representative Adam Schiff, whose district has more than 67,000 Armenians.[12] California Republican George Radanovich was the primary sponsor of the other Armenian Genocide Resolution introduced that year. Both resolutions call on the Turkish government to acknowledge the guilt of the Ottoman government for the extermination of the Armenians. While politicians' efforts to enact nonbinding legislation ought not to be taken too seriously, some of the claims made in these resolutions are worth noting for their audacity and the fact that some of their more dubious claims match those of other organizations concerned about the genocide. The Schiff Resolution calls upon the European Union (EU) to make Turkish acceptance of guilt for the Armenian genocide a condition for membership in the EU. The resolution requests that any Turkish government acknowledgment of its predecessor state's role in the genocide should be looked upon favorably by the EU. It is not clear, however, why the U.S. House of Representatives should recommend conditions for membership in the EU or any organization of which it is not a member. Interestingly, the resolution does not recommend that the United States impose any trade or other tangible sanctions on Turkey if it does not satisfactorily accept Ottoman guilt for the destruction of the Armenians. There have not been any resolutions condemning Turkish treatment of the Kurds, which, while not genocidal on the scale inflicted upon the Armenians, has been violent at times and involved such extreme measures as bans on using the Kurdish language in the media, speaking it in public, or giving children Kurdish names.[13]

Both the Schiff and Radanovich Resolutions give what might be called the most extreme Armenian version of events in that they ignore any suffering by Turkish Muslims in the breakup of the Ottoman Empire and use the highest possible estimates of Armenian deaths. (Both pieces of legislation estimate Armenian deaths at 1,500,000.) The Radanovich Resolution combines a rather sweeping generalization. For example, Article 30 states:

(30) Despite the international recognition and affirmation of the Armenian Genocide, the failure of the domestic and international authorities to punish those responsible for the Armenian Genocide is a reason why similar genocides have recurred and may recur in the future, and that a just resolution will help prevent future genocides.

Given that many genocides occurred after the Nuremburg tribunals, it is hard to argue persuasively that the failure to punish the Young Turk leaders has been a contributing factor to many subsequent genocides. It is difficult to imagine how a Turkish acknowledgment of genocide now would deter future genocides. Such resolutions are best seen as political gestures to placate voters and contributors rather than as efforts to establish a consistent stand on the acknowledgment of past genocide. The notion of inconsistency is buttressed by the ability of many lawmakers to ignore contemporary genocides while they call for recognition of an event that occurred decades ago, and by their willingness to disregard relatively recent cooperation between the United States and a variety of genocidal regimes. For example, the millions of deaths that have resulted from the wars in the Congo since 1994 have yet to be the subject of congressional resolutions.[14] Likewise, there has been little effort to condemn the administrations of Ronald Reagan and George H. W. Bush for their aid to Saddam Hussein in the 1980s. At the time, Saddam served a useful purpose for American policy by engaging in a protracted war with Iran. The U.S. government chose to disregard Saddam's use of poisonous gas on rebellious Kurds and Iranian troops.[15]

TURKEY AS AMERICAN ALLY: THE U.S. GOVERNMENT AND THE ARMENIAN GENOCIDE, 1919—2011

In the aftermath of World War I, Turkey, like the other defeated nations, was subjected to a harsh peace treaty. The Treaty of Sevres provided for the dismemberment of the Ottoman Empire and parts of Anatolia. The anger of nationalist Turks was fired by a treaty that would break apart Anatolia itself as a singular political entity. The British and French grabbed former Arab portions of the empire, with France taking the Cilicia region of Anatolia for a few years after the war (1918–1921). Istanbul itself was occupied by the Allies from 1918 to 1923. The Treaty of Sevres, concluded in 1920, granted key parts of Anatolia to two Turkish rivals with nationalist aspirations of their own. Greece was awarded the city of Izmir (Smyrna) and the region around it on at least a temporary basis as well as Edirne and the surrounding areas of Eastern Thrace. Greek Prime Minister Venizelos, a proponent of the irredentist Greek nationalist "*megali*" ideology that advocated the expansion of Greek sovereignty into parts of the former Ottoman Empire, hoped to grab as substantial a portion of western Anatolia as possible.[16]

The postwar victors decided that an Armenian Republic, its borders to be drawn by President Woodrow Wilson, was to be created in Eastern Anatolia; in late 1920, Wilson drew boundaries that gave the Armenians an extensive republic. Armenian genocide scholar Vahakn Dadrian describes the Treaty of Sevres as creating a "vast Armenia" that covered several provinces.[17] In a few short years, the provisions of Sevres would be wholly irrelevant as they applied to the partition of Anatolia. The U.S. government's policies, and indeed those of other Western powers, would change dramatically with respect to the Armenians.[18]

The change in the American government's attitudes toward the Armenian genocide is one of the less complicated aspects of the controversy surrounding the issue. Eventually the facts on the ground dictated changes in the geopolitical imperatives that motivated American foreign policy toward Turkey. The many territorial concessions imposed on Turkey under the Treaty of Sevres were rendered irrelevant by the Turkish nationalist triumphs on the battlefield. The Turks inflicted military defeats on the forces of the newly created Republic of Armenia in 1920, and the remnants of that Republic were soon absorbed into the Soviet Union. The Turkish nationalist forces commanded by Mustafa Kemal Ataturk defeated the Greek army, which had sought to conquer territory well beyond Izmir, and recaptured all of Anatolia by 1923. Robert L. Daniel described the full achievement of the Turkish nationalists when he said they had "…helped destroy the infant Armenian Republic, had repudiated the Treaty of Sevres, in which the allies had established spheres of influence in accord with secret war time agreements, had expelled the French, Italians, Greeks and British from Turkey, and had over thrown the Sultanate."[19]

The triumph of Ataturk and the Turkish nationalists was ratified by the 1923 Treaty of Lausanne, which resulted in the revision of most of the harsh terms and concessions to the Armenians mandated by the Treaty of Sevres. The Armenians were not ever mentioned in the Treaty of Lausanne. The United States, which contained strong Protestant interests that supported the Armenian cause, did not formally participate in the Lausanne conference, but it did send an observer delegation. In the same year as the Lausanne Treaty, the United States and Turkey signed the Turkish-American Treaty of Commerce and Amity. This treaty required nothing of the Turkish government with respect to the treatment of minorities. Although the treaty failed to receive the two-thirds Senate vote required for ratification when it came to a vote in 1927, it did signal a major shift in U.S. policy toward Turkey.[20] Dadrian has described the significance of the discarding of the Treaty of Sevres by noting that Kemalists had managed to turn military defeat into almost total triumph in just three years. Any future threats of prosecution for those responsible for the Armenian genocide were abandoned, and the prospect of a future Armenian nation was cast aside.[21]

There were multiple interests in the United States that preferred cordial diplomatic ties with Turkey to conflict over the treatment of the Armenians. (Among the most powerful of the lobbies desiring close relations with Turkey was the American oil industry.[22]) By the 1930s, the Turkish government had enough influence in the United States to stop the production of a film based on Franz Werfel's book *Forty Days of Musa Dagh.* Werfel's novel is the story of a group of five thousand Armenians who resist those Turkish forces that attempted to murder them. The Turkish government informed the U.S. State Department that MGM's plans to produce the film would be harmful to U.S.-Turkish relations and could lead to the restriction of American exports to Turkey, including a ban on all American films. The State Department lobbied MGM to discard plans to produce the film. Despite a series of negotiations there was no compromise, and MGM abandoned the film as it did again in 1938 when further consideration was given to the filming of *Forty Days of Musa Dagh.*[23]

In the post–World War II era, Turkey assumed a far more important role in U.S. foreign policy as a result of the emergence of the Cold War struggle between the United States and the Soviet Union. As they had in previous eras, the Dardanelles Straits and the Bosporus were of special importance in controlling Russian, or in this case Soviet, access to the Mediterranean Sea. As a NATO ally after 1952, Turkey was the site of U.S. military installations and was a most strategically located U.S. partner. The geopolitical value of Turkey under Ataturk's leadership was emphasized by Lewis Thomas and Richard Frye, American scholars who published a history of U.S.-Turkish relations in the 1950s. Thomas and Frye attributed Turkey's strength in significant measure to its homogeneous population (as they perceived it), and noted that this stable Turkey was an important ally of the United States.[24] It was not in the political interest of the United States to antagonize the Turks about a decades-old genocide when there was so much to be gained from an alliance with the strategically placed nation. On a number of occasions, resolutions that in one way or another commemorated the Armenian genocide were derailed in Congress, usually at the request of administrations that feared damage to U.S.-Turkish relations.[25] In 1985, Ronald Reagan explained his opposition to an Armenian genocide resolution to a Turkish journalist by stating that such a resolution would reward terrorism (Reagan was presumably referring to the bombing of Turkish diplomats and other parties viewed as pro-Turkish by radical Armenian groups) and could hurt relations with a vital ally.[26] Two years earlier, Reagan had refused to recognize the genocide and stated that "I can't help but believe that there's virtually no one alive today who was living in that era of terrible trouble."[27] (Of course, Reagan himself was born in 1911 and thus, although a small child, was alive during the Armenian genocide.)

The United States was hardly alone in placing political and economic interests over a desire for recognition of the Armenian genocide. Careful to protect its good relations with Turkey and desirous of protecting Jews in Turkey, the Israeli government scaled back its participation in a conference on the Armenian genocide that was held in Tel Aviv in 1982 because there were to be several presentations on the Armenian genocide.[28] (Turkey had comparatively good relations with Israel until the government of Prime Minister Erdogan, an Islamist by Turkish standards, distanced the country from Israel in 2009.) For nation-states, recognition of past atrocities is a minor concern, especially those that occurred elsewhere, compared to current strategic and economic objectives. Some Jewish scholars and activists on behalf of Israel were eager to protect the status of the Holocaust as a unique event, and their interests coincided with the Turkish government's refusal to acknowledge that anything approaching genocide had occurred with respect to the Armenians.[29]

In short, the American government's lack of interest in pursuing recognition of the Armenian genocide is rather simply explained. Ataturk's victories over the Armenians and the Greeks allowed the consolidation of the strategically located and highly populated state of Turkey. Turkey was far more important to the United States than an Armenian Republic would have been as an independent state and than it certainly was as a Soviet Republic. After the collapse of the Soviet Union, Turkey remained a far more important ally of the United States than the small and poor new state of Armenia. It is difficult to imagine nation-states being guided by humanitarian concern about the truth of a decades-old genocide where such a concern might conflict with present-day strategic interests. In fact, concerns about current human rights abuses rarely play a determining factor in the conduct of international relations. A morality that places the victims of genocide and other acts of violence at the core of foreign policy concerns would be regarded as a wonderful development by many people, but it would represent a revolution in the conduct of international relations.

THE TURKISH VIEW:
DEALING WITH TRAITORS AMID WAR

Successive Turkish governments have not been contented to simply use power politics to suppress recognition of the Armenian genocide. The Turkish government's view of the Armenian issue has remained remarkably consistent. In response to the 2005 resolutions introduced in the U.S. House of Representatives that called upon the Turkish government to acknowledge the responsibility of Turkey for the Armenian genocide, which it dated as occurring from 1915 to 1923, Egemen Bagis, foreign policy advisor to Prime Minster Erdogan, sent a letter to all members of the U.S. House of Representatives addressing the issues raised by the resolution. Bagis noted the long history of strategic cooperation between the United States and Turkey and emphasized the current challenges in the Middle East as well as other areas of the world. Bagis summarized the Turkish perspective in stark terms: "Tragic events of 1915 were triggered by a terrible political miscalculation of the Armenian citizens of the Ottoman Empire. Encouraged by the Czarist Russia's imperial policy of capturing Anatolia and reaching the warm waters of the Mediterranean, Ottoman Armenians allowed themselves to serve as a fifth column of Russia in Turkey. As a result they rebelled against the central government, triggered a civil war and paid a terrible price."[30] Interestingly, whatever his intentions, Bagis does not deny that there was an Armenian genocide. In fact, an ethnic group massacred in the course of a civil war—Bagis's version of the events of 1915—might well be the victims of state-perpetrated genocide.

Bagis argues that faced with treason on the part of the Armenians, the Ottoman government took measures that any government so situated would enact. According to Bagis, the Ottoman government was facing an armed rebellion by its own citizens, who happened to be members of an ethnic group that was collaborating with a foreign enemy during wartime.[31] Furthermore, the deportations from Anatolia were undertaken with careful preparation designed to promote the well-being of the Armenians. Such deaths as occurred were due to local ethnic tensions, climate, lack of food supplies, and harsh wartime conditions. In short, the traitorous population was to be well cared for and suffered losses due to factors largely beyond the control of the central government. Bagis does not provide any estimate for the Armenian deaths that he implies were inadvertent and argues that all deportations were ended in July 1916.

Among the most prominent scholars who supported the non-genocide theory of the Armenian tragedy proffered by the Turkish government are American academics, the late Stanford J. Shaw and his wife Ezel Kural Shaw of UCLA. The Shaws are the authors of a two-volume history of the Ottoman Empire that was published by Cambridge University Press in 1977. Professor Stanford J. Shaw was subjected to considerable harassment by Armenian activists and, at times, from terrorists who proclaimed their allegiance to the Armenian cause. His home was bombed, his office at UCLA was ransacked, and he was forced to cancel his classes. The executive vice-chancellor at UCLA stated that there was little the university could do in the face of an international terrorist organization.[32] The terrorists referenced by the UCLA administrator were from the Armenian Secret Army for the Liberation of Armenia (ASALA). ASALA conducted a number of bombings in the Los Angeles area, and the Shaws' reputation as pro-Turkish scholars drew the group's attention.

The Shaws' view of the deportations from Eastern and Central Anatolia in 1915 is best set out in the second volume of their history of the Ottoman Empire. It is worth quoting them at some length here. They argue that Armenian leaders declared their allegiance to the Russians and forced the hand of the Ottoman government:

> It would be impossible to determine which of the Armenians would remain loyal and which would follow the appeals of their leaders. As soon as spring came, then, in mid-May 1915, orders were issued to advance the entire Armenian population from the provinces of Van, Bitlis, and Ezurum, to get away from all the areas where they might undermine the Ottoman campaigns against Russia or against the British in Egypt with arrangements made to settle them in towns and camps of the Mosul area of Northern Iraq...Specific instructions were issued for the Army to protect the Armenians against nomadic attacks and to provide them with sufficient food and other supplies

to meet their needs during the march and after they were settled. Warnings were sent to the Ottoman military commanders to make certain that neither the Kurds nor any other Muslims used the situation to gain vengeance for the long years of Armenian terrorism. The Armenians were to be protected and cared for until they returned to their homes after the war. A supplementary law established a special commission to record the properties of some deportees and to sell them at auction at fair prices with the revenues being held in trust until their return. Muslims wishing to occupy abandoned buildings could do so only as renters, with the revenues paid to the trust funds and, with the understanding that they would have to leave when the original owners returned. The deportees and their possessions were to be guarded by the Army while in transit as well as in Iraq and Syria and the government would provide for their return once the crisis was over.[33]

In the Shaws' view, the major causes of Armenian deaths were the casualties and privations suffered when the Armenians retreated from the Van region with their Russian allies.[34]

The Shaws' version of the deportations defies historical common sense and would render the CUP or Young Turk regime led by Enver, Talat, and Djemal the saintliest government in human history. Stipulating to the Shaws' account of events leads to the following deductions. During a time of war, a government decided to expel an ethnic minority that had engaged in terrorism against the majority population and the state for many years. Furthermore, the leaders of the Armenian population declared their support for the nation's long-time enemy and current foe, Russia. Many Ottoman Armenians joined the Russian Army, which, in the spring of 1915, invaded Turkey. This army reached the important eastern Anatolian city of Van and carried out an indiscriminate massacre of the Muslim population. An Armenian state, based in Van, was created under Russian protection.

The Shaws ask their readers to believe that under the pressure of war, the CUP government confronted a minority that had a long terrorist history and was engaged in treasonous, armed collaboration with the enemy. One eventual goal of this armed treason was secession and creation of an Armenian state centered at Van. In the Shaws' version of events, the treasonous, secessionist terrorists were to be deported, but they were to be treated in the most humane manner possible even as Muslims—many of them *muhajirs* (Muslims who had been evicted from or fled former Ottoman territories) who had been victims of ethnic violence in the Balkans and the Caucasus—suffered severe privations due to the economic dislocations induced by the war. According to the authors, the property of the Armenians was to be protected in the most scrupulous manner. If there were any violations of the CUP regulations and intentions governing the deportations to Syria and Iraq, they are not mentioned by the Shaws. The Shaws' account of the Armenian deportations might be termed "touchy feely" ethnic cleansing. It is an almost inconceivable version of events in World War I Anatolia or anywhere else for that matter.

The reaction to the Shaws' work by scholars who argue that there was a Turkish genocide of the Armenians went well beyond the debate over evidence. Professor Richard Hovannisian, a colleague of Stanford Shaw's in the UCLA History Department and one of the premier scholars of Armenian history, wrote a lengthy review of the Shaws' book in 1977.[35] In addition to an analysis of the arguments and evidence in a book he clearly detests, Hovannisian argues that with the development of Turkish and Ottoman studies in the United States, some scholars who learned Turkish and lived in Turkey wished to dispel the Western myth of the barbaric Turks. In the process of this revision of uniformly negative depictions of Turks, Hovannisian believes that some scholars, especially the Shaws, went too far as they abandoned critical standards when they examined certain events in Turkish history. In short, Hovannisian argues that many of the Turkish scholars had become partisans of the present Turkish regime. Hovannisian's language is quite striking as he explains his views on the Shaws' work that was published by the very prestigious Cambridge University Press: "The fact that a strongly biased work such as *History of Ottoman Empire and Modern Turkey* has been authored by an individual enjoying such a considerable academic recognition and published by a highly reputable press causes deep consternation...One may speculate about why the work with such serious flaws in methodology and objectivity would emanate from the pen of Professor Shaw. What could have been—what should have been—a valuable text is instead an unfortunate example of non-scholarly selectivity and deceptive presentation."[36]

It should be noted that some Armenian organizations are not as reticent as Hovanissian in attributing more base motives to scholars who defend the Turkish perspective on the events of 1915–1923. They argue that such scholars are essentially paid shills for the government of Turkey. Sixty-nine scholars signed a statement that appeared as a paid advertisement in the *New York Times* and the *Washington Post* on May 19, 1985. The statement read in part as follows:

> As for the charge of "genocide," no signatory of this statement wishes to minimize the scope of Armenian suffering. We are likewise cognizant that it cannot be viewed as separate from the suffering experienced by the Muslim inhabitants of the region. The weight of evidence so far uncovered points in the direction of serious inter-communal warfare (perpetrated by Muslim and Christian irregular forces), complicated by disease, famine, suffering

and massacres in Anatolia and adjoining areas during the First World War. Indeed, throughout the years in question, the region was the scene of more or less continuous warfare…The resulting death toll among both Muslim and Christian communities of the region was immense…[37]

In response to this statement, Armenian organizations published lists of the signers with the grants they received from research institutions funded with Turkish government money.[38] The Armenian organizations essentially allege that the scholars, most of them Ottoman or Turkey specialists who deny that there was an Armenian genocide, have been compromised by Turkish money.

In response to criticism of their book on the Ottoman Empire, the Shaws were hardly reticent about attributing motives to scholars like Hovannisian. For them, the scholars of Armenian descent who argued that there had been a genocide in the 1915–1923 era were motivated by an excess of sentiment as well as ethnic and religious bias. In a reply to Hovannisian, the Shaws do not limit themselves to simply presenting a defense of their book.[39] They say of Hovannisian: "To those who are ethnically, politically, and emotionally committed to a particular cause…no amount of scholarship could produce conviction. Does Dr. Hovannisian really wish to perpetuate the biased image of the Terrible Turk that has its roots in the age of the Crusades? Does not his suspicion of Turkish source material, nay his complete disregard for it, reflect anti-Turkish and anti-Moslem propensities?"[40] The Shaws express empathy for Armenians: "We appreciate, understand, sympathize with the sensitivity of Professor Hovannisian and other Armenians on this issue. They and their friends and families have tragic memories of the past."[41] The Shaws go on to repeat their view that the violence in Anatolia was a case of mutual violence involving several ethnic groups. They also declare that the Armenians are emotionally overwrought about the whole question of genocide.

The Shaws were not the only scholars to argue that there was a strong anti-Turkish and anti-Muslim prejudice in much of the writing about the Ottoman Armenians. Historian Justin McCarthy believes that he has added considerable balance to the history of nationalism in the Balkans, Anatolia, Crimea, and the Caucasus by demonstrating that the ethnic and religious violence in these regions was not one dimensional, but rather that millions of Muslims were expelled from areas that were separated from the Ottoman Empire in the nineteenth and early twentieth centuries. Moreover, many Muslims were killed by nationalists in these regions.[42] Whatever position one takes on McCarthy's denial of the Armenian genocide, there is no doubt that the violent expulsion of Muslims from predominantly Christian regions of the Ottoman Empire is simply missing in much of the historical work on ethnic cleansing in the last decades of the empire. McCarthy's work is valuable in that it debunks the myth of the eternally innocent Christians forever pillaged by the demonic Turk that is present, explicitly or implicitly, in so much of the literature on the Armenian genocide.

On the issue of ethnic violence involving the Armenians during World War I, McCarthy adopts what might be called a "mutual destruction position." Arguing that eastern Anatolia devolved into a brief period of ethnic murder on the part of both Muslims and Armenians, McCarthy believes that the provocateurs of the violence were clearly the Armenians. As is usual with writers who reject the claim that a genocide was perpetrated against the Armenians, McCarthy is remarkably consistent in that all Turkish violence is inevitably presented as retaliatory. If the Turks are not innocents in his view, they are at the very least a uniquely patient people who resorted to violence only when provoked beyond endurance.

Like the Shaws, McCarthy argues that the Armenians were closely allied with the invading Russians and that Armenian collaboration with the enemy induced civil war in eastern Anatolia. In addition to mutual mass killings of civilians, he states that there were deportations of Muslims by the Armenians as well as deportations of the Armenians by the Ottoman government. McCarthy also differs from the Shaws in that he acknowledges that the Armenian deportees were not well protected by the Ottoman government and that many Armenians died from starvation.

McCarthy claims that the attacks against the ethnically cleansed Armenians were committed by those who were engaged "in a war to the death with the Armenians."[43] He does not present a comparable analysis of the relative strengths of the officially disarmed Armenians who were a minority and the Ottoman state with the power of a military, police force, and the thuggish gangs that were organized from *muhajirs*, released prisoners, and Kurds for the specific purpose of deporting Armenians.

Despite his contribution of missing perspectives to the entire debate on the ethnic violence in the Ottoman Empire, McCarthy's equivalence thesis falls short when one considers the imbalance of power between a minority group like the Armenians—who, according to McCarthy, constituted about a tenth of the population of Ottoman Anatolia—and a central state like the Ottoman Empire that, even as it weakened, had a much greater capacity to inflict violence and force deportations than did a legally disarmed minority group like the Ottoman Armenians. One does not need to adopt the Armenian innocence perspective so prevalent in the West to understand that the Ottoman Armenian conflict was not a battle of equals. McCarthy also neglects to include a serious consideration of Turkish nationalism in his analysis of the Armenian question, suggesting that only the Armenians had national aspirations in 1915. Like the writers they oppose, McCarthy and the Shaws, despite their contributions to the debates about the events of 1915, strain the reader's credulity when they present the actions of the Ottoman government as largely benign despite the decades-long conflict between the state and Armenian nationalists and the circumstances of wartime.

Certain assertions made by the Shaws and McCarthy receive support from Taner Akçam, a Turkish scholar living in exile in the United States who vehemently rejects their genocide denialist conclusions. In fact, Akçam has argued that there is clear evidence that the CUP government committed genocide against the Armenians beginning in 1915. Akçam also asserts that much of the championing of the rights of Christians in the Ottoman Empire was done by the Great Powers in the interest of grabbing parts of the Ottoman Empire for themselves rather than a genuine concern for the well-being of the Armenians.[44] Further, he notes that many claims about Christian massacres under the Ottomans were exaggerated. Furthermore, Western protests and Western media were extremely one-sided in that they ignored massacres against Muslims in the areas rebelling against Ottoman rule as well as the flight of refugees to Anatolia to escape Christian violence.[45] Of course, Akçam does not combine his conclusion about foreign hypocrisy about the Armenians with a denial of the genocide that began in 1915.

At times, scholarship and diplomacy have been intimately connected in the debates over the fate of the Armenians. The most bizarre case of scholarly defense of the Turkish position involves the activities of Princeton University professor Heath Lowry, holder of the Ataturk Chair of Turkish Studies in the Department of Near Eastern Studies. Prior to his appointment to chair, which was funded by a grant from the government of Turkey, Lowry was head of the Institute of Turkish Studies, a Washington-based organization funded by the Turkish government. In that capacity, Lowry advised the Turkish embassy on its defense against the charge of genocide. Lowry's activities were most peculiar in response to Robert Jay Lifton's book, *The Nazi Doctors*.[46] In the book, Lifton made several references to the Armenian genocide. In 1990, Lowry, the holder of a PhD in Ottoman history from UCLA, wrote a draft letter to the Turkish ambassador to the United States that the ambassador was to sign and forward to Professor Lifton. In an incidence of scholarly humility, in Lowry's draft memo from Ambassador Kandemir, he commends the works of two American experts in Turkish Armenian relations: Justin McCarthy and Heath Lowry. Ambassador Kandemir sent the letter to Professor Lifton and included Lowry's draft of the same letter as well as several talking points about the Armenian genocide and strategy for promoting the Turkish view of the events of 1915–1923.[47] Lowry's subsequent appointment to the Ataturk chair led to charges, which

Princeton denied, that through a large donation the Turkish government had purchased a faculty position that could be used to perpetuate genocide denial.[48]

Lowry's activities were exposed and denounced in an article in the journal *Holocaust and Genocide Studies* by Roger W. Smith, Eric Markusen, and Robert Jay Lifton.[49] This interesting article goes on to compare those who deny the Armenian genocide to those who deny the Holocaust. In summary, there has been a strong identification with the Turkish perspective on the Armenian genocide by the majority of the scholars of the Ottoman Empire. The reasons for this identification have been the subject of considerable speculation by some of those academics opposed to genocide denial. As we have seen, some are said to have been motivated by financial gain. As we shall see in the next section of this chapter, some writers have attributed skepticism about the Armenian genocide to the poor mental health of those who claim that there was no state-sponsored genocide of the Armenians.

THE PSYCHOLOGY OF DENIAL

Some scholars who are strong advocates of the position that there was an Armenian genocide have engaged in what might be called speculative psychology to explain why not everyone shares their views. Smith, Markusen, and Lifton question the professional ethics and the psychiatric state of those who would deny that there was a Turkish genocide of the Armenians. They cite with approval the work of genocide scholars and psychologists, Israel Charney and Daphna Fromer, who studied 69 academics who signed a statement denying the Armenian genocide. Charney and Fromer received just 17 "active responses" from the 69 signatories. Untroubled by their paltry response, Charney and Fromer devised a classification of the reasoning schemes that they called "thinking defensive mechanisms," which they believed "enabled" the scholars to deny the Armenian genocide.[50] One of these defense mechanisms is "scientism in the service of confusion" or the claim that there is insufficient evidence to claim with certainty that there was a genocide.[51] According to this line of reasoning, arguments over evidence may be indicators of mental defectiveness.

Another alleged defense mechanism is "definitionalism." This is the claim that killings occurred in some manner that does not constitute genocide.[52] Those who hold that there were indeed mass killings of Armenians, but that these acts did not constitute genocide, stand accused of mental deficiency, or at best psychological evasion. Smith, Markusen, and Lifton— after stating that the work of Charney and Fromer gives us clues to the mind-set of academics who deny the Armenian genocide—take a somewhat agnostic view of the theory they present: "Whether anyone is led into denial by such reasoning is an open question, but such thinking does serve to make denial easier thereafter while, at the same time, it preserves the appearance of objectivity."[53]

Charney has written several articles on the topic of denial mentalities. In addition to psychological analysis, he engages in what might be called the fallacy of "denial equivalence." According to this line of reasoning, since some people deny the Holocaust and the Holocaust did actually happen, those who deny the Armenian genocide must be wrong. This type of fallacious logic is interspersed between psychology, which serves to question the motives and/or the psychological well-being of those who do not accept that there was a Turkish genocide of the Armenians.[54]

In addition to scientism and defintionalism, Smith, Markusen, and Lifton proffer careerism as another motive for not sharing their views on the Armenian genocide. According to them, careerism "...is a complicated phenomenon, but for our purposes we would identify two (non-exclusive) forms that it may take: one that is oriented more toward material goals, and one that involves more the satisfactions that go with power. Both share the 'thoughtlessness' that Hannah Arendt saw as the essence of the 'banality of evils'":

> an imaginative blindness that prevents one from reflecting upon the consequences of one's actions. But elsewhere Arendt also speaks of a "willed evil," and the second type of careerism is not far removed from this: not simply the obliviousness to hurt, but the infliction of hurt. Intellectuals who engage in the denial of genocide may be motivated in part by either type of careerism, or by both. The more insidious form, however, is the second type of careerism. Here material rewards are important, but more so, the opportunity for certain psychological and social satisfactions: a sense of importance, of status, of being in control, all of which can come through identification with power, something we believe we have shown in the memorandum we have analyzed. The price for intellect in the service of denial, however, is a particular conception of knowledge, one in which knowledge not only serves the ends of those in power, but is defined by power. But to define truth in terms of power is to reveal the bankruptcy, irrationality, and above all, danger, of the whole enterprise of denial of genocide. Inherent in such a view of knowledge is both a deep-seated nihilism and an urge to tyranny.[55]

Here, the authors provide us with a psychological profile of all those who would argue that the events that led to the destruction of the Armenians in Anatolia were anything other than genocide. These deniers are said to be gripped by the need to identify with power. One wonders whether one would be engaging in the crime of scientism if one asked for some evidence to support this speculation on the ego needs of those who disagree with the authors' view of the Armenian genocide. The footnote that appears in the two quoted paragraphs refers to the work of Hannah Arendt whose principal work on genocide was her book on Adolf Eichmann. In the case of Eichmann, there is no doubt about his role in a genocide whose main objective—the desire of the Nazi regime to exterminate the European Jews—is not in doubt. Eichmann was a relatively high-ranking bureaucrat who served a government that dominated the European continent for a few years.[56] To liken those academics who deny that there was a genocide in Armenia to Eichmann is to engage in the overused tactic of constructing absurd Holocaust analogies.[57]

Employing the authors' notion of a need to identify with power, it is unclear how identification with Turkey feeds the ego. Imagine those who support the aims and actions of the foreign policy of the United States, a state far more powerful than Turkey. All those who supported the U.S. war against Serbia in 1999 in the dispute over Kosovo or the invasion of Iraq in 2003 must be yielding to the ego need to identify with the strong. The United States is so much more powerful than Turkey that one wonders whether the malady that afflicts supporters of U.S. actions is far deeper than the mental defects that afflict the deniers of the Armenian genocide. It is perhaps not a terrible thing if debate about genocide were not to descend to the level of unverified, and probably unverifiable, psychological speculation.

Finally, Smith, Markusen, and Lifton reach even more dramatic conclusions about those who would cast doubt on assertions that there was a genocide of the Armenians between 1915 and 1923. Again, a summary would not do justice to their sweeping conclusion:

> Where scholars deny genocide, in the face of decisive evidence that it has occurred, they contribute to a false consciousness that can have the most dire reverberations. Their message, in effect, is: murderers did not really murder; victims were not really killed; mass murder requires no confrontation, no reflection, but should be ignored, glossed over. In this way scholars lend their considerable authority to the acceptance of this ultimate human crime. More than that, they encourage—indeed invite—a repetition of that crime from virtually any source in the immediate or distant future. By closing their minds to truth, that is, such scholars contribute to the deadly psychohistorical dynamic in which unopposed genocide begets new genocides.[58]

Simply put, those who participate in one side of this debate argue that those who take the opposite position facilitate genocide. It is hard to imagine that the alleged academic indiscretions and immodesty of Heath Lowry or the selective use of evidence by Stanford Shaw or Justin McCarthy emboldened Saddam Hussein in his brutal campaigns against the Kurds. Nor is there a shred of evidence that writings denying the Armenian genocide played any role at all in the Hutu Power's decision to exterminate the Tutsis in Rwanda. No scholarly works on the Rwandan genocide mention Turkish denial of the Armenian genocide as an influence on the perpetrators of the horrible events that took place in Rwanda in 1994.[59]

PEOPLE OF INNOCENCE AND THE EVIL TURK

Those who support the Armenian perspective in the disputes over the genocide have long sought to buttress their case by indicting Turkish and, at times, Islamic culture. In the World War I era, many in the West held a deep hatred and contempt for the Turks. British Prime Minister David Lloyd George called the Turks "a cancer on humanity, a wound that has worked its way into the flesh of the earth that it has misruled." Lloyd George claimed that if the Turks won the war it would be " . . . the torch of pillage, cruelty and murder . . . that would be carried from Asia to Europe." Speaking of Mesopotamia in 1917, the British Prime Minister stated that this cradle of civilization should not be left to " . . . the incendiary and destructive brutality of the Turks."[60] Lloyd George was not alone in his deep contempt for the Turks.

Many scholars who argue that there was a genocide of the Armenians support the claim that much of the concern from the West about the fate of the Armenians was designed to promote territorial and other claims against the Ottoman Empire. As the empire weakened, various Christian powers could couch their claims against the Ottomans in terms of protecting the minority Christians from persecution. In World War I, the cause of the Armenians was to serve a similar purpose for the opponents of Turkey as it had in the preceding century. By the fall of 1915, British and French officials and the media attempted to use the massacres as war propaganda against the Germans. The slaughters were described as manifestations of German Kultur and depicted as a replication of the alleged German atrocities in Belgium.[61] According to historian Donald Bloxham, the actual aim of the pleading on behalf of the Armenians was to induce the Americans to enter the war against Germany. Bloxham argues that the Westminster propaganda contained specific, but patently false, accusations linking German diplomatic officials in Turkey to the genocide.[62]

Lloyd George and other British politicians of the World War I era were not alone in the West in despising the Ottomans in particular and Muslims in general. U.S. Ambassador Henry Morgenthau is regarded as a key source for the evidence of the intentional murder of the Armenians at the command of the CUP government. Morgenthau viewed the Turks as dull witted, evil, and lazy: "Such abstractions as justice and decency form no part of their conception of things.[63] We must realize that the basic fact underlying the Turkish mentality is its utter contempt for all other races."[64] Such contempt for Turks exemplifies the worldview often expressed by opponents of the Ottoman Empire in the decades preceding the Armenian genocide.

British diplomat Lord Bryce had championed the Armenian cause for many decades. He, too, viewed the Turks as a pestilence upon the earth. Bryce claimed that "wherever the Turk has ruled, he has spread desolation. The provinces of Asia Minor, once the scene of a brilliant civilization, had been emptied...by the lethargy, the incompetence, and the caprices of a barbarous master."[65] Again, contempt for Turkish civilization was a key component of the "weltanschauung" (worldview) of a defender of Christian minorities within the Ottoman Empire.

It is hardly surprising that Turks would be inclined to be skeptical of the charges of genocide. For almost two centuries, much of the criticism of the Ottomans/Turks and concern for the Armenians and other Christian minorities has been proffered as a ploy to gain territorial concessions or undermine the Turks. In the late twentieth and early twenty-first centuries, Turks were not just asked to acknowledge that the CUP ordered a genocide against the Anatolian Armenians beginning in 1915, but also that they are essentially an uncivilized people, descended from barbarians, who adhere to an inferior religion. The numerous atrocities that occurred in Christendom including the mass killings of non-Christians are not part of the worldview of many critics of the Ottomans. One would never know that much of Europe was "civilized" and Christianized under the threat or actual practice of extermination. Rather, for many of those who write about Turkey and the Armenians, barbarism is confined to those outside the realm of the West. Speaking to the allegedly inferior peoples in the eastern regions of the Habsburg Empire, Austrian diplomat Klemens von Metternich stated that the Orient begins on the *Landstrasse*. For many who write on the Armenian genocide, a lesser civilization begins just outside the center of Vienna.[66]

Some of the prominent contemporary writing about the Armenian genocide also appears to be rooted in the Western contempt for non-Westerners that characterized many late nineteenth and early twentieth century politicians' views of the Ottomans.[67] As will be demonstrated, the Ottoman Empire is often presented as uniquely intolerant when its actions and policies compared quite favorably to Western Europe. Islam is, at times, regarded as more likely to produce repression than Christianity despite the long history of religious persecution in Christian nations. Much of this contempt may be rooted in ethnic and religious superiority, but for some, it also adds to the righteousness of their cause by rendering Turks as hopelessly evil.

Peter Balakian's much-acclaimed book *The Burning Tigris* is a classic example of a work in the evil Turk/innocent Christian genre.[68] When discussing the violence in Bulgaria in the 1870s, Balakian refers only to the massacres of Christian Bulgarians and includes not a word on violence against Muslims there. Balakian goes so far as to label the killing of 15,000 Bulgarians as an unprecedented act of state sponsored murder.[69] This is a most ahistorical claim, whether one considers a few events in European history such as the Roman destruction of Carthage, the English conquest of Ireland, the Irish famine of the 1840s (largely a result of British government policy), various atrocities connected to the French Revolution such as the Terror or the suppression of counter-revolution in the Vendee, the sack of Jerusalem and the slaughter of Christians and Jews there by victorious crusaders, or the suppression of the Albigensians. Genocide historian Ben Kiernan notes that there were many settler genocides in nineteenth-century Africa and that half to 1 million Algerians perished in the first 30 years of the French conquest of Algeria.[70] Perhaps the Atlantic slave trade or the depopulation of the Americas by the European powers escaped Balakian's notice. His enthusiasm for making the Ottomans a uniquely brutal people leads him to make an astonishing claim.

Balakian presents starkly his view of benign European powers, innocent Christian minorities, and evil Turks. "At the heart of the problem—whether in the Balkans or in the Armenian provinces in the East—was the legal, political, and social status of Christians in the Ottoman Empire. On one front the fundamental question was: Can a Christian be the equal of a Muslim? The question was raised again and again by the Christian minorities and by the European powers, and in the end the answer from the ruling elite was a resounding no. And the Armenians as well as the Assyrians and the Greeks, all paid dearly for that answer."[71] Of course, at this very time, Europeans were establishing and perpetuating colonial regimes that were not based on equality, but brutal repression. In the United States, many Americans protested for the rights of the Armenians at a time when African Americans in the South had been stripped of most legal, political, and human rights either by law or actual practice. From the tone of Balakian's work, however, one would gather that the Ottomans were uniquely evil. (Donald Bloxham and Taner Akçam, both of whom firmly reject attempts to deny that there was a genocide of the Armenians, argue that Western governmental attempts to champion the rights of Christian minorities in the Ottoman Empire were often undertaken to promote geopolitical interests and not human rights.[72])

For Balakian, Islam is a major source of the sufferings of the Armenians. He relies upon the work of Vahakn Dadrian, one of the most prolific Armenian genocide scholars.[73] Dadrian cites numerous Quranic verses to argue that Islam teaches the subjugation and/or slaying of unbelievers. There are, of course, other interpretations that regard the Quran as a less-menacing document.[74] Even if one were to grant Dadrian's view of Islam, one would also have to concede that the Armenians and other Christians practiced a religion that preached its own exclusivity as the sole path to truth and salvation. One might recall Jesus teaching in the Gospel of John that "no man comes to the Father, but by me,"[75] or in the Gospel of Mark that "he that believes and is baptized shall be saved; but he that believes not shall be damned."[76] Dadrian argues that unlike Europe, the Ottomans could not separate church and state. He fails to note that the reduction of the role of religion in Western political affairs did not prevent any of the barbarism prevalent in the colonies held by the European nations during this period.

Dadrian, like other scholars of the Armenian genocide, wants Turks to believe that their state was founded on the basis of ethnic cleansing and mass murder. While his assertion is partly true, it is also true that many states are, in fact, founded on genocide and ethnic cleansing. The United States comes quickly to mind.[77] Few nations, however, are prepared to accept the facts about their origins. Still fewer are ever called upon to do so. Dadrian also implicitly wants the Turks to acknowledge that they belong to a defective religion. Even if there were no other political interests involved, it is not surprising that Turkey has so long resisted the call of Armenian activists and genocide scholars to acknowledge the genocide against the Armenians.

The Ottoman Empire is, for Balakian, unique in its discriminatory practices. The *millets* or semiautonomous organizations under which non-Muslims (*dhimmi*) existed in the Empire did, of course, relegate them to a second-class status. Without comparison to other existing regimes and their treatment of ethnic and religious minorities, one gets the impression that the Ottoman treatment of the dhimmi was unique in history. A comparative view of the treatment of minorities elsewhere would indicate that minorities were better treated under the Ottomans than in many places. Balakian relies heavily on the work of British diplomats who represented an empire that had wrought depredation and brutality to the far corners of the globe. None of those objecting to Turkish treatment of the Armenians seemed to have batted an eye over a famine that starved at least a million people in Ireland or the numerous other acts of brutality being committed around the world. The new round of colonization in Africa brought degradation that lasted into the 1950s when the British responded to Kenyan nationalist movements with a savage and murderous response to the Mau Mau insurgency.[78]

Dennis Papazian, of the Armenian Research Center at the University of Michigan at Dearborn, like some other advocates of the Armenian cause, falls into the practice of ethnic and religious castigation. Relying on the partisan Ambassador Morgenthau, Papazian argues that the CUP was pressured by the German Kaiser to declare a religious war or jihad against England, France, and Russia. Wilhelm II allegedly inspired a jihad such that "the religious passions evoked were expressed in the mass slaughter of Christian Armenians by a primitive and enraged population."[79] Bloxham, in a more balanced manner, argues that both sides in World War I used ethnic or national appeals to undermine their opponents with anti-imperial insurgencies.[80] Papazian's notion of the Turks as uniquely primitive is consonant with earlier descriptions of them as barbarians, which have been presented above. Papazian is more explicit in his embrace of Western superiority when he ends his essay with a reference to the attacks of September 11, 2001, and states, "The job of spreading enlightenment—to counter terrorism and genocide—is a difficult one and depends in some magnitude on the willingness of the West to have confidence in its fundamental values and to exhibit the will to stand up for them."[81]

In a web-based fact sheet on the Armenian genocide, Papazian makes clear his belief in Western cultural and ethical superiority. Papazian lists and corrects what he regards as a series of misconceptions about Turks. Point 14 is quite instructive:

14. The only reason that the Turks aren't allowed into the European Community is their Islamic religion.

What concerns the Europeans is not the religion of the Turks, but rather their *values*. Judeo-Christian culture, which characterizes the Western world, is dedicated to developing a moral society with civic institutions. Democracy and faith in the beneficent value of truth is the current manifestation of this aspiration. If the Turks were to thirst after justice and righteousness, values to which we in the West aspire, they would most certainly be welcomed in any society. As I said earlier, many Turks do, but they are hindered by their government. The first sign of this new morality would appropriately be for present-day Turkey to acknowledge the Ottoman genocide of the Armenians.[82]

Papazian's argument is that if Turks were better people, they might get into the EU. They could show that they were more moral human beings by acknowledging the Armenian genocide. It seems as though many problems could be solved by this one act that would render the Turks a more humane people. Pursuing this path, Papazian seems to believe that the Turks might even reach the lofty moral levels of the West. It should surprise no one that such a view is widely rejected in Turkey.

THE INTERNATIONAL ASSOCIATION OF
GENOCIDE SCHOLARS AND THE ARMENIAN GENOCIDE

If the Armenians have not done well in their appeals for the U.S. government to take up their cause, they have been much more successful in the academic community where many scholars have produced vast quantities of materials on the Armenian genocide. At the 6th biennial conference of the IAGS, the assembled scholars unanimously adopted and sent a letter about the Turkish government's call for further study of the question as to whether the Armenians were victims of genocide, to Turkish Prime Minister Recep Tayyip Erdogan. The following excerpts capture the essence of the claims made in the IAGS letter.[83]

> Dear Prime Minister Erdogan:
>
> We are writing you this open letter in response to your call for an "impartial study by historians" concerning the fate of the Armenian people in the Ottoman Empire during World War I.
>
> We represent the major body of scholars who study genocide in North America and Europe. We are concerned that in calling for an impartial study of the Armenian Genocide you may not be fully aware of the extent of the scholarly and intellectual record on the Armenian Genocide…
>
> The scholarly evidence reveals the following:
>
> On April 24, 1915, under cover of World War I, the Young Turk government of the Ottoman Empire began a systematic genocide of its Armenian citizens—an unarmed Christian minority population.
>
> The Armenian Genocide is corroborated by the international scholarly, legal, and human rights community.
>
> We note that there may be differing interpretations of genocide—how and why the Armenian Genocide happened, but to deny its factual and moral reality as genocide is not to engage in scholarship but in propaganda and efforts to absolve the perpetrator, blame the victims, and erase the ethical meaning of this history.
>
> We would also note that scholars who advise your government and who are affiliated in other ways with your state-controlled institutions are not impartial. Such so-called "scholars" work to serve the agenda of historical and moral obfuscation when they advise you and the Turkish Parliament on how to deny the Armenian Genocide.
>
> We believe that it is clearly in the interest of the Turkish people and their future as proud and equal participants in international, democratic discourse to acknowledge the responsibility of a previous government for the genocide of the Armenian people…as the German government and people have done in the case of the Holocaust.

The excerpts from the IAGS letter presented above and the full text of the 2005 resolution by the IAGS contain the very incomplete story of the genocide lamented in this chapter. There is no Armenian nationalism, no Armenian terrorism, and no Armenians who side with Russia during World War I. None of these factors remotely justifies genocide, but their omission indicates that those who seek recognition of the Armenian genocide feel that such facts might in some way offer some partial justification for Turkish actions against the Armenians. The other possible explanation for this one-sided version of events is that the anti-Turkish and anti-Muslim biases that are included in much writing on the Armenian genocide are present in the IAGS as well. Moreover, the resolution's tone smacks of condescension as the scholars worry that the Turks might not know the full extent of historical research on the Armenian genocide, and the IAGS offers gratuitous advice to the Turkish government on how the nation should proceed on the road to inclusion in the circle of democratic governments.

One must also be struck by the dedication of numerous individuals to single out the Turkish slaughter of the Armenians as an event for which an acknowledgment is required. For example, the IAGS produced no letters to George W. Bush demanding an apology or recognition of the genocide committed against Native Americans in the pursuit of the colonization and conquest of North America.[84]

As is discussed in greater detail in chapter 6, much of the writing about the Armenian genocide depicts the Armenians as a passive people. There is reluctance to discuss Armenian nationalism as a potential threat to the Ottoman Empire and later the Turkish state, and there is a tendency to neglect the Armenian collaboration with the Russians during World War I. While the degree of collaboration is a matter of considerable dispute, Mark Levene notes that collaboration or armed involvement with the opponent was not uncommon in the war.[85] The larger point about the presentation is what is most important here. Most genocides do not actually follow the model of the Holocaust where there was as in fact no dispute or enduring conflict between Germany and the European Jews.[86] Cambodia would be a second case in which there was no long-standing conflict between the perpetrators and the victims of genocide. Most genocides involve conflict between a state and a contending party. The Bengalis of East Pakistan desired, at the very least, greater autonomy from East Pakistan. The Hutus and the Tutsis had been contenders for power for several decades in Rwanda. Likewise, Armenian nationalism, like all nationalisms arising in the various multiethnic empires in Europe and the Near East in the nineteenth and early twentieth centuries, was a threat to the Ottoman Empire in the same manner as the Bulgarian, Serb, and Greek nationalisms. There is, however, a reluctance to focus on the actions of groups that are the victims of genocide. Levene states well the motivation behind the impulse to neglect the actions of the communal group that is ultimately victimized by a genocidal state: "One might appear to be apportioning blame equally between them. Worse still, as in the case of some pro-Turkish apologetics, there is the danger of placing the blame entirely on the victims' head, thereby claiming that, far from being genocide, the state's actions actually constitute legitimate self-defense."[87] Levene goes on to make what should be an obvious point: whatever the nature of communal conflict, genocide is never a justi-fied response. The reluctance to focus on the actions of the victim group seems to be greatest when accompanied by the cultural and religious biases that are found in so much writing about the Armenian genocide.

THE POLITICS OF A GENOCIDE DEBATE

It is hardly surprising that the Turkish government has declined to acknowl-edge the Armenian genocide. In this regard, the situation is similar to the Bangladesh genocide of 1971, and in both instances, the perpetrator regime was never removed from power. The nationalist principles of the Young Turks and especially Ataturk, who drove occupying powers out of the country, remain the guiding themes of the Turkish state. In fact, the Turks emerged in a stronger position than the Pakistanis, who, while retain-ing West Pakistan, were defeated in a brief war with India in 1971. The Turks emerged from a defeat in World War I and a humiliating Treaty of Sevres to military victory and a triumphant Treaty of Lausanne, which rati-fied Ataturk's victories on the battlefield. The Turks had ethnically cleansed their new state in a manner not unfamiliar to observers of nationalism in Europe. As Mark Levene puts it, "By adopting a Western formula of nation-alism, the leaders of post-Ottoman Turkey had punched their way towards modern nation-statehood."[88]

There were trials of some leaders of the CUP who were responsible for the Armenian genocide, but these Istanbul-based trials were short-lived and, to some Turks, not to be taken seriously as they were held under foreign occupation. They were also delegitimized because the Ataturk-led national-ists opposed them. While historians have learned a great deal from some of the evidence at the trials, they have become as much a part of the partisan arguments over the Armenian genocide as nearly every other aspect of the tragic destruction of the Armenians.[89]

There are few cases of nations simply admitting to genocide or other crimes against humanity. The Japanese have been notorious in refusing to acknowledge the many atrocities committed against fellow Asians in the 1930s and 1940s.[90] The U.S. government has never apologized for slavery and government officials, and even genocide scholars are reluctant to label the fate of the indigenous peoples of the Western Hemisphere as genocide.[91] One could point to numerous other examples, but the harder task is to find a case of a government willing to acknowledge a genocide that its own nation committed. Germany might be the prime case of a nation admitting to a genocide, though of course the Nazis were defeated. Still, the successor regime in the Bundesrepublik has gone further along the lines of contrition than is the international norm on such a sensitive matter. Of course, as a result of its defeat in World War II, modern Germany derived no material or territorial gains from exterminating the Jews. Many German Nazis and their military and civilian collaborators received relatively benign treatment in the postwar era, as anticommunism led the Allies to be more disposed to de-emphasize the Nazi past and rehabilitate or treat with lenience many individuals with very troubling records of criminality and complicity in mass murder between 1933 and 1945.[92]

The efforts of various scholars and especially the IAGS to seek an acknowledgment of the Armenian genocide ask the government of Turkey to take actions that depart from governmental norms. A departure from usual practices—in this case, the hardly admirable trait of moral myopia—is not a bad thing. What is more puzzling is the singling out of Turkey as if it were the only government in the world to whitewash its national past, whether that troubled history includes genocide or other actions that resulted in mass death and suffering. The resolutions of the IAGS are a tribute to the energy and dedication of the Armenian genocide scholars and activists in the United States and elsewhere. One must still acknowledge that the partisan nature of genocide scholarship is present here as well.

The actions of governments in the United States and Europe toward the Armenian genocide are wholly consistent with other cases of genocide and gross violations of human rights. In most instances, power matters; for nearly a century, the Turkish government has had more power than the Armenians, and for many decades it has simply been more important to American policymakers than issues about the mass murder of a minority. The case of the Iraqi Kurds, as explained by Samantha Power, illustrates well how a contemporary genocide can be caught up in realpolitik.[93] The Kurds were of no great interest to the U.S. government when Saddam Hussein was viewed as a useful counter to revolutionary Shia Islam in Iran. When Saddam invaded Kuwait, a U.S. ally in 1990, Iran seemed much less an expansionist threat than it had been a decade earlier. Saddam, who was now viewed as a threat to U.S. strategic interests, could be cast as a genocidal killer. It is therefore hardly surprising that a genocide that occurred ninety-five years ago is of no great concern to the U.S. government. This indifference is reinforced by the fact that there is no political or propaganda value to be gained by most politicians and academics from focusing on the genocide of the Armenians. In fact, as this chapter has demonstrated, the U.S. government has often regarded the question of the Armenians as a matter that could harm U.S. national interests. As is well known, the genocide of the Tutsis in Rwanda seemed to offend no particular strategic or political interest in the U.S. or

Europe and was allowed to proceed even as it was broadcast on television around the world.

The treatment accorded to the genocide of the Armenians by academics and politicians is no different than any of the other cases explored in other chapters. Moral outrage is displayed, in most cases, in a selective manner when it suits the political purposes of the government, scholar, or organization expressing righteous indignation. The degree of contempt for Muslims that is occasionally explicit, and implicit at other times, is what has distinguished the discussion of the Armenian genocide from other instances of genocide examined in this book.

CHAPTER 6

GENOCIDE PROVOCATION? THE CASE OF THE OTTOMAN ARMENIANS AND THE RWANDAN TUTSIS

PROVOCATION AND THE POLITICS OF STUDYING GENOCIDE

Academic and media interest in the study of genocide has grown significantly in recent years. The Holocaust is, of course, the most prominent genocide in both academic and popular culture. The fact that scholars and journalists pay attention to acts as horrific as genocide would not seem to be noteworthy or surprising. Yet, as the works of Peter Novick and Raul Hilberg demonstrate, there was comparatively little interest in the study of the Holocaust in the United States in the decades following World War II.[1] American Jews did not wish to emphasize the catastrophe that had been inflicted upon European Jews by the Nazis, or accentuate their cultural distinctiveness and vulnerability as a people. The political and historical circumstances that led to the intense interest in the Holocaust in the United States cannot be detailed here;[2] instead, this chapter will focus on the value many ethnic groups in the United States have come to place on the status of genocide victimhood in recent years. It is worth recalling Deborah Lipstadt's arguments about the value of victim status. Lipstadt claims that the world accords moral capital to genocide victims and those who would deny genocide victim status to a group may well deprive the group of a moral and political resource.[3] This is, of course, the reason Lipstadt argues so stridently against equating other genocides with the Holocaust and labels them "immoral equivalencies."[4]

The importance of victim status and the fear of legitimizing deniers of genocide make many scholars, writers, and political activists reluctant to acknowledge the complex role of victims, or political groups claiming to act in the interest of victims, in the conflicts that ultimately resulted in genocide. Writing about the Armenian genocide, Mark Levene states, "Some scholars have appeared anxious to play down the vitality of pre-1914 Armenian nationalism for fear that it will detract from their case and play into the hands of present-day Turkish government polemics. Robert Melson, for instance, has recently objected to drawing parallels between emerging Turkish and Armenian nationalism."[5] Levene notes that at the Paris Peace Conference after World War I, Armenian nationalists were resolute in demanding a large national state in eastern Anatolia and Cilicia that would be repopulated with Armenians following the expulsion of Turks and Kurds. Addressing the post-genocide timing of these demands, Levene argues that "recognizing that they were responding to victimhood does not require us to view all Armenians as innocents or plaster-cast saints...In most cases of modern genocide there is a genuine state-community contest."[6]

The desire to secure recognition of the massacre of the Ottoman Armenians beginning in 1915 has been described as a sine qua non for many Armenian Americans. Much as Novick suggests that the Holocaust has become part of the identity politics of Jewish Americans, Meline Toumani notes that third-generation Armenians in the United States are fiercely committed to the cause of genocide remembrance, and she poses the question "Is Turkey's denial the diaspora's lifeblood?"[7] (Toumani claims that in Armenia, Turkish denial of the genocide is not a great concern to an impoverished population.) In the strong language that characterizes much of the debate about the Armenian genocide, Toumani states of those who are three generations removed from the slaughters of the early twentieth century: "In the face of the distress of assimilation, the glory of a shared victim-hood is seductive indeed, especially when it can be attained without having actually suffered."[8] Some writers apparently fear that displaying even a hint of ambiguity about the causes of the Armenian genocide would serve to dilute its value as moral and identity capital in an era when victimhood is highly valued.

Alan J. Kuperman, one of the most prominent analysts and expositors of the concept of genocide provocation has written about the cases of Rwanda and the Darfur region of Sudan.[9] Kuperman argues that the Holocaust was exceptional in that there was no struggle for land or power between Germans and Jews. Most often, genocides involve a material conflict between victim and perpetrator and occur after a rebellion,

> often by an ethnically based group in the society, sometimes with a legitimate grievance of discrimination or poverty, other times...just wanting more

power or independence...States respond to these rebellions in a number of ways...one they sometimes choose, is to say 'well these rebels are supported by their ethnic group so we should target the civilians.' That can be done in a spectrum of ways, ranging from forcing the civilians to leave, which we typically call ethnic cleansing, all the way to actually killing all the civilians. With modern cases of genocide one often sees exactly those roots: first, there's a rebellion, then the government launches a brutal counterinsurgency campaign, which escalates to saying 'We have to kill all the civilians who are supporting the rebels.'[10]

For Kuperman, the actions of the victim group are more important than they are for the vast majority of genocide scholars. While Kuperman does not address the Armenian question and his mode of analysis is not central for most of those who study the Armenian genocide, it is argued in this chapter that considering the notion of genocide provocation provides useful insights into the Armenian genocide.[11] At the same time, some present-day Armenian activists and scholars fear, with some justification, that examining the provocative actions of some Armenian nationalists might be cited to legitimize the mass murder of Armenian civilians.

It is obvious that no rational group would wittingly seek to provoke total domestic genocide against its members, as it would then lack any population for the state it wished to create. Knowingly provoking a partial genocide that endangered a significant percentage of the population could be a self-defeating exercise. This qualification might be partially vitiated if there is a diaspora community similar in size to its ethnic compatriots within a country, as was the case in Rwanda. Even in this instance, it is far more likely that the insurgent group will have miscalculated the degree of repression that will be inflicted on the population whose interests it purported to champion.[12]

The genocide provocation claim that is made in the case of the Armenian nationalist groups (and also in a rather different manner about the Tutsi exile army, the Rwandan Patriotic Front (RPF)) is that they engaged in actions that facilitated genocide. In the case of the Armenians, the strategy that was allegedly employed was to provoke retaliation from the government that would spur intervention by the European powers who had long expressed a concern for the suffering of Armenians under the Ottoman government. A proponent of a genocide provocation thesis would claim that such actions—in this case, led by Turkey's Committee of Union and Progress CUP government, under conditions of war and presiding over an empire rife with previous secessions by ethnic nationalists—were taken when the CUP concluded that the Armenians posed a dire threat to the national security of Turkey. Long before the Maoist analogy of the revolutionaries being the fish and the people the water in which they swim, the CUP government had decided to drain the pond in which nationalist fish might swim. (The explicit analogy of draining the pond was made by U.S.–backed military regimes in Central America to justify the massacre and forced relocation of peasants who might side with leftist insurgencies in the 1980s.)

A corollary to the provocation thesis as formulated with regard to the Ottoman Armenians is that the Armenian nationalists, as distinguished from the mass of the Armenian people residing in the Ottoman Empire, placed their community in danger by aligning the Armenian interests so closely with the Great Powers that sought to encroach on Ottoman territory. The plight of Ottoman Christians was used by foreign powers as a pretext for intervening in the internal affairs of the Empire. The Armenian population was a de facto weapon of the empire's enemies. Despite the danger posed by a strategy of aligning with foreign powers, it is difficult to understand how those who sought Armenian autonomy or an Armenian state imagined that they could otherwise extract concessions from the Ottoman government given the vast disparity in coercive powers between the government and the nationalists. To assert that some Armenian nationalists pursued a strategy of provoking reprisals designed to attract external intervention does not require labeling the nationalists evil, but merely rational.

Genocide provocation can take more than one form. The role of the RPF in provoking a genocide against the Rwandan Tutsis in 1994 is also analyzed in this chapter. Here, the provocation claim is analytically distinct from that made in most other cases, though the moral capital argument about the manner in which a genocide is depicted is similar to that of the Ottoman Armenians. The provocation thesis here is simpler, but equally controversial. The argument is that the Tutsi-led RPF knew that its 1990 invasion of Rwanda from Uganda and pursuit of war against the regime of Hutu President Juvenal Habyarimana would likely lead to murderous reprisals against thousands of Tutsis residing in Rwanda. The RPF leaders never believed that this violence would reach the level of genocide, but they did believe that the deaths of tens of thousands of Tutsis were an acceptable price to pay for victory in the war against the Hutu regime.

Given the heated nature of nearly all discussion of genocide provocation, and of the Armenian genocide in particular, it is worth saying that a provocation thesis does not involve denial of the genocide that occurred; it does not and should not provide any moral justification for the genocide or any other repression of the Armenians or the Tutsis. This latter point is important because the threats or potential threats to the Ottoman state posed by Armenian nationalism are to this day used to justify the murder or, at the very least, deportation of the Armenians. As Taner Akçam summarizes, "The striking part of all these arguments is that they are used to justify the murder of eight hundred thousand people. No actions by gangs or individuals can justify the deaths of eight hundred thousand people...herein lies the problem in Turkey today. From this perspective, it becomes acceptable, when deemed necessary, for one ethno-religious group to carry out mass murder against another."[13] An analysis of an Armenian provocation strategy does not deny the repressive and lethal measures taken against Armenians in the decades preceding the genocide, and it also does not imply that the actions of the Armenian nationalists were the sole cause or even the primary cause of the genocide. The notion of provocation does imply that the actions of the Armenian nationalists are a part of the complex explanation for the origins of the genocide.

A similar note should be struck with regard to the Rwandan Tutsis. No acts of the RPF should be used to justify the 1994 genocide. Despite the fact that some apologists for genocide might use a provocation thesis as justification for horrific deeds, the study of provocation may lead to useful insights into the origins of genocide. Thus, it is worth pursuing an analysis of these two forms of genocide provocation as they have been applied to the cases of the Ottoman Armenians and the Rwandan Tutsis.

THE PROVOCATION THESIS
AND THE OTTOMAN ARMENIANS

Noted diplomatic historian William Langer was an early proponent of the provocation thesis. Langer claimed that Armenian revolutionary groups sought to provoke the Ottoman government to commit atrocities that would lead to intervention by the European powers that coveted territories controlled by the Ottomans.[14] Langer goes on to argue that the Armenian nationalist strategy was ineffective because the European powers never intervened on a sustained basis and thus, many Armenian lives were lost in vain.

Louise Nalbandian, a sympathetic historian of nineteenth-century Armenian revolutionary movements, has written that the initial plan of the nascent Hunchakian Revolutionary Party was for the Armenian people to profit geopolitically from the retaliatory actions of their oppressors. The early Hunchaks believed that the opportune moment to launch a rebellion would be when the Ottoman government was engaged in a war.[15] Nalbandian claims that the Hunchaks "relied in vain" on the European powers to force the Sultan to implement reforms. In Nalbandian's view, the rebellious activities of the Hunchaks in the 1890s "only helped to enrage Sultan Abdul Hamid II, who already hated the Armenians and feared that they, like the Balkan countries, would obtain their freedom."[16]

Taner Akçam notes that diplomats and other nationals of the Western countries that often championed the cause of the Armenians also believed that provoking violence was indeed a strategy of the Armenian nationalists.[17] American educator Dr. Cyrus Hamlin, the first president of Robert College, a private high school founded in Istanbul in 1863, quoted an Armenian revolutionary in an American newspaper: "The Hunchaks' armed bands...will look for the opportunity to kill Turks and Kurds and to raze their villages. The Muslims becoming wild enraged at this, will then revolt and go out and attack defenseless Armenians and kill them with such great savagery that Russia will be compelled to occupy the country in the name of humanity and Christian civilization."[18] Readers of Akçam will note that Hamlin's view nearly parallels that held by the Sultan Abdul Hamid II, who claimed that the revolutionaries were particularly seeking the support of England.

British historian Donald Bloxham rejects the crudest form of the provocation thesis with a specific rejoinder to Langer. It is worth noting that Bloxham states his rebuttal to Langer in a rather qualified manner: "There is no convincing evidence that the revolutionary leaders as a whole *desired* (emphasis in original) their actions to bring mass Armenian suffering as a way of attracting attention, though certain individuals did have this in mind. More importantly, it is clear that the parties were prepared to accept Armenian suffering as a probable by-product of their policies. The relationship between protection, agitation, and gesturing to the outside world would play itself out in a chain of calamitous events in the mid 1890s."[19] Bloxham goes on to describe Armenian nationalist resistance that resulted in huge massacres of Armenians.

An examination of the actions of Armenian revolutionary groups indicates that Bloxham is likely correct about the motives of the nationalist parties. After all, it was not only the early Hunchaks who advocated revolutionary action. The Armenian Revolutionary Federation (ARF), the Dashnaks, was also an advocate of violent action against the state. The first General Congress of the ARF met in Tiflis in 1892 and produced a document that delineated its program of a politically free Armenia and the methods by which it hoped to achieve that objective. Among the tactics to be employed were to "stimulate fighting and to terrorize government officials, informers, traitors, usurers, and every kind of exploiter; to establish communications for the transportation of men and arms; to expose government establishments to looting and destruction."[20]

On September 30, 1895, approximately 2000 Armenians demonstrated in the streets of Constantinople in support of the reform program for the eastern *vilayets* (provinces) of Anatolia. Levene argues that the charge that the September 30 demonstration by the Armenians, many of whom were armed, was designed to provoke a violent state reprisal and induce intervention by the major European powers is not proven. Still, Levene goes on to say that such a goal was likely, given that the march was organized by the Hunchaks, whom Levene calls "the most overtly revolutionary and unashamedly terroristic of the Armenian revolutionary groups."[21] The unique nature of the direct confrontation with the state in 1895 buttresses the provocation thesis. In Levene's opinion, "a more charitable view of the demonstration seems hardly plausible."[22] The armed demonstration did result in what appears to have been a state sanctioned pogrom against Armenians in Constantinople, followed by murderous assaults on Armenians in various parts of Anatolia in the months after the events in the capital.

Levene has also noted that the Dashnaks were inspired in part by the revolutionary strategies of the Russian group "Narodnaya Volya" (People's Will) that advocated terror to spark state repression, which would then engender rebellion among the masses. He goes on to argue that while this strategy was based on an ill-founded notion that state violence against the Armenians would spark Great Power intervention, it also exposed the Armenian masses to grave danger. Levene also makes the salient point that the Dashnaks confronted the state when they had no real military capacity and thus were wholly defenseless at the very time their articulation of themselves as an armed revolutionary organization permitted easy rationalization for the severe repression perpetrated by the Ottoman state.[23]

ETHNIC CLEANSING AND THE
LAST DECADES OF THE EMPIRE

Justin McCarthy has, along with other historians, provided a necessary corrective to much of the history produced by scholars of the Armenian genocide in the United States. McCarthy demonstrates that not all of the ethnic cleansing and ethnic killing in the Ottoman Empire in the late nineteenth and early twentieth centuries followed the model often posited in the West, whereby all the victims were Christian and all the perpetrators were Muslim.[24] McCarthy has shown that there were mass killings of Muslims and deportations of millions of Muslims from the Balkans and the Caucasus over the course of the nineteenth and early twentieth centuries.[25] McCarthy, who is labeled (correctly in this author's estimation) as being pro-Turkish by some writers and is a denier of the Armenian genocide, has estimated that about 5.5 million Muslims were killed in the hundred years from 1821–1922. Several million more refugees poured out of the Balkans and Russian conquered areas, forming a large refugee (*muhajir*) community in Istanbul and Anatolia.

In a review of McCarthy's book, Daniel Pipes uses these claims to argue that "it puts into perspective the deportation of Armenians in 1915 and turns this from an act of hatred into one motivated by fear (had the Armenians, with Russian support, rebelled, Ottoman Muslims could have expected to be slaughtered)."[26] Pipes postulates that what he is willing to call only the deportation (rather than genocide) of Armenians was in essence an act of preemptive self-defense. The CUP, in this view, had little choice but to kill those whose independence movement threatened the very existence of a substantial portion of the Turkish Muslims. Indeed McCarthy comes close to making this very argument as he attributes the deportations to the assistance given to the Russian army by Ottoman Armenians in World War I.[27] If one accepts fully the views put forth by McCarthy and Pipes then it would seem that ethnic cleansing was justified and thus undermines the view of Stanford Shaw and Ezel Kurel Shaw, who also deny that the Armenians were the victims of genocide, that the deportation of the Armenians was meant to be as gentle as could be expected in wartime.[28] The Shaws' account of the 1915 deportations of Armenians seems most unlikely, given that nation-states do not have a history of dispensing humane treatment to ethnic minorities that are perceived as mortal threats to their existence, especially when war places the state in grave peril.

THE WESTERN POWERS AND THE NEED FOR ALLIES

It is important to keep in mind the vast power disparities that existed between the Ottoman government and its Armenian subjects. Bloxham and most other students of the Armenian genocide have rightly rejected a two nations explanation for the genocide. The "two nations" theory posits that the Armenian genocide resulted from two nations that were locked in a mortal struggle over the same land. Justin McCarthy has provided a concise declaration of this position: "Imperialism and nationalism had created a state in which both Muslims and Armenians knew that they had the choice of killing or being killed."[29] McCarthy argues that the Armenians had armed themselves in a manner that made them a clear threat to the Ottoman government.[30] The comparison between a state such as the Ottoman Empire, battered and fragile as it might have been, and the Armenian nationalists, who were extraordinarily weak by comparison, is strained at best. If one were to add the admittedly inconsistent and self-interested support of nations such as Russia, Britain, and France to the Armenian cause, then of course the balance of power would look considerably different. The Armenian revolutionary groups would have been carrying a much larger stick than their opponents. Logic would indicate that the European powers were the best available allies for the Armenians.

If the Armenian nationalists were, in the main, not seeking to gain the support of the Western powers by provoking atrocities from the Ottoman government, then what could their strategic objective have been? If they were as hopelessly weak as most historians agree they were, then one must conclude that perhaps they did not realize just how great an imbalance of power there was between them and the state they opposed. It is possible that the revolutionary nationalists were simply delusional. In this sense, the Armenian revolutionaries who called for armed struggle against the state could be accused of reversing Theodore Roosevelt's most famous maxim and instead opted for speaking loudly and carrying a small stick. On the other hand, it would have seemed logical for an outnumbered and poorly armed minority to seek to gain the support of outside actors, the major world powers, who had an interest in weakening the Ottoman government. As noted above, such support, if consistently offered and sustained (and it clearly was not), would have altered the balance of power between the Armenians and the Turkish government. Arguing that the Armenian nationalists sought to provoke Great Power intervention is only to attribute rationality and a measure of perspicacity to insurgents who, within the Ottoman Empire, were hopelessly overwhelmed by the coercive powers of the central government.

As has been emphasized throughout this book, most genocides involve conflict between a state and a contending party that in some way poses a threat to that state. In many cases, the conflict involves a struggle over secession or control of the national government. As we saw in chapter 2, the Bengalis of East Pakistan desired, at the very least, greater autonomy from West Pakistan, and eventually independence. The Hutus and the Tutsis had been contenders for power for several decades in Rwanda before the horrific events of 1994.[31] Likewise, Armenian nationalism, to the extent that it was like all nationalisms arising in the various multi-ethnic empires in Europe and the Near East in the nineteenth and early twentieth centuries, was a potential threat to the Ottoman Empire in the same manner as the Bulgarian, Serb, and Greek nationalisms. There is, however, a reluctance to focus on the actions of victims of genocide or other lethal acts of state repression. Levene states well the motivation behind the impulse to neglect the actions of the communal group that is ultimately victimized by a genocidal state: "One might appear to be apportioning blame equally between them. Worse still, as in the case of some pro-Turkish apologetics, there is the danger of placing the blame entirely on the victims, thereby claiming that, far from being genocide, the state's actions actually constitute legitimate self-defense."[32] (Levene goes on to make what should be an obvious point, that whatever the nature of communal conflict, genocide is a never a justified response.)

Armenian nationalists had reason to believe that they could expect support from external powers in their struggle against the central government. Some scholars who argue that there was a genocide of the Armenians nevertheless support the claim that much of the concern from the West about the fate of the Armenians was designed to promote territorial and other claims against the Ottoman Empire. As the empire weakened, various Christian powers could couch their claims against the Ottomans in terms of protecting the Christian minority from persecution. In World War I, the cause of the Armenians was to serve a similar purpose for opponents of the Ottomans and their wartime allies, as it had in the preceding century. By the fall of 1915, British and French officials and the media in those nations attempted to use the massacres as war propaganda against the Germans. The slaughters were described as manifestations of German Kultur and depicted as a replication of the alleged German atrocities in Belgium.[33] According to Donald Bloxham, the actual aim of the pleading on behalf of the Armenians was to induce the United States to enter the war against Germany. Bloxham argues that the Westminster propaganda contained specific, but patently false, accusations linking German diplomatic officials in Turkey to the genocide.[34] The fact that British support for the Armenians was self-interested would not have made such aid unattractive to Armenian nationalists.

Much of the literature about the Armenians depicts them as a passive people, and there is a reluctance to discuss Armenian nationalism as a potential threat to the Ottoman Empire (and later, the Turkish state). There is also a tendency to neglect Armenian collaboration with the Russians during World War I. While the degree of collaboration is a matter of considerable dispute, Mark Levene notes that collaboration or armed involvement with the opponent of an oppressive government was a common strategy pursued by nationalist minorities during the war.[35]

Bloxham presents two important conclusions that are wholly ignored in various works on the Armenians published in the United States, including Peter Balakian's much-praised *The Burning Tigris*.[36] Bloxham argues, "First, strength of sentiment about 'suffering Christianity' only translated to policy when it coincided with material interest, as it did for Russia with the 'Bulgarian atrocities' of 1876. Secondly, atrocities against Muslims in and around the region—whether in the Crimea and the Caucasus from the time of the Crimean war, in Bulgaria in 1876 or during the Balkan wars of 1912–1913—were ignored by the Christian powers."[37] Western interest in the Ottoman Christians was clearly not motivated by purely humanitarian concerns. Nor was the killing in the declining decades of the empire as one-sided as Balakian presents it. Writers such as Balakian and Vahakn Dadrian neglect to mention the killing of Muslims in the Balkans, the wholesale deportation (and mass death) of the Muslim Circassians from the Caucasus, or the ethnic cleansing of Muslims anywhere else in the Russian empire.[38]

ROBERT MELSON: CRITIQUING THE PROVOCATION THESIS

Robert Melson argues against proponents of the provocation thesis in the case of the Armenians, stating that the thesis is fundamentally flawed given its failure to focus on the political and ideological motives of the perpetrators. In the case of the Armenians, Melson points to Turkish nationalism as a causal factor in the genocide. The identity of Muslim Ottomans was transformed as the multi-ethnic empire collapsed into a nation of Turks who could not tolerate the presence of a nationalist minority community. Pan-Turkism is the second and related factor that Melson claims motivated the CUP to eliminate the Armenians of Anatolia.[39]

Melson also dislikes the provocation thesis because, in his words, it links the victim to the perpetrator or, put slightly differently, it establishes a direct line "from the provocateur to the provoked."[40] In other words, something in the actions of the Armenians was a factor in the decision of the CUP to promote a genocidal campaign against them. Melson refutes this view by employing a Holocaust analogy, arguing that supporting the provocation thesis is the equivalent of blaming the Holocaust on the Jews, "had there been fewer Jewish Communists, or bankers, or department store owners, or journalists, or beggars there would have been no Holocaust."[41] As we have seen repeatedly, Holocaust analogies are frequently invoked when genocides are studied or debated. Yet in most cases, genocide does not resemble the circumstances of the Holocaust but actually involves more overt conflict. The resistance of the indigenous peoples in the Western Hemisphere or Africa likely contributed to a more aggressive response from those who wished to displace them. Passivity in the face of aggression might have rendered the victims less vulnerable to a murderous onslaught. The desire of the Bengalis in East Pakistan for autonomy and eventual independence was undoubtedly a factor in the genocide that left so many Bengalis dead.[42] The secessionist and nationalist aspirations and actions of various nationalities in the former Yugoslavia certainly played a role in the genocidal policies of the Milosevic regime. By comparison, the German conflict with the Jews was an invention of Nazi ideology that attributed control of world finance capital and responsibility for Bolshevism to the Jews.[43] Paradoxically, the Holocaust is the most used, and often least apt, point of comparison for group conflict that ends in genocide. Its mere assertion for purposes of comparison proves nothing.

For Melson, the actions of the victims are not irrelevant when studying genocide. Rather he argues that the "motives, perceptions, constructions, and actions both of the attackers and their targets as well as the circumstances under which they interact, must be examined for a complete explanation."[44] Despite his deep reservations about the provocation hypotheses, Melson clearly allows for agency by those who would ultimately become victims of genocide.

Melson considers Bernard Lewis's conception of the Armenian threat to the Ottoman state to be an attempt at fairness and also a succinct statement of a common perspective on the Armenian genocide. Lewis writes in his classic study, *The Emergence of Modern Turkey*,[45] of the particular threat that Armenian nationalism posed to the aspirations of Turkish nationalists:

> For the Turks, the Armenian movement was the deadliest of all threats. From the conquered lands of the Serbs, Bulgars, Albanians, and Greeks, they could, however reluctantly, withdraw, abandoning distant provinces and bringing the Imperial frontier nearer home. But, the Armenians, stretching across Turkey-in-Asia from the Caucasian frontier to the Mediterranean coast, lay in the very heart of the Turkish homeland—and to renounce these lands would have meant not the truncation, but the dissolution of the Turkish state. Turkish and Armenian villagers, inextricably mixed, had for centuries lived in neighbourly association. Now a desperate struggle between them began—a struggle between two nations for the possession of a single homeland, that ended with the terrible holocaust of 1915, when a million and half Armenians perished.[46]

For Melson, Lewis's statement implies, in the absence of other information, that the struggle was between two comparably equal forces rather than an Ottoman state with military and police forces against the Armenians, who at best had some poorly armed irregular forces. In short, Melson claims that the Armenians lacked the arms or other resources to be a credible threat to the Turkish government. What is clearly missing from this account of the balances of forces, which is indisputably correct on its face, is a fact acknowledged by Melson elsewhere in his book. Various foreign powers were, as always, ready to intervene diplomatically and rhetorically on behalf of the Armenians under the guise of humanitarian concern. This willingness was clearly demonstrated in February 1914 when the Turkish government was confronted with Western demands for the establishment of European supervision in the six eastern vilayets that had comparatively high percentages of Armenians.[47]

As Mark Levene notes, a similar arrangement had been proposed by the European powers and accepted by the Ottoman government in 1895, and only a very vulnerable state would have agreed to such a demand.[48] Levene is surely correct in viewing these interventions on behalf of the Armenians as a pretext for self-interested motives, as none of the foreign powers pressing the Ottomans were distinguishing themselves as supporters of self-determination in their policies toward subject and colonized peoples around the world. As had been the case for two decades, in the months before the outbreak of World War I, Armenians were again a pretext for foreign intervention in the already truncated Ottoman Empire. Summing up the entire Great Power policy with respect to the Ottomans and the Armenians, Levene states of the Western powers: "By giving the Armenians, for instance every incentive to see themselves as a separate nationality under Great Power protection they in effect poured a bucket of poison into Turkish-Armenian relations, yet without any intention of coming to the rescue when the Turks predictably overreacted."[49] Levene attributes the reluctance of the Western powers to intervene in a more forceful manner to their goal of gaining concessions from the Ottoman Empire without actually coming into armed conflict with one another.

Even as he seeks to refute a provocation thesis explanation of the Armenian genocide, Melson acknowledges that the appointment of external supervision in the Ottoman vilayets must have induced feelings of "humiliation" and "rage" in Turkish nationalists.[50] Still Melson argues that the peasant masses of Armenians in eastern Anatolia were not supportive of more radical nationalist goals. As was the case with many nondiaspora Tutsis residing in Rwanda in the years just prior to 1994, many Anatolian Armenians were not enthusiastic about policies or political actions that could place them in grave peril. The fact of passivity by many Armenian peasants does not demonstrate that the actions of Armenian nationalists could not have helped to provide a pretext for foreign intervention in Turkey or that the nationalists did not actively seek to provoke intervention by external powers even if they were aware of the risks to the Armenian population. The revolutionary groups might have been willing to sacrifice some substantial portion of the Armenian population to achieve their larger political goals.[51]

Feroz Ahmad has argued that the various interventions on behalf of Christian minorities were part and parcel of the Great Powers domination of the Ottoman state. Indeed, Ahmad claims that the Young Turks threatened these arrangements and their reforms undermined the great infringements on Turkish sovereignty that were imposed upon them by the imperial powers: "The Porte could not pass most laws without having them vetoed by the European embassies. Every piece of legislation was carefully vetted by legal staff of the embassies to see that it did not infringe on treaty rights of the foreigners."[52] Foreign intervention on behalf of Ottoman Christians made the putative beneficiaries of the Great Powers accomplices to the practices that the Young Turks and other nationalists regarded as humiliating violations of Turkish sovereignty. Ahmad also notes that some subjects of the Ottomans could purchase foreign protection with near immunity.

Melson writes that despite the CUP's notion that the Armenians were the deadliest of the enemies facing the Ottomans, this belief may not have been objectively true. He does not dispute, however, that the Young Turks perceived the Armenians to be a deadly threat. For Melson, the key question was whether the Young Turks' apprehensions about the Armenians rose out of the actions of the Armenians or what Melson describes as the Young Turks' "desperate situation" or Turkish nationalism.[53] Of course, the explanation for the genocide perpetrated against the Armenians need not be one dimensional. Describing the CUP's increased hostility toward the Armenians, Melson states, "Since the radical change in the perceptions of the Young Turks cannot be derived only from Armenian behavior it is entirely possible that this transformation had its origins in the altered worldview and perceptions of the CUP itself."[54] By seeming to argue that a provocation thesis is not valid unless it can provide a comprehensive explanation for the genocide of the Armenians, Melson sets a very stringent standard for historical explanation that precludes many worthwhile contributions to historical understanding. Melson's own thesis about the importance of Pan-Turanism or integral Turkish nationalism as the major cause of the Armenian genocide would likely be undermined by his own standard of valid explanation.

Noting that the great majority of the Armenian population resided in Eastern Anatolia, a region that bordered Turkey's enemy, Russia, Melson writes that "across the border was a sizable Armenian population that evinced irredentist sentiments…But by 1912, they [the Young Turks] had become integral nationalists for whom the identity and situation of the Armenians were sufficient proof of their treachery and potential threat to the continuity of the empire. This was the decisive factor in the genocide."[55] Melson makes this claim with a certainty that is probably not warranted in explaining a complex situation that would ultimately result in a wartime genocide. Furthermore, Melson's acknowledgment of a coincidence of Russian strategic interests with Armenian nationalist aspirations further weakens his claim of a primacy of nationalist or racist ideology in explaining the motivation of the genocide. It is very difficult to determine the primary causal factor in a complex series of events and, despite his contributions of our understanding of the Armenian genocide, Melson does not actually write anything that would lead one to dismiss provocation as a significant causal factor in the genocide.

WAR, NATIONALISM, AND GENOCIDE

Michael Mann provides a synthesis of much of the very highly contested literature on the genocide that facilitates some assessment of the provocation thesis. According to Mann, "This was an asymmetric clash between two rival and predominantly ethno-nationalist movements claiming ideologically plausible and practically achievable sovereignty over the same territory…Armenian nationalists were beginning to claim their own state, asserting historical legitimacy rooted in past Armenian states…they were aided by an invading great power in whose territories millions of Armenians lived. Russia was a quasi-homeland state stiffening the will of the weaker side to fight."[56] On the events of 1914–1915, Mann claims that the CUP wanted Armenian nationalists to foment insurrection within the territory of its Russian enemy in exchange for an autonomous Armenian region under CUP rule. This offer was rejected by the nationalists on the ostensible grounds that Armenians on each side of the border should remain loyal to the state under which they resided. Mann argues that, were they forced to choose, most Armenians would have chosen Russia rather than Turkey, where they had experienced severe repression. Indeed, Mann states that some Armenian memoirs recall the belief that liberation from the Ottomans would come from the Russians.[57] Mann goes on to note that while the number of Ottoman Armenians who volunteered to fight for Russia in World War I is disputed, 5,000–8,000 seems the most plausible number. While comparatively few in number, such troops were valuable because of their knowledge and contacts in eastern Anatolia.[58] (Mann's ruminations point to a fundamental contradiction in many Armenian accounts of the sources of the genocide. Readers are asked to believe that Armenians had experienced severe repression at the hands of the Ottoman regimes, but remained intensely loyal citizens of a murderous government.)

Like nearly every aspect of the deportation and killing of the Armenians that began in 1915, the degree of Armenian cooperation with the Russians is a matter of great contention. What is indisputable is that there was war in eastern Anatolia between the Russians and Ottomans, and the Russian army did advance to the city of Van. The invading army included Russian Armenians and some number of Ottoman Armenians.[59] Thus, at some level, the fears of the Sultan and later the CUP government, that Armenian nationalism was a security threat to the Ottoman state, were vindicated at least in part.

The memoir of U.S. Ambassador Henry Morgenthau in Istanbul is one of the sources most often cited as evidence of the genocidal intent of the ruling CUP. "The great trouble with the Armenians is that they are separatists." Enver Pasha the Minister of War, justified the killing and deportation of the Armenians: "They are determined to have a kingdom of their own, and they have allowed themselves to be fooled by the Russians. Because they have relied upon the friendship of the Russians, they have helped them in this war. We are determined that they shall behave just as Turks do... We don't want the Americans to feed the Armenians. That is one of the worst things that could happen to them. I have already said that it is their belief that they have friends in other countries which leads them to oppose the Government and so brings down upon them all their miseries. If you Americans begin to distribute food and clothing among them, they will then think that they have powerful friends in the United States. This will encourage them to rebellion again and then we shall have to punish them still more."[60]

Morgenthau goes on to state that "Foreign Minister Halil gave a similar explanation for refusing to allow the Americans to provide any food aid for the Armenians. Enver says that the Armenians are idealists, and that the moment foreigners approach and help them, they will be encouraged in their national aspirations. He is utterly determined to cut forever all relations between the Armenians and foreigners."[61] Based on the oft-cited Morgenthau diary, it is clear that leading perpetrators of the genocide believed that Armenian nationalist aspirations were a mortal threat to the Ottomans, especially in wartime.

In his foreword to Melson's book, the eminent genocide scholar Leo Kuper argues that the provocation thesis implies that "Armenians by reason of their revolutionary and provocative behavior were in fact the agents of their own destruction, [and that it] offers a parallel to the Nazi ideology of Jews engaged in an international conspiracy against the Third Reich."[62] It is a considerable oversimplification to argue that the provocation hypothesis must lead us to the conclusion that the Armenians were the agents of their own destruction. Kuper also makes a fallacious analogy with the Holocaust. There was no conflict between Germany and the Jews. There were no Jewish revolutionary organizations seeking independence from Germany. Nearly all parties to the disputes about the fate of the Armenian genocide admit there was ongoing conflict between the Armenians and the Ottoman regime. Kuper, too, engages in the very common practice, already discussed in this chapter, of analogizing all genocide to the Holocaust. As has been noted, the Holocaust was very different than most other genocides precisely because of the lack of any previous history of ideological, political, or territorial dispute between the perpetrators and the victims. At a minimum, it would seem fair to conclude that a thesis about genocide provocation is not refuted by referencing the Holocaust.

RWANDA: ANOTHER THEORY OF PROVOCATION

The argument for genocide provocation in the case of Rwanda is considerably different than that for the Ottoman Armenians. Unlike the Ottoman Armenians who had no organized military capacity, the Tutsis, or rather the diasporic Tutsis, had an army that was capable of fighting and ultimately defeating the military of the Hutu-dominated Rwandan government led by Juvenal Habyarimana and his National Republican Movement for Development and Democracy (MRND) party.[63] Proponents of the provocation thesis claim that the Tutsi army, the RPF, launched an invasion of Rwanda in 1990 from its base in Uganda and persisted in seeking to win an armed conflict even when presented with evidence that the continuation of combat and demands for political power would likely lead to the slaughter of tens of thousands of Tutsi living in Rwanda. Proponents of the provocation thesis assert that the RPF simply decided that the deaths of thousands of Tutsi noncombatants were an acceptable price of victory. Such a claim is not in conflict with research that focuses on the development of racist ideologies regarding the differences between Hutus and Tutsis largely rooted in colonial practices that constructed racial categories from precolonial ethnic differences.[64] Nor does it in any way obviate complex arguments that are based in political economy.[65] Proponents of provocation arguments do differ from those writers of the Rwandan genocide literature that focus almost exclusively on the actions and ideologies of the Hutu Power movement, especially those who became genocidaires, and who present the RPF as a benign political force liberating an oppressed people.[66]

Alan Kuperman has provided a clear statement of a provocation thesis with respect to Rwanda.[67] Kuperman begins with a strong version of a basic proposition about genocide and other atrocities that was introduced when examining the Ottoman Armenians, but bears repeating here in a vastly different context. In his opening paragraph, Kuperman states that "in most instances of mass killing since World War II, unlike the Holocaust, the victim group has triggered its own demise by violently challenging the authority of the state."[68] He considers several explanations for the aggressive policy of war pursued by the RPF from 1990 to 1994 that eventually ended in genocide. He rejects the notion that the RPF did not weigh the possible consequences of their actions or that they did not expect that their actions would lead to the murder of civilian Tutsis. Kuperman also rejects the notion that the RPF believed that the Tutsis in Rwanda were unlikely to suffer violent attacks irrespective of the actions of the Tutsi invaders from Uganda. Based on his interviews with many RPF officials and his analysis of the logic of their actions, Kuperman argues that the evidence points to another conclusion: well in advance of the genocide that commenced in early April 1994, the RPF fully expected that their actions might incite violence of genocidal proportions, but they regarded this horrific outcome as an acceptable price to pay for gaining power in Rwanda. Kuperman argues that at numerous points in the power struggle in Rwanda, the RPF refused to compromise on its demands even though its actions regularly provoked retaliatory violence against Tutsis residing in Rwanda, and that in the persistent drive to seize power, the RPF's own estimates of the number of atrocities committed against Rwandan Tutsis by Hutu militants grew. Referring to the early days of the genocide, Kuperman writes that "in the first two weeks alone, they killed approximately 200,000 Tutsi. Despite this the RPF clung to its strategy, refusing to compromise its demands for political power, while accepting retaliation against Tutsi civilians as the price of achieving that goal, even as the price climbed much higher than expected."[69]

In late April, the RPF reacted to the speed of the murders of the Tutsis by offering a ceasefire, but by that time the Hutu militants directing the genocide were determined to exterminate all the Rwandan Tutsis and were not interested in any compromise, but rather in completing their task of eradicating the Tutsi population in Rwanda. Kuperman notes that the indigenous Tutsis had often remarked that the RPF was willing to fight to the last Tutsi living in Rwanda. Distinguished Africa scholar Mahmood Mamdani notes, "The more sober advice offered by a wise old Tutsi man to a young RPF fighter who had come to liberate him in Ruhengeri in January, 1991: 'You want power? You will get it. But here we will all die. Is it worth it to you?'"[70]

In his book, *Africa's World War*, Gerard Prunier has provided further evidence for the provocation thesis offered by Kuperman.[71] Referring to the Tutsis killed in the genocide perpetrated by the Hutu Power, Prunier speaks of the "apparent global disdain of the RPF for the safety of the Tutsi victims."[72] He notes that the RPF military operations were never primarily aimed at stopping the killings of Tutsis and that the RPF was adamantly opposed to any external intervention to halt the genocide. (Such an intervention might have prevented a complete military victory by the Tutsi insurgents.) According to Prunier, the RPF knew since 1992 that the ideological fervor of the Hutu Power militants might result in mass killings. In Prunier's view, some RPF members regarded Tutsis residing in Rwanda as *Interahamwe* (those who fight together) collaborators and at least one RPF ideologue argued that "internal" Tutsi deserved whatever fate befell them.[73]

Mahmood Mamdani's account of the genocide provides further reason to grant credence to the Kuperman thesis. Mamdani argues that when the RPF invaders advanced, most Hutu civilians fled. Furthermore, each RPF success on the battlefield seemed to strengthen the Hutu Power elements in Rwanda. The advance of an army of Tutsi exiles could plausibly be portrayed as a restoration of the Tutsi domination that many Hutus had come to resent and that had endured longer in neighboring Burundi where President Melchior Ndadaye, a Hutu, had been assassinated by the Tutsi dominated army in 1993. In the words of Mamdani, "For the first time since the *inyenzi* (cockroaches) raids of the early 1960s, the 1990 invasion raised the specter of Tutsi power inside Rwanda. This unsurprisingly is how the Rwandan government portrayed the invasion to the population inside and to the world outside...And the fact was that many inside the country agreed that RPF rule would mean nothing but the return of Tutsi domination. The irony was that the more successful the RPF was on the battlefield, the more this came to define the political center stage, bringing the Hutu Power back from a fringe preoccupation to the mainstream of respectable politics."[74]

Kuperman's article is, like many pieces advocating such a strong point of view, somewhat selective in its focus. There is little discussion of the development of the racial theory, the Hamitic hypothesis that postulates that unlike the indigenous Hutus, the alien Tutsis are originally from the Horn of Africa. The Hamitic hypothesis was a staple of the militant Hutu ideologies.[75] Hutu activist Leon Mugesera's incendiary racist exhortation to his fellow Hutus to kill the "foreign" Tutsis, discussed below, is absent from Kuperman's article. Still, the degree of Hutu militancy and the vitriolic rhetoric that accompanied it does not detract from a provocation thesis such as that proffered by Kuperman. Indeed the very virulence of Hutu Power rhetoric and the propagation of racist theories of Rwandan history by some Hutu politicians should have served as a warning to the RPF of the possible consequences of continued military action that might restore Tutsis to power in Rwanda.

Mugesera's November 21, 1992 speech is often cited for its ominous threat to send the alien Tutsis back to Ethiopia by way of the Nyabarongo River. Scott Straus places the speech in greater perspective by citing the many passages from the address that indicate the degree of threat that Hutus felt, or in Mugesera's view, the danger they should fear from the invaders. Referring to the RPF as "*inyenzi*," Mugesera warns, "These people called *inyenzi* are on their way to attack us...Are we really waiting till they come to exterminate us? If justice is no longer serving the people as written in our constitution which we voted ourselves, this means at that point we who make up the population whom it is supposed to serve, we must do something ourselves to exterminate this rabble."[76] Repeatedly Mugesera refers to the threat facing the Hutus as he incites violence. He concludes with a reminder that even the most violent act might be self-defense: "Do not be afraid, know that anyone whose neck you do not cut is the one who will cut your neck."[77] Mugusera's words uttered more than sixteen months before the genocide commenced clearly demonstrated that at least some in the MRND were threatening the most horrific violence for Tutsis residing in Rwanda (and those who might be less than enthusiastic supporters of the Hutu Power agenda.) Whatever his actual motivation for hatred of the Tutsis, Mugesera clearly frames his speech as a response to the mortal threat to Hutus posed by the invaders.

Mamdani also believes that in the historical and political context of Rwanda in the early 1990s, the Hutus who became participants in the genocide viewed themselves as potential victims. Analyzing the masses as well as the elites who perpetrated the genocide, Mamdani observes that "if it is the struggle for power that explains the motivation for those who crafted the genocide, then it is the combined fear of a return to servitude and of retribution thereafter that energized the foot soldiers of the genocide. The irony is that…the perpetrators of the genocide saw themselves as the true victims of an ongoing political drama, victims of yesterday who may become victims of tomorrow. That moral certainty explains the easy transition from yesterday's victims to killers the morning after."[78] Surely, the RPF invasion enhanced the fears of ordinary Hutus and made the spurious claims of close identification of Rwandan Tutsis with the RPF more credible in the eyes of many of those who participated in or supported the genocide.

THE PRESIDENTIAL PLANE
CRASH AND GENOCIDE PROVOCATION

The provocation theory is further strengthened by the likely identity of the culprits in the fateful plane crash that precipitated the genocide. On April 6, 1994, the plane carrying Rwandan president Juvenal Habyarimana and the president of Burundi, Cyprien Nytaritamara, was shot down over Kigali. More than a decade after the genocide, there is still heated debate over the perpetrators of the assassination of two Hutu presidents of neighboring nations both of which had seen decades of conflict between majority Hutus and minority, but often politically dominant, Tutsis. The two primary suspects in the assassination of the two presidents would appear to be those who had the most to gain by destroying the power sharing agreement negotiated in 1993 at Arusha, Tanzania. Radical Hutu elements opposed the accord because they did not support any division of power with the Tutsi. The Committee for the Defense of the Republic (CDR), though allied to the ruling MRND, was bitterly opposed to the concessions made to the RPF in the Arusha Accords. CDR supporters or dissidents within the MRND are thought by some to have been responsible for killing Habyarimana to prevent the implementation of power sharing concessions to the RPF.

The RPF itself is the other prime suspect in the downing of the presidential plane. The RPF is thought, by those who accuse it of complicity in the duel assassination, to have had an interest in undermining the Habyarimana government and, hence the Arusha agreement, because it preferred to win complete power by military conquest rather than entering into the negotiated power sharing arrangement. A French court investigating the downing of Habyarimana's plane, because the flight crew was French, concluded that the RPF was responsible for the incident. A United Nations (UN) document, originally disclosed by the *National Post* of Canada, claimed that RPF informants acknowledged their role in the destruction of the presidential aircraft.[79] In a January 2007 interview with BBC journalist Fergal Keane, President Kagame was evasive and seemingly indifferent as to whether or not the RPF had downed Habyarimana's plane: "I care that there was a genocide here. A million people died—people have been persecuted for decades here in Rwanda. I was a refugee for nearly 30 years out of my country as result of that. Would I care that bloody Habyarimana died, someone who was president of a country that discriminated, that persecuted its own people? That Judge Bruguiere says this or France says that—I don't give a damn."[80] While not an affirmation of the charge that the RPF assassinated Habyarimana, the response was hardly a denial of the allegation.

Tensions over French allegations about the RPF were such that Rwanda broke off diplomatic relations with France in November 2006. In August 2008, a Rwandan government report claimed that the French had aided in planning the genocide and participated in massacres, and that its Operation Turquoise military deployment in the summer of 1994 had done nothing to aid the victims of the Hutu genocidaires.[81] The French government rejected the report, noting that the Rwandan government commission that produced the 500-page document had been given the explicit charge to demonstrate French complicity in the 1994 genocide.[82] As the dominant power in the Rwandan government since 1994, the RPF devotes substantial effort to denying any involvement in the events that led to the genocide that now legitimates their power. Tutsi claims to victim status would be weakened if the RPF were proved to have assassinated the Hutu president in 1994.

Scott Straus has provided a concise and clear summary of the most significant reasons why the radical Hutus and the RPF may or may not have been the culprits in the fateful events of April 6, 1994. Straus notes that the militant hard-line Hutus had some key officials on the plane and thus would have had to have been willing to kill some of their own leaders in the course of assassinating Habyarimana. Other prominent Hutu militants in the government, including the defense minister and the chief of military intelligence, were out of the country at the time. These two factors would not have made the downing of the presidential airplane the optimal method of launching the genocide of the Tutsis in April 1994. Straus further notes that neither the RPF nor the International Criminal Tribunal for Rwanda (ICTR) has produced any concrete evidence linking the Hutu extremists to the attack on the presidential plane, though each has incentives to do so.[83]

Straus sees one flaw in attributing the downing of the plane to the RPF: "The main problem with the theory is that the assassination triggered the genocide. If the theory is correct, then the RPF leadership must have miscalculated their ability to win the war quickly, the impact of the president's assassination, or the depravity of their opponents or some combination of the three."[84] The points raised by Straus do not, of course, disprove the theory that the RPF was behind the downing of the plane. Straus also does not consider explicitly the possibility that the RPF was prepared to risk widespread and violent retaliation against the Rwandan Tutsi population as an acceptable cost of winning complete political power in Rwanda.

There is some evidence for the view that the callousness of the RPF is underestimated by some writers on the 1994 genocide. The commander of the United Nations Assistance Mission for Rwanda (UNAMIR), Canadian General Romeo Dallaire, has described his meeting with Kagame in early May, a month into the genocide. Speaking of the threat to the moderate Hutus and Tutsis who were holed up in the Hotel Milles Collines in Kigali, and whose lives had been threatened in retaliation for the shelling of Kigali by the RPF, Kagame responded by denouncing the Hutus and asserting that "they are practicing their age-old black mail methods and it won't work anymore. There will be many sacrifices in this war. If the refugees have to be killed for the cause, they will be considered as having been part of the sacrifice."[85] Dallaire believed that Kagame was willing to pay any price to win the war that had been initiated in 1990. Straus, while aware of the conversation between Dallaire and Kagame, does not fully consider the possibility that the RPF was prepared to accept extensive massacres of the indigenous Tutsi as a cost of winning the war. It is likely that the RPF downed the presidential aircraft knowing that the probable outcome would be mass killings by the Hutu militants. Confident of military victory, the RPF was determined to seize power and avoid the power-sharing mandated by the Arusha Accords. Tutsis residing in Rwanda were simply collateral damage in a power struggle.

HUMANITARIAN INTERVENTION AND GENOCIDE PROVOCATION

Those who write about the Rwandan genocide with a focus on the actions—or more accurately, the inaction of the international community in response to the genocide—tend to present the RPF in a very different manner than Kuperman, and indeed the RPF is sometimes regarded as the voice of reason and moderation.[86] Samantha Power gained considerable renown with her book on American government indifference to genocide. In *A Problem from Hell: America and the Age of Genocide,* Power chronicles the largely ineffectual or often delayed actions of the U.S. government as horrific atrocities occurred in Cambodia, Iraq, the Balkans, and Rwanda.[87] For Power, the RPF was essentially an exile army that wanted only to return to its homeland and live in peace. In Power's analysis, there was no divergence of political interest between the exile Tutsis and those Tutsis who had lived within Rwanda since independence. In her presentation of the situation in 1993, only the militant Hutus had anything to lose from the Arusha Accords, and Habyarimana and the militants did indeed lose a great deal in the agreements of 1993. The incumbent could remain president until elections were held, but his was to be a symbolic role. The RPF, claiming to speak for the Rwandan Tutsis (about 15 percent of the population), were to receive 50 percent of the officer positions in the army and 40 percent of the regular soldiers were also to be Tutsi.[88] The RPF also had reasons to proceed with a war, even in the face of the well-documented mortal threat that the war posed for Tutsis in Rwanda. If there had been genuinely democratic elections in Rwanda as a result of the Arusha Accords, the RPF could never have obtained the near total power that they gained from victory in war. Power gives no consideration to the possibility that the RPF might have sought to maximize its political power. In the political struggles of Rwanda, we are left to assume that the RPF is essentially a benevolent organization. (Of course, Power is certainly correct that the RPF's victory in the war eventually halted the genocide.)

Philip Gourevitch was one of the writers to bring the Rwandan genocide into the consciousness of many readers in the United States with a series of articles in the *New Yorker* and later a book with the chilling title *We wish to inform you that tomorrow we will be killed with our children: Stories from Rwanda*.[89] Like Power, Gourevitch is appalled by the failure of UNAMIR in particular, and of the international community in general, to save the Tutsis from the murderous onslaught of the Hutu Power militants. He also presents the RPF as an army representing a people who want to come home and live in peace. The aspirations of the long-exiled Tutsis were blocked by President Habyarimana and his military regime that Gourevitch labels "totalitarian."[90] Gourevitch also takes RPF official Tito Ruteremara at his word when he says that the RPF only sought to fight its way to a negotiated peace such as that agreed to at Arusha. Ruteremara asserts that inclusion in the political process was the only goal of the RPF. Like Power, Gourevitch does not mention atrocities committed by the RPF or even consider that the RPF might have sought to impose its own dictatorial regime on the country, and that such a regime would not have been possible with a system of UN-monitored elections and a peace enforced by UNAMIR. The situation in Rwanda was never as Manichean as presented by writers such as Power and Gourevitch. (The possibility of retaliatory violence against Tutsis in response to exile invasions was evident to all with a passing knowledge of modern Rwandan history.) Mahmood Mamdani reports that Tutsi exiles launched cross-border attacks on Hutu officials in the early 1960s and that the Rwanda government of President Gregoire Kayibanda, a Hutu, responded with massacres of Tutsis living in Rwanda.[91]

Power and Gourevitch present substantial evidence that the RPF had ample reason to believe there was a danger of genocide or at the very least a mass killing of Tutsis. Both mention Leon Mugusera's explicitly genocidal speech delivered in 1992. Power also reports on the 1993 visit to Rwanda by the International Commission of Investigation that included Alison Des Forges, a long-time scholar of Rwanda. The commission reported in March 1993 that 10,000 Tutsis had been detained since the RPF invasion in 1990 and that 2,000 had been murdered. In addition, there was an increase in militias and racist rhetoric. The commission explicitly warned of the potential for genocide in Rwanda.[92] Power and Gourevitch both documented that media outlets controlled by, or sympathetic to, Hutu extremism conveyed threats against the Tutsi population.

Gourevitch presents evidence that in the years preceding the genocide, the threats against the Tutsis were extraordinarily explicit. In 1992, Stanislas Mbonampeka, the justice minister of Rwanda and a member of the Liberal Party rather than the dominant MRND, issued an arrest warrant for Leon Mugusera after the latter demanded that the Tutsis be returned to Ethiopia by way of the Nyabarongo River. Mugusera escaped arrest and eventually immigrated to Canada. Mbonampeka was dismissed from his cabinet post. A year later, Mbonampeka had, in effect, switched sides and addressed the RPF on Radio Rwanda: "Stop fighting this war if you do not want your supporters inside Rwanda to be exterminated."[93] In 1995, Mbonampeka explained his position to Gourevitch: "In a war you can't be neutral. If you are not for your country, are you not for its attackers? . . . Personally I don't believe in the genocide. This was not a conventional war. The enemies were everywhere. The Tutsis were not killed as Tutsis, only as sympathizers of the RPF."[94] Gourevitch provides ample evidence that the RPF had many reasons to believe that the Hutu Power militants were contemplating extensive killing.

Not all those who indict the West or the international community for not preventing or ending the Rwandan genocide have a comparatively benign view of the RPF. Linda Melvern issued a strong indictment of the various international actors in a book published in 2000.[95] Melvern claims that the RPF offensive of February 8, 1993 was very successful with the rebel army coming within twenty-three miles of Kigali, the Rwandan capital. The Tutsi rebels might have taken the city had it not been for French troops bolstering the Habyarimana government. Hundreds of civilians were killed and many thousands fled the advancing RPF. At this point, nearly a million people, about one seventh of the population had been displaced by the war.[96] Melvern reports that the RPF asserted that it had to launch the attack to prevent the killing of more Tutsi civilians. She also states that many in the diplomatic corps in Kigali believed that the purpose of the February offensive was to strengthen the RPF's hand at the negotiating table in Arusha.

Melvern argues that the impact of the 1993 RPF offensive greatly heightened tensions and further polarized Rwandan society. In her blunt words,

"The 1993 RPF attack had terrible consequences for the people of Rwanda."[97] She notes that the attack gave credence to those in the government who had claimed that the RPF was really interested in seizing power. "Suddenly it seemed as though all those who had warned that the RPF was acting not just for the refugees but was intent on seizing power had been right after all. All the Tutsi inside Rwanda were now labeled accomplices...and Hutu members of opposition parties were called traitors to the nation."[98] Melvern goes on to note that RPF killings, which included civil servants and women and children, harmed the RPF image among liberal opposition groups. Prime Minister Dismas Nsengiyarimye, who had viewed the RPF as moderate, began to change his views in a manner that placed him in partial agreement with more militant elements of the government and the MRND. The prime minister now supported the distribution of weapons for civil defense as long it was done in a systematic fashion. Melvern is among those who see RPF atrocities prior to 1994 as one source of the systematic violence that would erupt in 1994.

THE ARGUMENTS CONTINUE

The debate over the RPF's actions in 1994 has spilled into some very public forums. The film *Hotel Rwanda* called public attention to the genocide, highlighting the actions of Paul Rusesabagina, the manager of the Hotel des Milles Collines in Kigali who sheltered more than a thousand Tutsis in the hotel during the genocide. For saving so many lives, Rusesabagina, a Hutu married to a Tutsi woman, was hailed as an African Oskar Schindler and received numerous international awards. Rusesabagina has, however, become disillusioned with the post-genocide government of Paul Kagame, which he regards as a dictatorship benefiting the Tutsi elite.[99] In recent years, he has been very critical of the regime, calling attention to allegations that the RPF shot down Habyarimana's plane and also to killings committed by the RPF in the course of the 1990–1994 war.[100] Rusesabagina requested that the ICTR prosecutor in Arusha indict Kagame and other high-ranking RPF military officers for crimes committed against civilians in the course of the war.[101] While the Kagame government had expressed its disdain for the film before Rusesabagina became such a public and strident opponent of the regime, the government took further measures to discredit him including publishing a book entitled *Hotel Rwanda or the Tutsi Genocide as Seen by Hollywood*.[102] The book alleges that the film exaggerates Rusesabagina's role in rescuing Tutsis, but it is interesting that it also claims that it was the RPF and UN peacekeepers who saved the lives of the refugees in the Hotel des Milles Collines. More than a decade after the genocide, it is obviously important to Kagame and the RPF that the organization's reputation be unsullied and that it be seen as the sole benefactor of the Rwandan Tutsis, as it rules a de facto one-party state in Rwanda. (Kagame was re-elected with 93.08 percent of the vote after a campaign that included the unsolved murders of several opposition figures.)[103]

The RPF government deems it important to keep its reputation clean with respect to foreknowledge of the possibility that genocide might result from its invasion of Rwanda, and it is hardly surprising that it does not wish to call attention to the atrocities it committed in the pursuit of power. It is not the least bit unusual for a government to be concerned about its public image and when the question at hand is genocide, the issue engenders a great deal of emotion and passion. This is especially true in Rwanda, where the proclaimed representatives of the victim group rule over the majority in a virtual dictatorship.[104] The notion that the RPF acted with the knowledge that its actions would result in mass death or, at the very least, that it should have known of the potentially deadly consequences of its actions might undermine the moral legitimacy of the RPF government. The genocide is the moral capital and source of legitimacy for the RPF dictatorship and it is quite important to the Kagame regime that this capital be preserved.

It is worth noting that this chapter has not examined some of the unsubstantiated and more dubious claims made about the Rwandan genocide. The notion of a double genocide has been proffered by some apologists for the Hutu genocide.[105] There is no evidence that the Tutsis planned a wholesale extermination of the Hutus. A desire for political or economic domination is simply not genocide. Likewise, claiming that calling attention to Tutsi atrocities committed in the course of the civil war is a form of genocide denial, as Deborah Lipstadt does, is simply not an analytically credible claim.[106]

Finally, in the past few years, Edward S. Herman and David Peterson, consistent critics of U.S. foreign policy, have argued that the 1990 RPF incursion into Rwanda was a United States' intervention by Uganda, the Americans' alleged proxy state in the region. Furthermore, these writers claim that the RPF was responsible for more killings than Hutu Power.[107] The controversies over the sources of the mass killings of 1994 have only begun.

PROVOCATION SHOULD NOT
BE ALL THAT PROVOCATIVE

In a controversial revisionist account of what he terms the Armenian massacres (as opposed to genocide), Gunter Lewy discusses widespread rejection of the provocation thesis by many Armenian scholars and other writers sympathetic to what might be called the standard version of these events among genocide scholars in the United States. Lewy labels their rejections of the provocation thesis as "needlessly defensive."[108] Lewy rightly notes that to account for the strategies of the Armenian nationalists does not deny any malevolent intent or violent actions by the Ottoman state. An examination of the historical circumstances and the balance of power in the Ottoman Empire would indicate that it was fully rational for those seeking greater autonomy or independence for the Armenians, to pursue outside intervention. In fact, given the location of the majority of the Armenian population, it is hard to imagine that any other strategy would have succeeded. It has been argued in this chapter that following a provocation strategy would have only rendered the Armenian nationalists rational and strategic. Given the increasingly harsh measures imposed by the government of Abdul Hamid II, even the likely repressive consequences of pursuing a "provocation" strategy might have seemed less costly, in net terms, than it had previously.

It is well worth noting that even Taner Akçam, a scholar as firmly in the "Armenian camp" on the issue of whether there was a state-ordered genocide committed against the Armenians, has claimed that the CUP movement was driven by fear of partition by the European powers. Akçam also argues that the CUP opposition to Christian minorities' quest for autonomy was rooted in a fear that granting concessions would ultimately result in separatism.[109] There seems to be at least some agreement—no matter how vehement differences may be on the question of genocide—that the CUP, like the regime it succeeded, feared a further dissolution of what remained of the empire as a result of further demands by the Armenians and others.

Debates about the Armenian genocide will undoubtedly continue indefinitely, and political interests will probably determine many of the positions adopted. The one lesson that can be taken from this case is that provoking state authority from a position of weakness is a very dangerous strategy. In theory, external intervention might even the odds in an asymmetrical political struggle, but in practice, self-interested external powers may not intervene as the weaker party hoped or such intervention may arrive too late to prevent massive killing. Protests about the condition of the Armenians may have helped create a genocide in Anatolia. Such protests whether by governments, missionaries, newspapers, or churches certainly did little to aid the Ottoman Armenians.

The most provocative aspect of the provocation thesis may be that Armenians concerned about the genocide and securing official recognition of it from Turkey were willing to court deadly violence from the state. The considerable evidence that some Armenians sought to provoke violent retaliation from the central government is apparently viewed as somehow justifying genocide or at least reducing the Armenians' moral capital. From an academic perspective, dismissing a provocation analysis, because of its political implications in present politics, does not enhance understanding of the Armenian genocide or other genocides for that matter.

Research and analysis of the ethnic cleansing campaigns in the Balkans provide evidence for the notion that provoking state repression is a strategy that an insurgent or secessionist ethnic group can use to induce external intervention that can grant it parity and even better, superiority on the battlefield. Alan Kuperman asserts that Croats and Muslims in Bosnia declared independence knowing that the response from Belgrade would likely be war and violence of genocidal proportions.[110] Several Bosnian Muslim leaders interviewed by Kuperman acknowledged that provoking violence that would lead to Western intervention on their behalf was their strategy. Likewise, the Kosovo Liberation Army (KLA) rebelled against the central government in Belgrade with the full knowledge that it could not defeat the armed power of the Yugoslav state with its own arms. Rather, several of the leading figures in the KLA or the Albanian nationalist movement in Kosovo have stated that their goal was to provoke violence that would lead to NATO intervention. Emrush Xhemajli, a leading KLA officer, admitted, "We knew our attacks would not have any military value. Our goal was not to destroy the Serb military force [but to make it] become more vicious…We thought it was essential to get international support to win the war."[111] In a sense, the KLA was, in the spring of 1999, able to obtain a rather powerful air force (NATO) that enabled it to advance its political goals.

For the RPF, the provocation thesis is much more damaging than it is for the Armenian scholars and activists of the present era. Since 1994, Rwanda has been a de facto Tutsi dictatorship.[112] Moral capital accrues to the RPF as the party that stopped one of the most horrific genocides of modern times. The charge that the RPF knew there would be severe violence against the Rwandan Tutsis if they persisted in their invasion from Uganda reduces the moral stature of the RPF immensely. The charges that have emerged from the 1995 Gersony Report and from other sources, that the RPF committed numerous atrocities against Hutu civilians during their military campaign for power and against Hutu refugees in the Democratic Republic of Congo in the years afterward, while not an allegation of genocide provocation, further reduces the moral capital of the RPF.[113]

For Western advocates of humanitarian intervention in various corners of the globe, a discussion of RPF provocation, foreknowledge of genocide, and atrocities against Hutus complicates their efforts to make a case for external intervention to save lives. As has been emphasized repeatedly in this book, motive is difficult to discern, let alone to prove with certainty. Still, it would seem that a fairly clear morality tale of two opposing sides, one good and the other evil, is the best way to convince a distracted and often apathetic world that it is worth expending blood and treasure to save human lives in faraway and unknown places.

Genocide provocation should not be all that provocative as a purely academic concept. When however, victimization status is a source of legitimacy for historical or contemporary claims to recognition, restitution, or political power, the charge of genocide provocation in either form discussed in this chapter is most provocative.

CHAPTER 7

FINAL THOUGHTS

STILL OTHERS SEEK THEIR DUE

Many diaspora communities remain deeply committed to securing official and quasi-official recognition that their ancestors were victims of genocide. Former Ukrainian President Viktor Yuschenko, who left office in 2010, devoted considerable amounts of time and effort to promoting the claim that the famine in Ukraine in 1932 and 1933 was a deliberate act of genocide by the Soviet government. (Not surprisingly, there is significant debate over claims of genocide in Ukraine in academic and political circles.) The cause of Ukraine genocide recognition has been backed vigorously in Canada where there is a large population (in excess of 1 million people) of Ukrainian descent.[1] On a visit to Canada in 2008, Yuschenko focused primarily on two issues: NATO membership for Ukraine and official recognition of the famine as genocide.[2]

In 1932 and 1933, millions of Ukrainians starved to death because of a famine that was a result of government policy. There are no rational reasons to doubt that what is known as the *Holodomor* ("death by hunger" in Ukrainian) occurred. There is fierce academic debate, however, about whether the famine in Ukraine was a genocide directed against those of Ukrainian ethnicity or an indirect consequence of Soviet economic policy. This distinction mattered a great deal to the Ukrainian government when Yuschenko was in power, and it is of great importance to many of those of Ukrainian origin, the Ukrainian diaspora, around the world. Questions about the famine are not pressing issues for Yuschenko's successor and long-time rival, Viktor Yanukovich, whose political base is among Russians in Ukraine and who is also committed to close political ties with Russia.

Many diaspora groups seek recognition of their view that the deaths of millions of Ukrainians by famine was a deliberate attempt by Stalin and the Bolshevik regime to murder Ukrainians, rather than the result of policies of agricultural collectivization and forced rapid industrialization that were being imposed on the Soviet Union by the communist government.[3] In the words of Yaroslav Bilinsky, a strong advocate of the view that the Holodomor was genocide, "Stalin hated the Ukrainians...Stalin decided to collectivize Soviet agriculture and under the cover of collectivization, teach the Ukrainians a bloody lesson. Had it not been for Stalinist hubris and the incorporation of the more nationalistically minded and less physically decimated Western Ukrainians after 1939, the Ukrainian nation might have never recovered from the Stalinist offensive against the main army of the Ukrainian national movement, the peasants."[4] Bilinsky's view of the famine as an instrument of deliberate ethnic murder is not shared by all historians who study Stalin's policies with regard to agricultural collectivization.

Some scholars have argued that the mass death in Ukraine was the result of Stalinist economic policies that forcibly requisitioned grain from peasants to feed urban industrial workers and not a consequence of a deliberate attempt to suppress Ukrainian nationalism by murdering Ukrainians. Historian Barbara Green states this perspective in a succinct manner: "The purpose was not to exterminate Ukrainians simply because they were Ukrainians...The famine was the result of Stalin's effort to totally reconstruct Soviet society through rapid industrialization. The burden of industrialization, of necessity, fell most heavily on the peasants. Since Ukrainians were overwhelmingly a peasant people they suffered disproportionately."[5] For Green, and others who argue a similar economic policy case regarding the primary cause of the famine in Ukraine in the early 1930s, the mass death by famine was a consequence, rather than the intent, of Soviet actions. Similarly, Timothy Snyder argues that during the famine, the vast majority of deaths in Ukraine were in the rural areas and that mortality in cities, while high, was much lower than in the countryside.[6]

For many Ukrainians and members of the Ukrainian diaspora, recognition of the Holodomor as genocide is essential. Upon opening the website of the Holodomor education page, sponsored by the Ucrainica Research Institute in Canada, one is greeted with a tolling bell and the phrase "Holodomor, Death by Genocide." Further down the page are the words and numbers "10,000,000 Ukraine 1932-1933."[7] (Snyder believes that there were 3.3 million deaths as a result of the famine).[8] The cause of having the Holodomor officially recognized as a genocide was furthered in 2009 when the Ontario Provincial Legislature unanimously proclaimed that the fourth Saturday in November would be Holodomor Memorial Day in the province.

The League of Ukrainian Canadians (LUC) has long urged that the Holodomor, labeled as a genocide-famine, should be a compulsory component of education in each province. In the words of the LUC, "An education and human rights agenda in Canada that fails to address the *Holodomor* falls short of its goal."[9] Like many groups that advocate recognition of genocides or alleged genocides of the past, the LUC argues that there is much good to be gained from the recognition of the Holodomor, especially its alleged cautionary impact on future state actors. A pamphlet published by the LUC states that "awareness and education about this horrific man-made famine that took as many as 10 million lives in Ukraine, is crucial to preventing atrocities like this in the future."[10] It is not at all clear how such knowledge will deter future regimes that might wish to commit mass murder against a population. As with Congressional resolutions about the Armenian genocide in the United States, no evidence or even argumentation is provided in support of the assertion of the salutary impact Holodomor education would have on the world. To this point in human history, it would appear that unfortunately, the dissemination of knowledge of atrocities and genocide in various parts of the world has not prevented their recurrence in many other locales.

It is obvious that Ukrainian organizations in the United States and Canada regard Holodomor recognition and its acknowledgment as genocide, and not simply state-induced mass death, a matter of considerable importance. Like many advocates for genocide recognition in other nations, Ukrainian organizations tend to use the highest estimates of 10 million victims. Other estimates of the number of Ukrainian deaths fall in the 3 to 6 million range.[11] It would seem that there is a feeling among many who focus on their group's victim status that more moral capital accrues if the number of victims is as high as can be credibly, or even perhaps not so credibly, claimed. It is perhaps true, as Peter Novick argues, that there is a vigorous pursuit of a symbolic gold medal in suffering and that victimhood is increased by the total number of dead.[12] (Ukrainians are not the only group to seek the highest possible number of victims. For example, Novick believes that about five to ten thousand homosexuals were killed by the Nazis, yet gay activists claim that the Nazis murdered as many as a million gays.)[13] An unsettling competiveness often emerges in the study of genocide and other mass atrocities.

For Ukrainians, the notion of victimhood especially at the hands of Russians, or in the name of Russian chauvinism (Stalin was, of course, a Georgian), might be useful as moral capital, as Ukraine engages in disputes with a more powerful Russia in the early decades of the twenty-first century. Ukraine's relationship with Russia under the Yuschenko government was strained by its pursuit of NATO and EU membership, Ukrainian objections to the price Russia charges for natural gas, the disputed status of a Russian naval base at the port of Sevastopol on the Black Sea, and Russian claims that Ukraine provided arms to Georgia, which engaged in a brief war with

Russia over the breakaway regions Abkhazia and South Ossetia in the summer of 2008.[14] Claims of moral innocence and of being victims of genocide perpetrated by Russians, even decades ago, may be perceived as an aid to the image of Ukraine. Invoking the Holodomor also presents opportunities for politicians in Ukraine who wish to mobilize Ukrainian nationalist sentiment in a country with a substantial Russian minority.

GENOCIDE AND SELECTIVE INTEREST

The ongoing struggle over the classification of the Ukrainian Holodomor illustrates many of the themes explored in the preceding chapters and demonstrates that these controversies are likely to continue indefinitely. The analysis presented in this book might be viewed as terribly cynical. Scholars, activists, politicians, and ethnic organizations are depicted as acting from political or self-righteous motives. It may be that each of these groups pursues the truth as it sees the truth. The selectivity and cultural biases that are attributed to many of those who focus on the Armenian genocide are very common human traits. In most instances, the motives that have been attributed to various academics, politicians, and activists in this book are inferred, but cannot be proven. Yet, the confluence of historical perspectives and political interest occur too frequently to be mere coincidence.

In a sense, there is nothing new about an analysis that argues that the words and deeds of political actors reflect their political and economic interests. Those with an exalted view of the academy might well argue that scholars are not politicians and that their deeds are rooted in loftier motives. In the field of genocide studies, like so many other academic disciplines, some scholars may at times select only the facts that fit their worldview. Such a claim entails no imputation of particular mendacity to academics, but only asserts that they possess the same foibles as other human beings. (This claim of fallibility may not sit well with all members of the academy.)

Because of the extreme nature of genocide, we might ask those who examine it in the past, and especially those who analyze it as it occurs in the present, to strive to rise above the normal human impulse to adopt explanations of events that fit ideological predispositions, but instead allow these explanations to evolve and accommodate available evidence. In his insightful book *Facing the Extreme: Moral Life in the Concentration Camps*, Tzvetan Todorov argues that it is not reasonable to expect human beings to be morally pure, but that we might rise to a more elevated ethical dimension when confronted with a crime as horrible as genocide: "Only the saint can live in perfect truth, renouncing comfort and consolation. We can, however, set for ourselves a more modest and accessible goal: in peacetime, to care about those close to us, but in times of trouble, to find within ourselves, to expand this intimate circle beyond its usual limits and recognize as our own even those whose faces we do not know."[15] Todorov's exhortation might be applied, albeit in modified form, to scholarly, political, and journalistic discourse about genocides past and present. In this case, scholars and politicians might recognize victims of genocides as fellow human beings and aid them, where possible, with less regard for the geopolitical and ideological consequences of their actions. Such a hope is not likely to be realized, but we should not forget that idealism and aspiration are also very common human traits.

NOTES

1 A MOST SENSITIVE MATTER

1. Bernhard Schlink, *The Reader* (New York: Vintage, 2008).
2. Jacob Heilbrunn, "Telling the Holocaust Like It Wasn't," *New York Times*, January 11, 2009, WK. 5.
3. For a critique that takes the novel *The Reader* to task for presenting Schmitz as an illiterate, see Cynthia Ozick, "The Rights of History and the Rights of Imagination," *Commentary*, March 1999, 22–27.
4. The idea that Eichmann was essentially a vain, but dull, cipher who was committed to obedience was presented by Hannah Arendt in *Eichmann in Jerusalem* (New York: Viking Press, 1963). For a different perspective that depicts Eichmann as more committed to Nazi ideology, see David Caserani, *Becoming Eichmann: Rethinking the Life, Crimes, and Trial of a Desk Murderer* (New York: Da Capo Press, 2007). The well-known debate about whether the men of Police Battalion 101 were ordinary men, or more specifically ordinary Germans, is found in part in the 1998 edition of Christopher R. Browning, *Ordinary Men: Police Battalion 101 and the Final Solution in Poland* (New York: Harper Collins, 1992). For a rejoinder to Browning and an argument that eliminationist anti-Semitism was the cultural consensus in Germany for several decades preceding the Holocaust, see Daniel J. Goldhagen, *Hitler's Willing Executioners: Ordinary Germans and the Holocaust* (New York: Vintage, 1996).
5. Christopher R. Browning, *The Path to Genocide: Essays on Launching the Final Solution* (Cambridge: Cambridge University Press, 1992), 85.
6. On the Bielski brothers, see Peter Duffy, *The Bielski Brothers: The True Story of Three Men Who Defied the Nazis, Built a Village in the Forest, and Saved 1,200 Jews* (New York: Harper Perennial, 2004). Also see, Nehama Tec, *Defiance: The Bielski Partisans* (New York: Oxford University Press, 2008).
7. There were two concerts held on August 1, 1971, which were designed to raise funds to aid refugees from both the November 1970 cyclone that devastated East Pakistan and caused several hundred thousand deaths and the atrocities that commenced with the army repression in Dhaka in March 1971.
8. Private communication of August 16, 2004, in the author's possession.
9. Private communication of November 5, 2004, in the author's possession.
10. Ibid.

11. E-mail of December 3, 2004, in the author's possession.
12. Samantha Power, *A Problem from Hell: America and the Age of Genocide* (New York: Harper Perennial, 2007).
13. It should be noted, the events of 1971 are the subject of a novel by Tahmima Anam, a Bangladeshi-born woman educated in the United States and Great Britain. See Tahmima Anam, *A Golden Age* (New York: Harper Collins, 2007). Anam includes the targeting of Hindus by the Pakistani army as a major theme in her novel.
14. The controversial Bangladeshi writer Taslima Nasrin, who as of 2010 lived in exile in Sweden, has written about the more recent oppression of Hindus in Bangladesh in her polemical novel, *Shame*. See Taslima Nasrin, *Shame: A Novel* (New York: Prometheus Books, 1997).
15. For the third edition of the book that addresses this issue most directly, see Alan S. Rosenbaum, ed., *Is the Holocaust Unique?* 3rd ed. (Boulder, CO: Westview Press, 2008).
16. See other essays in Rosenbaum, *Is the Holocaust Unique?*
17. International Association of Genocide Scholars Resolutions & Statements, http://www.genocidescholars.org/resolutionsstatements.html/ (accessed July 19, 2009).
18. The case that there was a state-sponsored genocide of the Ottoman Armenians is made most persuasively in Taner Akçam's *A Shameful Act: The Armenian Genocide and the Question of Turkish Responsibility* (New York: Henry Holt, 2007).
19. Tzvetan Todorov, *Facing the Extreme: Moral Life in the Concentration Camps* (New York: Henry Holt, 1997), 156.
20. Donald Bloxham, *The Final Solution: A Genocide* (New York: Oxford University Press, 2009), 31.
21. See the first academic study of the topic, Leo Kuper, *Genocide: Its Political Use in the Twentieth Century* (New Haven, CT: Yale University Press, 1982).
22. Mahmood Mamdani, "The Politics of Naming: Genocide, Civil War, Insurgency," *London Review of Books*, March 8, 2007, http://www.lrb.co.uk/v29/n05/mamd01.html. Mamdani also presents his views on Darfur in Mahmood Mamdani, *Saviors and Survivors: Darfur, Politics, and the War on Terror* (New York: Doubleday, 2009). Mamdani argues that Darfur has experienced considerable loss of life from civil war and violence, but that no party to the conflict is guilty of genocide. He further asserts that Western governments and human rights activists have labeled the conflict "genocide" for political purposes.
23. Ibid.

2 THE POLITICS OF GENOCIDE SCHOLARSHIP: THE CASE OF BANGLADESH

1. Quoted in Leo Kuper, *Genocide: Its Political Use in the Twentieth Century* (New Haven and London: Yale University Press, 1982), 78–79.
2. East Timor was a third case of an Asian genocide that did not receive much attention in the American media. The Indonesian government was

a close Cold War ally of the United States. This interesting case will not be explored here. On East Timor, see Edward S. Herman and Noam Chomsky, *Manufacturing Consent: The Political Economy of Mass Media* (New York: Pantheon, 2002).

3. While there has been little attention paid to the Bangladesh genocide elsewhere in the West, this article focuses on the United States.

4. http://cie.kean.edu:16080/~bdgenostudy/archive/Site/Welcome.html/ (accessed August 6, 2009).

5. By 2007, a group was formed in North America to study the Bangladesh genocide. It was known as the Bangladesh Genocide Study Group and based at Kean University in New Jersey. It held a short first seminar in December 2007. http://cie.kean.edu:16080/~bdgenostudy/archive/Site/Welcome.html/ (accessed August 6, 2009). It planned a conference for October 2009.

6. Adam Hochschild, *King Leopold's Ghost: A Story of Greed, Terror, and Heroism in Colonial Africa* (Boston: Houghton Mifflin, 1998).

7. Raul Hilberg, *The Politics of Memory: The Journey of a Holocaust Historian* (Chicago: Ivan R. Dee, 2002).

8. Raul Hilberg, *The Destruction of the European Jews,* 3rd ed., 3 vols (New Haven and London: Yale University Press, 2003).

9. Hilberg, *The Politics of Memory.*

10. Peter Novick, *The Holocaust in American Life* (Boston: Houghton Mifflin, 1999).

11. Tom Segev, *The Seventh Million: Israelis and the Holocaust,* trans. from Hebrew by Haim Watzman (New York: Henry Holt, 2000).

12. Norman Finkelstein, *The Holocaust Industry: Reflections on the Exploitation of Jewish Suffering* (London: Verso, 2000).

13. Tim Cole, *Selling the Holocaust: From Auschwitz to Schindler: How History is Bought, Packaged, and Sold* (New York: Routledge, 1999).

14. George Orwell, "Notes on Nationalism," in *The Collected Essays, Journalism and Letters of George Orwell. Vol. 3: As I Please, 1943 1945*, ed. Sonia Orwell and Ian Angus (New York: Harcourt Brace Jovanovich, 1968), 370.

15. Ben Kiernan, "Cover up and Denial of Genocide: Australia, the USA, East Timor and Aborigines," *Critical Asian Studies* 34, no. 2 (June 2002): 163–92.

16. Leo Casey, "Questioning Halabja: Genocide and the Expedient Political Lie," *Dissent* (Summer 2003): 61–65.

17. Ibid.

18. Ibid.

19. Richard Sisson and Leo E. Rose, *War and Secession: Pakistan, India, and the Creation of Bangladesh* (Berkeley: University of California Press, 1990).

20. Anthony Mascarenhas, *The Rape of Bangla Desh* (New Delhi: Vikas Publications, 1971).

21. Robert Payne, *Massacre: The Tragedy of Bangladesh and the Phenomenon of Mass Slaughter throughout History* (New York: Macmillan, 1973).

22. Ibid.

23. Mascarenhas, *The Rape of Bangla Desh.*

24. Sisson and Rose, *War and Secession.*

25. A. M. A. Muhith, *Bangladesh: Emergence of a Nation* (Dhaka: University Press, 1992).

26. Rounaq Jahan, "Genocide in Bangladesh," in *Century of Genocide: Eyewitness Accounts and Critical Views,* ed. Samuel Totten, William S. Parsons, and Israel W. Charny (New York: Garland Publishing, 1997), 291–316.

27. R. J. Rummel, *Death by Government* (New Brunswick, NJ: Transaction Publishers, 1997).

28. Kalyan Chaudhuri, *Genocide in Bangladesh* (Bombay: Orient Longman, 1972).

29. Sydney H. Schanberg, "Bengalis' Land a Vast Cemetery," *New York Times,* January 24, 1972, 1.

30. Wardatul Akmam, "Atrocities against Humanity during the Liberation War in Bangladesh: A Case of Genocide," *Journal of Genocide Research* 4, no. 4 (December 2002): 543–59.

31. Eric Weitz, *A Century of Genocide: Utopias of Race and Nation* (Princeton, NJ: Princeton University Press, 2003).

32. "Convention on the Punishment and Prevention of the Crime of Genocide," December 9, 1948, available on the Office of the United Nations High Commissioner for Human Rights website at www.ohchr.org/english/law/genocide.htm (accessed June 14, 2007).

33. Robert Melson, "Modern Genocide in Rwanda: Ideology, Revolution, War, and Mass Murder in an African State," in *The Specter of Genocide: Mass Murder in Historical Perspective,* ed. Robert Gellately and Ben Kiernan (Cambridge: Cambridge University Press, 2003).

34. Robert Melson, *Revolution and Genocide: On the Origins of the Armenian Genocide and the Holocaust* (Chicago: University of Chicago Press, 1992).

35. Rohde's letter is reprinted from the Record of the U.S. Senate as "Recent Events in East Pakistan" in Sheelendra Kumar Singh et al. (eds), *Bangladesh Documents,* vol. 1 (Madras, India: B. N. K. Press, 1971), 349–51.

36. Ibid., 351.

37. Reprinted from the Record of the U.S. House of Representatives in ibid., 357.

38. James A. Michener, "A Lament for Pakistan," *New York Times Magazine,* January 9, 1972.

39. Mascarenhas, *The Rape of Bangla Desh,* 117.

40. Anthony Mascarenhas, "Genocide," reprinted from *The Times* (London), June 13, 1971, in Singh et al., *Bangladesh Documents,* 358–72.

41. Ibid.

42. Mascarenhas, *The Rape of Bangla Desh,* 116–17.

43. Jahan, "Genocide in Bangladesh," 299.

44. Mascarenhas, *The Rape of Bangla Desh.*

45. Rummel, *Death by Government.*

46. Mascarenhas, "Genocide," 371.

47. Mascarenhas, *The Rape of Bangla Desh*, 117–18.

48. Sydney H. Schanberg, "Dacca is Still Gripped by Fear 3 Months after Onslaught," *New York Times*, June 26, 1971, 1.

49. Sydney H. Schanberg, "West Pakistan Pursues Subjugation of Bengalis," *New York Times*, July 14, 1971, 1.

50. Ibid.

51. Muhith, *Bangladesh*.

52. Sydney H. Schanberg, "A Pakistani Terms Bengalis 'Chicken-hearted,'" *New York Times*, July 17, 1971.

53. Sydney H. Schanberg, "Foreign Evacuees from East Pakistan Tell of Grim Fight," *New York Times*, April 7, 1971, 1.

54. Ibid.

55. Jahan in "Genocide in Bangladesh" provides eyewitness testimony of mass rape camps established by the Pakistani army.

56. Susan Brownmiller, *Against Our Will: Men, Women and Rape* (New York: Simon & Schuster, 1975).

57. Ibid.

58. Ibid. In 2011, the rapists in Bangladesh were incorrectly identified as members of the Indian Army in *The Economist*. See "War's Overlooked Victims." *The Economist*, January 15, 2011, 63–65.

59. Muhith, *Bangladesh*.

60. Schanberg, "Dacca is Still Gripped by Fear." See also Robert Laporte, Jr., "Pakistan in 1971: The Disintegration of a Nation," *Asian Survey* 12, no. 2 (February 1972): 97–108.

61. Michael Stohl, "Outside of a Small Circle of Friends: States, Genocide, Mass Killing and the Role of Bystanders," *Journal of Peace Research* 24, no. 2 (June 1987): 151–66.

62. Akmam, "Atrocities against Humanity."

63. Ian Talbot, *Punjab and the Raj, 1849-1947* (New Delhi: Manohar Publications, 1988).

64. Ian Talbot, *Pakistan: A Modern History,* revised edition (London and New York: Palgrave Macmillan, 2005).

65. Philip Oldenburg, "'A Place Insufficiently Imagined': Language, Belief, and the Pakistan Crisis of 1971," *Journal of Asian Studies* 44, no. 4 (1985): 711–33.

66. Tariq Rahman, "Language and Politics in a Pakistan Province: The Sindhi Language Movement," *Asian Survey* 35, no. 11 (November 1995): 1005–16.

67. Paul R. Brass, "The Partition of India and Retributive Genocide in the Punjab, 1946–47: Means, Methods, and Purposes," *Journal of Genocide Research* 5, no. 1 (2003): 71–101. See also Anders Bjorn Hansen, "The Punjab 1937–1947: A Case of Genocide?" in *Genocide: Cases, Comparisons and Contemporary Debates,* ed. Steven L. B. Jensen (Copenhagen: Danish Center for Holocaust and Genocide Studies, 2003).

68. Brass, "The Partition of India." Violence between Hindus and Muslims had occurred on a smaller scale in Calcutta in 1946; see Larry Collins and Dominique Lapierre, *Freedom at Midnight* (New York: Simon & Schuster, 1975).

69. Quoted in Oldenburg, "A Place Insufficiently Imagined," 724.

70. Nazis often referred to areas that were free of Jews as a result of deportations as *judenrein,* implying that they had been cleansed of Jews.

71. Oldenburg, "A Place Insufficiently Imagined."

72. Ibid.

73. Jahan, "Genocide in Bangladesh."

74. Quoted in Oldenburg, "A Place Insufficiently Imagined," 724.

75. For Bangladesh, see Ali Riaz, *God Willing: The Politics of Islamism in Bangladesh* (Lanham, MD: Rowman & Littlefield, 2004). Indian Hindu nationalist violence against Indian Muslims is analyzed in Martha C. Nussbaum, "The Gujarat Massacre," *Dissent* (Summer 2003): 15–23.

76. There has been no investigation into the numbers of Hindus and Muslims killed in 1971, though there were obviously many victims from each religion.

77. Akmam, "Atrocities against Humanity," 553.

78. For a discussion of war as an influence on perpetrators of genocide, see Christopher R. Browning, *Ordinary Men: Reserve Police Battalion 101 and the Final Solution in Poland* (New York: Harper Collins, 1992). Placing the Holocaust in the context of World War II is a major theme in Christopher R. Browning, *The Origins of the Final Solution: The Evolution of Nazi Jewish Policy, September 1939–March 1942* (Lincoln: University of Nebraska Press, 2004).

79. Melson, *Revolution and Genocide.*

80. Stanley Wolpert, *A New History of India* (New York: Oxford University Press, 1977).

81. Secretariat of the International Commission of Jurists, *The Events in East Pakistan, 1971. A Legal Study* (Geneva: International Commission of Jurists, 1972), 9.

82. Weitz, *A Century of Genocide.*

83. Although the Pakistani army also eliminated many Bengali Muslims.

84. Henry Kissinger, *The White House Years* (Boston: Little, Brown, 1979), 855.

85. Ibid., 914.

86. Christopher Van Hollen, "The Tilt Policy Revisited: Nixon-Kissinger Geopolitics and South Asia," *Asian Survey* 20, no. 4 (April 1980): 339–61.

87. Kissinger, *The White House Years,* 854.

88. Christopher Hitchens, *The Trial of Henry Kissinger* (London and New York: Verso, 2001).

89. Quoted in Lawrence Lifschultz, *Bangladesh: The Unfinished Revolution* (London: Zed Press, 1979), 158.

90. Dennis Kux, *The United States and Pakistan, 1947–2000: Disenchanted Allies* (Washington, D.C.: Woodrow Wilson Center Press, 2001).

91. Ibid., 203.

92. Sisson and Rose, *War and Secession.*

93. Siddiq Salik, *Witness to Surrender* (Karachi: Oxford University Press, 1978).

94. Ibid., 298n9.

95. Ibid., 306n24.

96. Akmam, "Atrocities against Humanity."

97. See, for example, Gareth Porter and George C. Hildebrand, *Cambodia: Starvation and Evolution* (New York: Monthly Review Press, 1977). While they are not uncritically supportive of the policies of the Khmer Rouge, Chomsky and Herman are skeptical of claims about its atrocities. Noam Chomsky and Edward S. Herman, *After the Cataclysm: Postwar Indochina and the Reconstruction of Imperial Ideology* (Boston: South End Press, 1979). Support for the Khmer Rouge by the American Left is discussed in Samantha Power, "*A Problem from Hell: America in the Age of Genocide* (New York: Basic Books, 2002), and also in Peter Maguire, *Facing Death in Cambodia* (New York: Columbia University Press, 2005).

98. Power, *A Problem from Hell.*

99. The controversy over the Cambodian genocide is well summarized in Eyal Press, "Unforgiven: The Director of the Cambodian Genocide Program Rekindles Animosities," *Lingua Franca* (April/May 1997): 66–75.

100. David Chandler, *Voices from S-21: Terror and History in Pol Pot's Secret Prison* (Berkeley: University of California Press, 1999).

101. Ibid.

102. Alex Alvarez, *Governments, Citizens, and Genocide: A Comparative and Interdisciplinary Approach* (Bloomington: Indiana University Press, 2001).

103. Levon Chorbajian and George Shirinian, eds., *Studies in Comparative Genocide* (Basingstoke: Macmillan and New York: St Martin's Press, 1999).

104. Gellately and Kiernan, *The Specter of Genocide.*

105. Rummel, *Death by Government;* Totten, Parsons, and Charny, *Century of Genocide.*

106. Henry R. Huttenbach, "The Psychology and Politics of Genocide Denial: A Comparison of Four Case Studies," in Chorbajian and Shirinian, *Studies in Comparative Genocide.*

107. Hitchens, *The Trial of Henry Kissinger.*

108. For a critical view of Mujib's government from an author who chronicled Pakistani army atrocities in Bangladesh, see Anthony Mascarenhas, *Bangladesh: A Legacy of Blood* (London: Hodder & Stoughton, 1986).

109. Lawrence Ziring, *Bangladesh: From Mujib to Ershad: An Interpretive Study* (Karachi and Oxford: Oxford University Press, 1992).

110. Mark Levene, "The Chittagong Hill Tracts: A Case Study in the Political Economy of "'Creeping' Genocide," *Third World Quarterly* 20, no. 2 (1999): 339–69.

111. See the website of the Liberation War Museum at www.liberationwarmuseum.org (accessed June 26, 2007).

112. The issue is reported in an article in an English-language newspaper by an unidentified staff correspondent, "Zia First Proclaimer of Independence, Reprinted Liberation War History Says," *Daily Star,* July 9, 2004.

113. Riaz, *God Willing,* 20.

114. Ibid.

115. Ibid.

116. For developments in 2010, see Sebastian Strangio, "War Crimes and Bangladesh," *The Diplomat,* July 22, 2010, http://the-diplomat.com/2010/07/22/war-crimes-and-bangladesh/ (accessed July 24, 2010).

117. Novick, *The Holocaust in American Life.*

118. Frank Sysyn, "The Ukrainian Famine of 1932-3: The Role of the Ukrainian Diaspora in Research and Public Discussion," in Chorbajian and Shirinian, *Studies in Comparative Genocide.*

119. Peter Balakian, *The Burning Tigris: The Armenian Genocide and America's Response* (New York: Harper Collins, 2003).

120. The claim here is not that all academic research seeks to score political points, but that there are few political gains to be had in focusing on Bangladesh.

121. The atrocities committed during the attempt to suppress Bengali nationalism are a major focus of *A Golden Age*, a novel by Bangladeshi writer Tahmima Anam published in Britain in 2007. Anam devotes considerable attention to the very controversial topic of the violence directed against Hindus by the Pakistani army. Tahmima Anam, *A Golden Age* (New York: Harper, 2008).

3: Arguing about Cambodia: Genocide and Political Interest

1. Samantha Power, *A Problem from Hell: America in the Age of Genocide* (New York: Basic Books, 2002).

2. Ben Kiernan, "The Demography of Genocide in Southeast Asia: The Death Tolls in Cambodia, 1975–1979 and East Timor, 1975–1980," *Critical Asian Studies* 35, no. 4 (2003): 587.

3. The events in Bangladesh are discussed in chapter 2. A good summary of the genocide in Bangladesh can be found in Rounaq Jahan, "Genocide in Bangladesh," in *Century of Genocide: Eyewitness Accounts and Critical Views,* ed. Samuel Totten, William S. Parsons, and Israel W. Charny (New York: Garland, 1997).

4. Jamie Frederic Metzl, *Western Responses to Human Rights Abuses in Cambodia, 1975–1980* (New York: St. Martin's, 1996), 29.

5. Political and economic groups were excluded from protection of the genocide convention after considerable debate, likely due to Soviet objection to terming the killing of oppositional groups as genocide. See Leo Kuper, *Genocide: Its Political Use in the 20th Century* (New Haven, CT: Yale University Press, 1981).

6. Genocide as defined by the 1948 Convention of the UN General Assembly constituted various harms perpetrated against a national, ethnic, racial, or religious group. In addition to Power, *A Problem from Hell,* see Kuper, *Genocide: Its Political Use.*

7. Mark Levene, *Genocide in the Age of the Nation State: The Meaning of Genocide* (London: I. B. Taurus, 2005), 83.

8. Ibid., 84.

9. Eric D. Weitz, *A Century of Genocide: Utopias of Race and Nation* (Princeton, NJ: Princeton University Press, 2003).

10. Manus I. Midlarsky, *The Killing Trap: Genocide in the Twentieth Century* (Cambridge: Cambridge University Press, 2005).

11. Ben Kiernan, *How Pol Pot Came to Power: Colonialism, Nationalism, and Communism in Cambodia, 1930–1975* (New Haven, CT: Yale University Press, 2004).

12. Ben Kiernan, "The Cambodian Genocide," in Totten, Parsons, and Charny, *Century of Genocide,* 343. Kiernan estimated that about 10,000 urban and 10,000 rural Vietnamese were killed by the Khmer Rouge. Indeed, Pol Pot and Democratic Kampuchea radio exhorted citizens to kill as many Vietnamese as possible. More than 100,000 Vietnamese were expelled from the country. Kiernan wrote that in a year's research in Cambodia, he was unable to identify a single Vietnamese remaining in the country after the reign of the Khmer Rouge; p. 341.

13. Power, *A Problem from Hell,* 100–02.

14. Ibid.

15. Ibid.

16. Gareth Porter and George C. Hildebrand, *Cambodia: Starvation and Revolution* (New York: Monthly Review Press, 1976).

17. Ibid., 56.

18. Ibid., 97.

19. Ibid., 104.

20. Ibid., 9.

21. Hearing before the Subcommittee on International Organizations of the Committee on International Relations, House of Representatives, May 3, 1977 (Washington, D.C.: U.S. Government Printing Office, 1977), 32.

22. A classic articulation of the underdevelopment thesis appears in Andre Gunder Frank, *Capitalism and Underdevelopment in Latin America: Historical Studies of Brazil and Chile* (New York: Monthly Review Press, 1967).

23. For example, Samir Amin, *Accumulation on a World Scale: A Critique of the Theory of Underdevelopment* (New York: Monthly Review Press, 1974).

24. Samir Amin, *Imperialism and Underdevelopment* (Sussex, UK: Harvester Press, 1977).

25. Ibid.

26. Amin is quoted in Kiernan, "The Cambodian Genocide," 457.

27. Andrew Anthony, "Lost in Cambodia: The Life and Death of Malcolm Caldwell, *The Observer*, January, 10, 2010, http://www.guardian.co.uk/lifeandstyle/2010/jan/10/malcolm-caldwell-pol-pot-murder   (accessed January 21, 2011).

28. Caldwell might have considered the fate of the landlord class as presented in a well-known book highly sympathetic to the Maoist revolution as it unfolded immediately following establishment of the People's Republic of China. William Hinton, *Fanshen: A Documentary of Revolution in a Chinese Village* (New York: Vintage, 1966).

29. Malcolm Caldwell, "Revolutionary Violence in a Peoples' War," *Social Scientist* 3 (1975): 43–52.

30. Ibid., 50.

31. Ibid., 47.

32. Bob Hering and Ernst Utrecht, eds., *Malcolm Caldwell's Southeast Asia* (Townsville, Australia: Committee of South-East Asian Studies, James Cook University of North Queensland, 1979), 23; Caldwell notes that the *Reader's Digest* book was serialized on Hanoi radio. For Barron and Paul, see n. 41 below.

33. Ibid., 27.

34. Ibid., 42.

35. Ibid., 46.

36. Ibid., 49–50.

37. Ibid., 103.

38. Elizabeth Becker, *When the War Was Over: Cambodia and the Khmer Rouge Revolution* (New York: Public Affairs, 1998), 427–31.

39. See for example his *American Power and the New Mandarins: Historical and Political Essays* (New York: Vintage, 1969).

40. One of Chomsky's most recent works is *Hegemony or Survival: America's Quest for Global Dominance* (New York: Metropolitan, 2004), which was praised by Venezuelan president Hugo Chavez in the same speech that likened George W. Bush to the devil.

41. Noam Chomsky and Edward S. Herman, "Distortions at Fourth Hand," *The Nation*, June 6, 1977, 789–94.

42. John Barron and Anthony Paul, *Murder in a Gentle Land: The Untold Story of a Communist Genocide* (New York: Thomas Y. Crowell, 1977).

43. Ibid., xv.

44. Francois Ponchaud, *Cambodia: Year Zero* (New York: Henry Holt, 1978).

45. "Let's Look Out for No. 1," *New York Times Magazine*, May 1, 1977.

46. The American bombing of Cambodia is richly detailed in William Shawcross, *Sideshow: Nixon, Kissinger, and the Destruction of Cambodia* (New York: Simon & Schuster, 1979).

47. Chomsky and Herman, "Distortions," 792.
48. Ibid.
49. Ibid., 790.
50. Noam Chomsky and Edward S. Herman, *After the Cataclysm: Postwar Indochina and the Reconstruction of Imperial Ideology* (Boston: South End Press, 1979).
51. Ibid., 146.
52. Peter Maguire, *Facing Death in Cambodia* (New York: Columbia University Press, 2005). Maguire cites DC Cam document 16147 in making this assertion; 204n69.
53. Aleksandr I. Solzhenitsyn, *A World Split Apart: Commencement Address Delivered at Harvard University, June 8, 1978* (New York: Harper & Row, 1978).
54. Jean Louis Margolin, "Cambodia, the Country of Disconcerting Crimes," in *The Black Book of Communism: Crimes, Terror, Repression*, ed. Stéphane Courteois et al. (Cambridge, MA: Harvard University Press, 1999).
55. Walter Lafeber, *Inevitable Revolutions: The United States in Central America* (New York: W. W. Norton, 1993).
56. Stephen J. Morris, "The Left's Selective Outrage," *Wall Street Journal*, August 15, 1984.
57. Serge Thion, "Genocide as a Political Commodity," in *Genocide and Democracy in Cambodia*, ed. Ben Kiernan (New Haven, CT: Yale University Southeast Asia Studies, 1993), 163–90.
58. Ibid.
59. Power, *A Problem from Hell*, 146–48.
60. Ibid.
61. Becker, *When the War Was Over*, 435.
62. Kenton Clymer, "Jimmy Carter, Human Rights and Cambodia," *Diplomatic History* 27, no. 2 (April 2003): 245–78.
63. Ibid., 278.
64. Power, *A Problem from Hell*, 154
65. William Shawcross, *The Quality of Mercy: Cambodia, Holocaust and Modern Conscience* (New York: Simon & Schuster, 1984).
66. See the web page of the Yale Cambodian Genocide Project at http://www.yale.edu/cgp (accessed April 23, 2009).
67. Ibid.
68. For an example of Kiernan's early writing in support of the Khmer Rouge government, see his "Social Cohesion in Revolutionary Cambodia," *Australian Outlook* 30, no. 3 (December, 1976). Kiernan briefly discusses his change of perspective in "Bringing the Khmer Rouge to Justice," *Human Rights Review* (April–June 2000): 92–108.
69. Shawcross, *The Quality of Mercy*.
70. "The Case for U.S. Military Aid in Cambodia," *The Age* (Melbourne), October 2, 1985, http://www.abbc.net/totus/CGCF/file38arms.html/ (accessed April 13, 2009).

71. Stephen J. Morris, "The Wrong Man to Investigate Cambodia," *Wall Street Journal*, April 17, 1995.

72. Ben Kiernan, letter to the editor, *Wall Street Journal*, May 30, 1995.

73. Ibid.

74. Nancy de Wolf Smith, "America's Cambodia Coda," *Wall Street Journal*, December 19, 1996.

75. Kiernan, "Bringing the Khmer Rouge to Justice."

76. Opposing the Khmer Rouge was politically unacceptable to many U.S. conservatives from 1979 until the collapse of the Soviet Union. Those who fought against Franco in the Spanish Civil War were labeled "prematurely anti-fascist" in the McCarthy era.

77. Eyal Press, "Unforgiven: The Director of the Cambodian Genocide Program Rekindles Cold War Animosities," *Lingua Franca*, April/May 1997, 66–75.

78. Kiernan, "Bringing the Khmer Rouge to Justice," 103.

79. Shawcross, *Quality of Mercy, 358*.

80. David Chandler, *Voices from S-21: Terror and History in Pol Pot's Secret Prison* (Berkeley: University of California Press, 2000).

81. Ibid.

82. Steve Heder, "Hun Sen and Genocide Trials in Cambodia: International Impacts, Impunity, and Justice," in *Cambodia Emerges from the Past: Eight Essays*, ed. Judy Ledgerwood (DeKalb, IL: Southeast Asia Publications, 2002), 221.

83. Peter Maguire, *Facing Death in Cambodia*.

84. Ibid., 96.

85. Ibid., 97.

86. Ben Kiernan claimed in 2000 that some academics, notably Bunrouen Thach and Sorpong Peou, had written with sympathy for the Khmer Rouge during the 1990s. See "Bringing the Khmer Rouge to Justice."

87. Referring to the so-called genocidists in comments on Kiernan; book review essay, *Holocaust and Genocide Studies* 11, no. 3 (1997): 414.

88. Ibid., 417.

89. Ibid., 424.

90. For the response, see "Ben Kiernan Replies to Sorpong Peou," *Holocaust and Genocide Studies* 12, no. 1 (1998): 213–14.

91. Michael Vickery, *Cambodia: 1975–1982* (Boston: South End Press, 1984).

92. Ibid.

93. Ben Kiernan, *The Pol Pot Regime: Race, Power, and Genocide in Cambodia under the Khmer Rouge* (New Haven, CT: Yale University Press, 1996), 26.

94. Ibid., 27.

95. Stephen Heder, "Racism, Marxism, Labeling and Genocide in Ben Kiernan's *The Pol Pot Regime*," *South East Asia Research* 5, no. 2 (1997): 101–53.

96. Ibid., 103.

97. Ibid., 146.

98. Steve Heder, "Reassessing the Role of Senior Leaders and Local Officials in Democratic Kampuchea Crimes" in *Bringing the Khmer Rouge to Justice: Prosecuting the Mass Violence before the Cambodian Courts*, ed. Jaya Ramji and Beth Van Schaack (Lewiston, NY: Edward Mellen Press, 2005), 379.

99. Ibid., 407.

100. David Chandler, *Brother Number One: A Political Biography of Pol Pot* (Boulder, CO: Westview Press, 1992).

101. Ben Kiernan, review of *Brother Number One: A Political Biography of Pol Pot*, by David P. Chandler, *Journal of Asian Studies* 52, no. 4 (1993): 1076–77.

102. David Chandler, review of *The Pol Pot Regime: Race, Power and Genocide in Cambodia under the Khmer Rouge, 1975–1979*, by Ben Kiernan, *Journal of Asian Studies* 44, no. 4 (1996): 1063–64.

103. Stephen Heder, review of *Genocide and Democracy in Cambodia*, ed. by Ben Kiernan, *Phnom Penh Post*, June 16–29, 1995, 18–19.

104. Sophal Ear, "The Khmer Rouge Canon, 1975–1979: The Standard Total Academic View on Cambodia" (undergraduate political science honors thesis, University of California, Berkeley, 1995).

105. Metzl, *Western Responses*, 113.

106. Ear, "The Khmer Rouge Canon"

107. Sophal Ear, "One Side of the Two Sided Switch: Ben Kiernan and the Khmer Rouge," *Khmer Conscience* IX, no. 9 (Winter 1995), http://www.csua.berkeley.edu/~sophal/twoside.html/ (accessed September 21, 2007).

108. Metzl, *Western Responses*, 113.

109. George Orwell, "Notes on Nationalism," in *As I Please, 1943–1945: The Collected Essays, Journalism, and Letters of George Orwell*, ed. Sonia Orwell and Ian Angus (New York: Harcourt, Brace, Jovanovich, 1968), 370.

110. On the issue of rescue, see Arthur Morse, *While Six Million Died: A Chronicle of American Apathy* (New York: Random House, 1968); and David S. Wyman, *The Abandonment of the Jews: America and the Holocaust, 1941–1945* (New York: Pantheon, 1984). For a contrasting view that claims that it was not possible to bomb Auschwitz or do much else for most of Europe's Jews, see William Rubenstein, *The Myth of Rescue: Why the Democracies Could Not Have Saved More Jews from the Nazis* (London: Routledge, 1997). For interesting reflections on morality and genocide, see Tzvetan Todorov, *Facing the Extreme: Moral Life in the Concentration Camps* (New York: Phoenix, 2000).

111. Ibid. Todorov argues that humans ought to strive for a heightened moral standard when other people face a situation as dire as genocide.

4   WHO SUFFERED THE MOST? GENOCIDE STUDIES AND THE POLITICS OF VICTIMIZATION

1. For a concise argument by a uniqueness advocate, see the chapter by Steven T. Katz, "The Uniqueness of the Holocaust," in *Is the Holocaust Unique?*

Perspectives on Comparative Genocide, ed. Alan S. Rosenbaum (Boulder, CO: Westview Press, 2001).

2. Ian Hancock, "Responses to the Porrajamos: The Romani Holocaust," in Rosenbaum, *Is the Holocaust Unique?* 87.

3. Deborah Lipstadt, *Denying the Holocaust: The Growing Assault on Truth and Memory* (New York: Plume, 1994).

4. For accounts of the Irving-Lipstadt case, see D. D. Guttenplan, *The Holocaust on Trial* (New York: W. W. Norton, 2002); Richard J. Evans, *Lying about Hitler: History, Holocaust and the David Irving Trial* (New York: Basic Books, 2002); Deborah Lipstadt, *History on Trial: My Day in Court with David Irving* (New York: Ecco, 2005).

5. See all three of the books in the preceding reference.

6. Lipstadt, *Denying the Holocaust,* 212.

7. Ibid.

8. Deborah Lipstadt, "Not Facing History?" *The New Republic*, March 6, 1995.

9. It is worth recalling that in his 1984 presidential campaign, Jesse Jackson would not directly repudiate Farrakhan despite the controversial Nation of Islam leader's anti-Semitic comments and death threat against a black *Washington Post* reporter. Jackson received the bulk of his support from African Americans and was reluctant to alienate his political base.

10. Lipstadt, *Denying the Holocaust,* 7–8.

11. Evan Burr Bukey, *Hitler's Austria: Popular Sentiment in the Nazi Era* (Chapel Hill: University of North Carolina Press, 2000). Among the Austrians playing a prominent role in the Final Solution were Adolf Eichmann, Ernst Kaltenbrunner, and Franz Stangl.

12. See Christopher Browning, *The Origins of the Final Solution: The Evolution of Nazi Jewish Policy, September 1939–March 1942* (Lincoln: University of Nebraska Press, 2004). Also see Alexander B. Rossino, *Hitler Strikes Poland: Blitzkrieg, Ideology, and Atrocity* (Lawrence: University Press of Kansas, 2003). As for harvesting Aryan elements of the Polish population, see Himmler's memo, "Some Thoughts on the Treatment of the Alien Population in the East," in *Nazism: A History in Documents and Eyewitness Accounts*, ed. J. Noakes and G. Pridham (New York: Schocken Books, 1990), 932–34.

13. Browning, *Origins of the Final Solution,* 14.

14. Ibid., 15.

15. The killing of Poles by both the Nazis and the Soviet Union is discussed in Timothy Snyder, *Bloodlands: Europe between Hitler and Stalin* (New York: Basic Books, 2010).

16. Michael Burleigh, *The Third Reich: A New History* (New York: Hill & Wang, 2000).

17. It is worth recalling that the definition of genocide approved by the UN General Assembly in 1948 refers to killing and other acts of destruction against a group, "in whole or in part." See Leo Kuper, *Genocide: Its*

Political Use in the 20th Century (New Haven, CT: Yale University Press, 1981).

18. Deborah Dwork and Robert Jay Van Pelt, *The Holocaust: A History* (New York: W. W. Norton, 2002).

19. Ibid.

20. Snyder, *Bloodlands.*

21. Browning, *The Origins of the Final Solution,* 259.

22. Lipstadt, *Denying the Holocaust,* 212.

23. The vast literature on Ottoman Armenians cannot be considered here. It is analyzed in chapter 5. Two insightful recent works on the genocide are Donald Bloxham, *The Great Game of Genocide: Imperialism, Nationalism, and the Destruction of the Ottoman Armenians* (New York: Oxford University Press, 2005), and Taner Akçam, *A Shameful Act: The Armenian Genocide and the Case of Turkish Responsibility* (New York: Metropolitan Books, 2006). For an argument that many Armenians were killed, but most likely not a result of central government direction, see Gunter Lewy, *The Armenian Massacres in Ottoman Turkey: A Disputed Genocide* (Salt Lake City: University of Utah Press, 2005).

24. Akcam, *A Shameful Act.*

25. Lipstadt, *Denying the Holocaust,* 212.

26. Moshe Lewin, *Russian Peasants and Soviet Power: A Study in Collectivization* (New York: W. W. Norton, 1975).

27. J. Otto Pohl, *Ethnic Cleansing in the USSR, 1937–1949* (Westport, CT: Greenwood Press, 1999). See also, chapter 3 in Norman Naimark, *Fires of Hatred: Ethnic Cleansing in Twentieth Century Europe* (Cambridge, MA: Harvard University Press, 2002). The destruction of the kulaks and those perceived as political opponents of the regime is a focus of much of the work of Aleksandr Solzhenitsyn. See for example, Aleksandr Solzhenitsyn, *The Gulag Archipelago: An Experiment in Literary Investigation, I–II* (New York: Harper & Row, 1973).

28. Barbara B. Green, "Stalinist Terror and the Question of Genocide: The Great Famine," in Rosenbaum, *Is the Holocaust Unique?*

29. Lipstadt, *Denying the Holocaust,* 212.

30. Ben Kiernan, "The Cambodian Genocide: 1975–1979," in *Century of Genocide: Eyewitness Accounts and Critical Views,* ed. Samuel Totten, William Parsons, and Israel W. Charny (New York: Garland, 1997). There is, of course, a great deal of literature on the Cambodian genocide. See for example, Ben Kiernan, *The Pol Pot Regime: Race, Power and Genocide under the Khmer Rouge, 1975–1979* (New Haven, CT: Yale University Press, 1996).

31. Ibid.

32. See Richard J. Evans, *In Hitler's Shadow: West German Historians and the Attempt to Escape from the Nazi Past* (New York: Pantheon, 1989).

33. Arno Mayer, *Why Did the Heavens Not Darken? The Final Solution in History* (New York: Pantheon, 1990), 365.

34. See the review of Mayer's book in Christopher R. Browning, *The Path to Genocide: Essays on Launching the Final Solution* (Cambridge: Cambridge University Press, 1992).

35. Ibid., 82.

36. Mayer, *Why Did the Heavens Not Darken?* 452.

37. Lipstadt, *Denying the Holocaust,* 215.

38. Peter Novick, *The Holocaust in American Life* (New York: Houghton Mifflin, 1999).

39. "Birnbaum vs. Deborah Lipstadt," *The Morning News,* May 4, 2005, http:// www.themorningnews.org/ (accessed August 22, 2007).

40. Ibid.

41. Deborah Lipstadt, "Jimmy Carter's Jewish Problem," *Washington Post,* January 20, 2007, A20.

42. Ibid.

43. Similar allegations are made about the book by John J. Mearsheimer and Stephen M. Walt, *The Israel Lobby and U.S. Foreign Policy* (New York: Farrar, Straus & Giroux, 2007). For a negative assessment of this book, see William Grimes, "A Prosecutorial Brief against Israel and Its Supporters," *The New York Times,* September 6, 2007, E7. Also see Leslie H. Gelb's review, "Dual Loyalties," *New York Times Book Review,* September 23, 2007, 18–20. For an argument that Mearsheimer and Walt's argument is monocausal, see the review of Nils Minkmar, "Israel Unter Verdachtcht," *Frankfurter Allgemeine Zeitung,* September 8, 2007, 33.

44. Benny Morris demonstrates that the Palestinians often resisted the Zionist project. Benny Morris, *Righteous Victims: A History of Arab-Zionist Conflict, 1880–2001* (New York: Vintage, 2001).

45. Michael Massing, "The Storm over the Israel Lobby," *New York Review of Books,* June 8, 2006, 64.

46. Robert Satloff, *Among the Righteous: Lost Stories from the Holocaust's Long Reach into Arab Lands* (New York: Public Affairs Books, 2006).

47. Ibid., 164–65.

48. Ibid., 199.

49. For a discussion of selective and opportunistic concern about Kurdish victims of Saddam Hussein by the U.S. government and its critics, see Leo Casey, "Questioning Halabja: Genocide and the Expedient Political Lie," *Dissent* (Summer 2003): 61–65.

50. Ron Grossman, "DePaul, Embattled Professor End Dispute," *Chicago Tribune,* September 5, 2007.

51. For an account of Finkelstein's inability to secure employment after his tenure denial at DePaul and the tale of some professors' unsuccessful efforts to secure a job for him at California State University at Northridge, see David Klein, "Why is Norman Finkelstein Not Allowed to Teach?" http://www. csun.edu/~vcmth00m/finkelstein.html (accessed January 16, 2011).

52. Norman Finkelstein, *The Holocaust Industry: Reflections on the Exploitation of Jewish Suffering* (New York: Verso, 2000).

53. Ibid., 32.
54. Ibid., 37.
55. Ibid., 127.
56. Ibid., 68.
57. Ibid., 69.
58. Finkelstein cites an article by historian Gordon Craig that appeared in the *New York Review of Books* in 1988, a dozen years before the verdict in the Lipstadt/Irving case.
59. In addition to the incorrect claim that more Jews died of natural causes than were murdered in the years 1939–1945, Mayer also claims that the Nazi hatred of the Jews was rooted in anti-communism rather than anti-Semitism.
60. Ibid., 72.
61. *Remembering Raul Hilberg,* www.Normanfinkelstein.com (accessed August 15, 2007).
62. Guttenplan, *The Holocaust on Trial.* Lipstadt's major publications were on the American media's coverage of the Nazi persecution of the Jews and, of course, Holocaust denial.
63. Novick, *The Holocaust in American Life,* 216.
64. Edward T. Linenthal, *Preserving Memory: The Struggle to Create America's Holocaust Museum* (New York: Viking Press, 1995).
65. "Carter and the Jews," *Time,* June 21, 1976, http://www.time.com/time/printout/0,8816,918186,00.html (accessed August 23, 2007).
66. See the exit poll results for presidential elections from 1976 to 2000 in "Who Voted: A Portrait of American Politics, 1976–2000," *New York Times,* November 12, 2000, section 4, 4.
67. See "Carter and the Jews," for the 1960, 1964, and 1968 elections. Ibid. for the 1976 election.
68. Linenthal, *Preserving Memory,* 18.
69. Ibid., 27.
70. "Who Voted," *New York Times,* section 4, 4. In losing by wide margins in 1984 and 1988, Walter Mondale and Michael Dukakis won 67 and 64 percent of the Jewish vote, respectively.
71. Novick, *The Holocaust in American Life,* discusses the quote and the reasons for believing that the most likely order of victims was listed by Niemoller is the communists, the Social Democrats, the trade unionists, and the Jews.
72. Richard J. Evans, *The Third Reich in Power* (New York: Penguin Press, 2005). Burleigh, *The Third Reich.*
73. Novick, *The Holocaust in American Life,* 221.
74. Linenthal, *Preserving Memory.*
75. See Gunter Lewy, *The Nazi Persecution of the Gypsies* (New York: Oxford University Press, 2001).
76. Ian Hancock, *Responses to the Porrajamos.*
77. Linenthal, *Preserving Memory,* 238.
78. Ibid.

79. David E. Stannard, "Uniqueness as Denial: The Politics of Genocide Scholarship," in Rosenbaum, *Is the Holocaust Unique?*

80. Ibid., 250.

81. Ibid., 249–50.

82. Stannard, "Uniqueness as Denial." See Stannard's main work on Native American genocide, *American Holocaust: The Conquest of the New World* (New York: Oxford University Press, 1993). Also, Ward Churchill, *A Little Matter of Genocide: Holocaust and Denial in the Americas* (San Francisco: City Lights Books, 1998).

83. Gavriel D. Rosenfeld, "The Politics of Uniqueness: Reflections on the Recent Polemical Turn in Holocaust and Genocide Scholarship," *Holocaust and Genocide Studies* 13, no. 1, 28–61.

84. Ibid.

85. The Karaites, who resided in several places in Eastern Europe (Lithuania, Galicia, and Crimea), specifically denied that they were Jews. Raul Hilberg, *The Destruction of the European Jews, Third Edition* (New Haven, CT: Yale University Press, 2003). There was considerable debate and disagreement among the Nazi elites about how to treat Jews of mixed lineage. Mark Roseman, *The Villa, The Lake, The Meeting: Wannsee and the Final Solution* (London: Allen Lane, 2002).

86. Hilberg briefly discusses the Karaites in Raul Hilberg, *The Destruction of the European Jews,* vol. 1 (New Haven, CT: Yale University Press, 2003).

87. Roseman, *The Villa, The Lake, The Meeting.*

88. Churchill, *A Little Matter of Genocide.*

89. Ward Churchill, *Some People Push Back: On the Justice of Roosting Chickens,* http://www.kersplebedeb.com/mystuff/s11/churchill.html (accessed January 18, 2011).

90. T. R. Reid, "Professor under Fire for 9/11 Comments: Free Speech Furor Roils over Remarks," *Washington Post,* February 5, 2005, C01.

91. The committee's report on Churchill is entitled "Report of the Investigative Committee of Standing Committee on Research Misconduct at the University of Colorado at Boulder Concerning Allegations of Academic Misconduct against Professor Ward Churchill" and is available at http://www.colorado.edu/news/reports/churchill/churchillreport051606.html (accessed January 18, 2011).

92. Ibid., 4. The committee also said that the investigation was "perhaps" in response to the attacks on Churchill's "controversial publications," 3.

93. Ward Churchill, "Forbidding the G-Word: Holocaust as Judicial Doctrine in Canada," *Other Voices* 2, no. 1 (February 2000), http://www.othervoices.org/2.1/churchill/denial.html (accessed January 18, 2011).

94. Ibid.

95. Churchill, "Forbidding the G-word."

96. Ibid., FOL refers to Friends of the Lubicon, a support group for the Lubicon who are a small indigenous tribe in Alberta.

97. David Art, *The Politics of the Nazi Past in Germany and Austria* (Cambridge: Cambridge University Press, 2007).

98. "Ward Churchill Says Deborah Lipstadt is the Same as Adolf Eichmann," http://lipstadt.blogspot.com/search/label/Ward%20Churchill (accessed January 18, 2011).

99. Churchill, *A Little Matter of Genocide,* 11.

100. Peter Fritzsche, *Life and Death in the Third Reich* (Cambridge, MA: Harvard University Press, 2008). Also see George Clare, *Before the Wall: Berlin Days, 1946–1948* (New York: Dutton, 1989).

101. See the special 130-page issue of *Der Spiegel* published in 2002 as *Die Flucht der Deutschen (The Flight of the Germans). Der Spiegel* has devoted hundreds of articles to the crimes of the Nazis over many years.

102. From an anti-imperialist perspective or from a Palestinian perspective in particular, the Balfour Declaration must seem like a case of the British government promising something that they did not have a legitimate right to award.

103. Recall that the fertility comment is from Finkelstein, *The Holocaust Industry.*

104. The Iranian president made his claim about homosexuals in Iran at Columbia University in September 2007. Sewell Chan, "Iranian Leader, Calling Introductory Remarks Insulting, Addresses Columbia," http://cityroom.blogs.nytimes.com/2007/09/24/protests-at-columbia-over-iran-leaders-speech/ (accessed January 18, 2011).

5 THE DISPUTED FATE OF THE OTTOMAN ARMENIANS

1. Donald Quataert, "The Massacres of the Ottoman Armenians and the Writing of Ottoman History," *Journal of Interdisciplinary History* 27, no. 2 (2006): 249–59. For his book, see Donald Quataert, *The Ottoman Empire, 1700–1922,* 2nd ed. (Cambridge: Cambridge University Press, 2005).

2. Quataert, "The Massacres of Ottoman Armenians," 251–52.

3. Suna Erdem, "Author May Be Jailed for Speaking of Kurd Deaths," *TimesOnline,* www.Timesonline.co.uk.

4. Amberin Zaman, "Nationalists and Islamic Conservatives Stoke the Anti-European Passions," *Daily Telegraph,* September 9, 2005, www.telegraph.co.uk.

5. Arant Dink's case is discussed in Sebnem Arsu, "Turks Angry over House Armenian Genocide Vote," *New York Times,* September 12, 2007.

6. Leo Kuper, *Genocide: Its Political Use in the Twentieth Century?* (New Haven, CT: Yale University Press, 2001).

7. Heath W. Lowry, "The U.S. Congress and Adolf Hitler and the Armenians," *Political Communication and Persuasion* 3, no. 2 (1985). There is no reference to the Armenian quote in Ian Kershaw's authoritative biography of Hitler. See Ian Kershaw, *Hitler: 1936–1945: Nemesis* (New York: W. W. Norton, 2000).

8. Edward T. Linenthal, *Preserving Memory: The Struggle to Create America's Holocaust Museum* (New York: Viking Press, 1995).

9. Ibid., 232.

10. Ibid.

11. Ibid.

12. The politics of the Armenian genocide in the 29th district of California are discussed in Michael Barone and Richard Cohen, *The Almanac of American Politics, 2006* (Washington, D.C.: The National Journal, 2005).

13. Ken Dilanian, "Turkey Eases Repression of its Kurds," *Philadelphia Inquirer,* October 4, 2004, www.philly.com.

14. On the Congo wars, see Gerard Prunier, *Africa's World Wars: Congo, the Rwandan Genocide, and the Making of a Continental Catastrophe* (New York: Oxford University Press, 2008).

15. Samantha Power, *A Problem from Hell: America in the Age of Genocide* (New York: Basic Books, 2002).

16. Margaret MacMillan, *Paris, 1919: Six Months that Changed the World* (New York: Random House, 2001).

17. Vahakn H. Dadrian, *The History of the Armenian Genocide: Ethnic Conflict from the Balkans to Anatolia to the Caucasus* (Providence, RI: Berghahn Books, 1995), 356.

18. The complex relationship between the international and ethnic politics of the Ottoman Empire is covered well in Donald Bloxham, *The Great Game of Genocide: Imperialism, Nationalism, and the Destruction of the Ottoman Armenians* (New York: Oxford University Press, 2007).

19. Robert L. Daniel, "The Armenian Question and American-Turkish Relations," *The Mississippi Valley Historical Review* 46, no. 2 (September 1959): 266.

20. Mark Malkasian, "The Disintegration of the Armenian Cause in the United States, 1918–1927," *International Journal of Middle East Studies* 16 (1984): 349–65.

21. Dadrian, *The History of the Armenian Genocide.*

22. Malkasian, "The Disintegration of the Armenian Cause."

23. Richard Hovanissian, "The Armenian Genocide and Patterns of Denial," in *The Armenian Genocide in Perspective*, ed. Richard Hovanissian (New Brunswick, NJ: Transaction Publishers, 1997).

24. Lewis V. Thomas and Richard N. Frye, *The United States and Turkey and Iran* (Cambridge, MA: Harvard University Press, 1951).

25. Torben Jorgensen, "Turkey, the U.S., and the Armenian Genocide," in *Genocide: Cases, Comparisons, and Contemporary Debates*, ed. Steven L. B. Jensen (Copenhagen: The Danish Center for Holocaust and Genocide Studies, 2003).

26. Linenthal, *Preserving Memory.*

27. Ibid., 237–38.

28. Ibid.

29. Ibid.

30. Bagis's letter was distributed on H-Genocide@H-Net.MSU.edu on July 19, 2005.
31. Ibid.
32. Michael M. Gunter, *Pursuing the Just Cause of Their People: A Study of Contemporary Armenian Terrorism* (New York: Greenwood Press, 1986).
33. Stanford J. Shaw and Ezel Kural Shaw, *History of the Ottoman Empire and Modern Turkey: Volume II: Reform, Revolution and Republic: The Rise of Modern Turkey, 1808–1975* (Cambridge: Cambridge University Press, 1977), 315.
34. Ibid.
35. Richard G. Hovanissian, "The Critics View: Beyond Revisionism," *International Journal of Middle East Studies* 9 (1978): 379–88.
36. Ibid., 387–88.
37. *New York Times*, May 19, 1985.
38. See for example, *The Armenian Encyclopedia*, "Recipients of Turkish Government Money," www.armeniapedia.org. According to the Encyclopedia, 59 of the 69 scholars had received grant money from a Turkish-funded institute.
39. Stanford J. Shaw and Ezel Kural Shaw, "The Authors Respond," *International Journal of Middle East Studies* 9 (1978): 388–400.
40. Ibid., 388.
41. Ibid., 400.
42. McCarthy's view can be found in his general history of the Ottoman Empire. See Justin McCarthy, *The Ottoman Turks: An Introductory History to 1923* (London: Addsion, Wesley, Longman Limited, 1997).
43. Ibid., 365.
44. Taner Akçam, *From Empire to Republic: Turkish Nationalism and the Destruction of the Ottoman Armenians* (London: Zed Books, 2004).
45. Ibid.
46. Robert Jay Lifton, *The Nazi Doctors: Medical Killing and the Psychology of Genocide* (New York: Basic Books, 1986).
47. This entire incident is discussed at length in Roger W. Smith, Eric Markusen, and Robert Jay Lifton, "Professional Ethics and the Denial of the Armenian Genocide," *Holocaust and Genocide Studies* 9, no. 1 (1995): 1–22.
48. William H. Honan, "Princeton is Accused of Fronting for the Turkish Government," *New York Times*, May 22, 1996, B1.
49. Smith, Markusen, and Lifton, "Professional Ethics." In an interview with a Swiss newspaper in February, Mr. Pamuk said, "Thirty thousand Kurds and one million Armenians were killed in these lands and nobody but me dares to talk about it." He was referring to the conflict between the Turkish Army and Kurdish separatists and the slaughter of Armenians, which Turkey denies was genocide.
50. Israel W. Charney and Daphna Fromer, "Denying the Armenian Genocide: Patterns of Thinking as Defence-Mechanisms," *Patterns of Prejudice* 32, no. 1 (1998): 39–49.

51. Ibid., 46.
52. Ibid., 47.
53. Smith, Markusen, and Lifton, "Professional Ethics," 14.
54. Israel W. Charney, "The Psychological Satisfaction of Denials of the Holocaust or Other Genocides by Non-Extremists or Bigots, and Even by Known Scholars," *Idea: A Journal of Social Issues* 6, no. 1 (2001).
55. Smith, Markusen, and Lifton, "Professional Ethics," 14–15.
56. Hannah Arendt, *Eichmann in Jerusalem: A Report on the Banality of Evil* (New York: Penguin Books, 1994). Eichmann can be depicted in an organizational chart as heading section IV B4 of the Reich Main Security Office (RSHA or *Reichssicherheittshauptamt*), but he had a major role in the persecution of the Jews, from the German occupation of Vienna in 1938 to the murderous actions against Hungarian Jews in 1944. He was also present at the Wannsee Conference of January 20, 1942, where the implementation of the Holocaust was discussed.
57. Peter Novick, *The Holocaust in American Life* (Boston: Houghton Mifflin: 1999).
58. Smith, Markusen, and Lifton, "Professional Ethics," 15.
59. Mahmood Mamdani, *When Victims Become Killers: Colonialism, Nativism, and Genocide in Rwanda* (Princeton, NJ: Princeton University Press, 1984). See also Gerard Prunier, *The Rwanda Crisis: History of a Genocide* (New York: Columbia University Press, 1997).
60. Akçam, *From Empire to Republic,* 67.
61. Bloxham, *The Great Game of Genocide.*
62. Ibid., 128.
63. Robert Morgenthau, *Ambassador Morgenthau's Story* (New York: Doubleday, 1918) 334, 337. Quoted in Gunter, *Pursuing the Just Cause.*
64. Ibid., 276.
65. Hal Fisher, *James Bryce,* vol. 1 (New York: Macmillan, 1927), 187. Quoted in Gunter, *Pursuing the Just Cause.*
66. The mass atrocities committed by the crusaders in pursuit of Jerusalem are well known as are the persecution and expulsion that followed the unification of Spain. The conquest of Eastern Europe and Ireland is chronicled in Robert Bartlett, *The Making of Europe: Conquest, Colonization, and Cultural Change, 950–1350* (Princeton, NJ: Princeton University Press, 1993). The Albigenisan or Cathari heretics were largely exterminated in the thirteenth century. See Norman Davies, *Europe: A History* (Oxford: Oxford University Press, 1996).
67. The classic statement on the Western view of "the other" is by Edward Said in *Orientalism* (New York: Vintage, 1979).
68. Peter Balakian, *The Burning Tigris: The Armenian Genocide and America's Response* (New York: Harper Collins, 2003).
69. Ibid., 5.
70. Ben Kiernan, *Blood and Soil: A World History of Genocide and Extermination from Sparta to Darfur* (New Haven, CT: Yale University Press, 2007).

71. Ibid., 45.

72. Bloxham, *The Great Game of Genocide,* and Akçam, *From Empire to Republic.*

73. Dadrian, *The History of the Armenian Genocide.*

74. See for example, Khaled Abu El Fadl, *The Place of Tolerance in Islam* (Boston: Beacon Press, 2002).

75. John 14:6, *Holy Bible. New Revised Standard Version* (New York: Oxford University Press, 1989).

76. Mark 16:16. Ibid.

77. One might also consider the case of Australia. For a comparative study, see Ashley Riley Sousa, "They Will Be Hunted Down like Wild Beasts and Destroyed: A Comparative Study of Genocide in California and Tasmania," *Journal of Genocide Research* 6, no. 2 (2004): 193–209.

78. Caroline Elkins, *Imperial Reckoning: The Untold Story of Britain's Gulag in Kenya* (New York: Henry Holt, 2005).

79. Dennis R. Papazian, "Modern Genocide: The Case of the Nation State and Ideological Political Parties: The Armenian Case," *Idea: The Journal of Social Issues* 7, no. 1 (2002): 8.

80. Bloxham, *The Great Game of Genocide.*

81. Ibid.

82. Dennis R. Papazian, "Useful Answers to Frequent Questions about the Armenian Genocide," http://www.umd.umich.edu/dept/Armenians/facts/answers/html (accessed January 10, 2011).

83. The full text of the letter may be found on the IAGS website at http://www.genocidescholars.org/about-us/iags-resolutions-statements/ (accessed December 5, 2010).

84. On Native Americans, see the work of David Stannard, "Uniqueness as Denial: The Politics of Genocide Scholarship," in *Is the Holocaust Unique? Perspectives on Comparative Genocide, Second Edition,* ed. Alan S. Rosenbaum (Boulder, CO: Westview Press, 2001). Also David Stannard, *American Holocaust: The Conquest of the New World* (New York: Oxford University Press, 1993).

85. Mark Levene, "Creating a Modern Zone of Genocide: The Impact of Nation and State Formation on Eastern Anatolia, 1878–1923," *Holocaust and Genocide Studies* 12 (1998): 393–433.

86. See the extended discussion of Rwanda in chapter 6.

87. Levene, "Creating a Modern Zone of Genocide," 395.

88. Ibid., 421.

89. The trials are discussed briefly in Dadrian, *The Armenian Genocide,* and Bloxham, *The Great Game of Genocide.*

90. For perhaps the worst of Japanese atrocities, see Iris Chang, *The Rape of Nanking* (New York: Penguin, 1998).

91. On Native Americans, see Stannard, "Uniqueness as Denial." For an interesting comparison of the Holocaust and the Atlantic slave trade, see Seymour Drescher, "The Atlantic Slave Trade and the Holocaust: A Comparative Analysis," in Rosenbaum, *Is the Holocaust Unique?*

92. Donald Bloxham, *Genocide on Trial: War Crimes, Trials and the Formation of Holocaust History and Memory* (Oxford: Oxford University Press, 2001). Bloxham does not see the emerging conflict with the Soviet Union as the sole reason why so many prominent officials in Nazi Germany were released from custody or had sentences reduced. Interestingly, he argues that some Allied officials were not wholly unsympathetic with the crusade against Judeo-Bolshevism as the Nazis termed their murderous Operation Barbarossa campaign against the Soviet Union. U.S. and British business interests had reservations about the trial of the large industrial corporation I. G. Farben.

93. Power, *A Problem from Hell.*

6 GENOCIDE PROVOCATION? THE CASE OF THE OTTOMAN ARMENIANS AND THE RWANDAN TUTSIS

1. Raul Hilberg, *The Politics of Memory: The Journal of a Holocaust Historian* (Chicago: Ivan R. Dee, 1996). Peter Novick, *The Holocaust in American Life* (Chicago: Houghton Mifflin, 1999).

2. For a more controversial and very tendentious analysis of economic and political interest and purported exploitation of the Holocaust, recall the work discussed in chapter 4: Norman G. Finkelstein, *The Holocaust Industry: Reflection on the Exploitation of Jewish Suffering*, 2nd ed. (London: Verso, 2003).

3. Deborah Lipstadt, *Denying the Holocaust: The Growing Assault on Truth and Memory* (New York: Plume, 1994).

4. Ibid., 212.

5. Mark Levene, "Creating a Modern Zone of Genocide: The Impact of Nation and State Formation in Eastern Anatolia, 1878–1923," *Holocaust and Genocide Studies* 12 (1998): 393–433.

6. Ibid., 418.

7. Meline Toumani, "The Burden of Memory," *The Nation*, September 20, 2004, 29–42.

8. Ibid., 40.

9. Alan J. Kuperman, "Strategic Victimhood in Sudan," *New York Times*, May 31, 2006, 19; "Provoking Genocide: A Revised History of the Rwandan Patriotic Front," *Journal of Genocide Research* 6, no. 1 (2004): 61–84.

10. Alan J. Kuperman, "Genocide: The Cases of Rwanda and Sudan," *SperoNews*, May 22, 2007, http://www.utexas.edu/lbj/news/summer2007/kuperman_spero.php (accessed January 28, 2007).

11. Genocide provocation and the prospect of humanitarian intervention are explored in the essays in Timothy W. Crawford and Alan J. Kuperman, eds., *Gambling on Humanitarian Intervention: Moral Hazard, Rebellion, and Civil War* (New York: Routledge, 2006).

12. Kuperman, "Provoking Genocide," 61–84.

13. Taner Akçam, *A Shameful Act: The Armenian Genocide and the Question of Turkish Responsibility* (New York: Picador, 2007), 202–03.

14. William Langer, *The Diplomacy of Imperialism: 1890–1902*, vol. 1 (New York: Alfred A. Knopf, 1935).

15. Louise Nalbandian, *The Armenian Revolutionary Movement: The Development of Armenian Political Parties through the Nineteenth Century* (Berkeley and Los Angeles: University of California Press, 1967).

16. Ibid., 128.

17. Taner Akçam, *From Empire to Republic: Turkish Nationalism and the Armenian Genocide* (New York: Zed Books, 2004).

18. Ibid., 99.

19. Donald Bloxham, *The Great Game of Genocide: Imperialism, Nationalism, and the Destruction of the Ottoman Armenians* (New York: Oxford University Press, 2007), 51.

20. Nalbandian, *The Armenian Revolutionary Movement*, 168.

21. Mark Levene, *Genocide in the Age of the Nation State, Volume 2: The Rise of the West and the Coming of Genocide* (London: I.B. Taurus, 2005), 305.

22. Ibid.

23. Ibid.

24. Justin McCarthy, *Death and Exile: The Ethnic Cleansing of the Ottoman Muslims, 1821–1922* (Princeton, NJ: Darwin Press, 1995). McCarthy estimates that as many as 5 million Muslims were killed in the ethnic cleansing that occurred as the component parts of the Ottoman Empire gained independence or some measure of autonomy and as the Russian empire encroached on Ottoman territory in the century that he studied. Vahakn Dadrian is among the historians of the genocide who see the Turks as uniquely violent due to their Islamic faith and warrior culture. See Vahakn Dadrian, *The Armenian Genocide: Ethnic Conflict from the Balkans to Anatolia to the Caucasus*, rev. ed. (New York: Berghan Books, 2004). For a work in a similar vein, see Peter Balakian, *The Burning Tigris: The Armenian Genocide and America's Response* (New York: Harper Collins, 2003).

25. Ibid.

26. Review of McCarthy's book, *Death and Exile* in *Middle East Quarterly*, 1996. It should be noted that Pipes regards the assertion that the CUP leadership was involved in a genocide against the Armenians as evidence of bias against Turkey.

27. McCarthy, *Death and Exile*. For a western academic proffering of the view long advanced by the Turkish government that the Armenian deportations were a military necessity and that the central government ordered that great care be taken to secure the well-being of the deportees, see Stanford Shaw and Ezel Kurel Shaw, *The History of the Ottoman Empire and Modern Turkey: Reform, Revolution and Republic: The Rise of Modern Turkey, 1808–1975* (Cambridge: Cambridge University Press, 1977).

28. Shaw and Shaw, *The History of the Ottoman Empire*.

29. Justin McCarthy, *The Ottoman Peoples and the End of Empire* (London: Arnold, 2001).

30. McCarthy, *Death and Exile*. McCarthy has continued to argue in this vein in *The Armenian Rebellion at Van* (Salt Lake City: University of Utah Press, 2006).

31. Scott Straus, *The Order of Genocide: Race, Power and War in Rwanda* (Ithaca, NY: Cornell University Press, 2006).

32. Levene, "Creating a Modern Zone of Genocide," 395.

33. Bloxham, *The Great Game of Genocide.*

34. Ibid., 128.

35. Levene, "Creating a Modern Zone of Genocide."

36. Balakian, *The Burning Tigris.*

37. Bloxham, *The Great Game of Genocide,* 16.

38. On the killing of Muslims as well as Christians in Bulgaria and the fate of the Circassians, which Levene classifies as genocide, see Mark Levene, *Genocide in the Age of the Nation State, Volume 2: The Rise of the West and the Coming of Genocide* (London: I. B. Taurus, 2005).

39. Robert Melson, *Revolution and Genocide: On the Origins of the Armenian Genocide and the Holocaust* (Chicago: University of Chicago Press, 1992), 12.

40. Ibid.

41. Ibid.

42. See chapter 2.

43. In the threatening speech of January 30, 1939 that he later called his prophecy, Hitler conflated Judaism with both Bolshevism and capitalism ("international finance Jewry") in just a few sentences as he also promised that a new world war would result in the destruction of Europe's Jews. The speech is quoted in many sources. See for example, Saul Friedlander, *Nazi Germany and the Jews: The Years of Persecution, 1933–1939* (New York: Harper & Collins, 1997), 309–10.

44. Melson, *Revolution and Genocide,* 12.

45. Bernard Lewis, *The Emergence of Modern Turkey* (New York: Oxford University Press, 1961).

46. Ibid., 356.

47. Bloxham, *The Great Game of Genocide.*

48. Levene, *Genocide in the Age of the Nation State.*

49. Ibid., 225.

50. Melson, *Genocide in the Age of the Nation State,* 157.

51. Consider the case of Rwanda in the 1990s. See Kuperman, *Provoking Rebellion.* Also Scott Straus, *The Order of Genocide: Race, Power and War in Rwanda* (Ithaca, NY: Cornell University Press, 2006). Also, Romeo Dallaire, *Shake Hands with the Devil: The Failure of Humanity in Rwanda* (Toronto: Random House Canada, 2003).

52. Feroz Ahmad, *The Making of Modern Turkey* (New York: Routledge, 1993).

53. Melson, *Genocide in the Age of the Nation State,* 155.

54. Ibid., 159.

55. Ibid., 162.

56. Michael Mann, *The Dark Side of Democracy: Explaining Ethnic Cleansing* (Cambridge: Cambridge University Press, 2005), 176.

57. Ibid., 134–35.

58. Ibid., 136.

59. Donald Quataert, *The Ottoman Empire, 1700–1922* (New York, Cambridge University Press, 2000).

60. *Ambassador Morganthau's Story*, http://net.lib.byu.edu/~rdh7/wwi/comment/morgenthau/Morgen26.htm (accessed January 21, 2011).

61. Ibid.

62. Leo Kuper, "Forward," in Melson, *Revolution and Genocide*, xi.

63. The MRND was the Mouvement Nationale Revolutionaire pour Development.

64. The fact that the Tutsis held power over Hutus in precolonial times and that colonialists, especially the Belgians, built their system of control on these differences is discussed in virtually all the literature on the Rwandan genocide. A good overview of the background to genocide is Gerard Prunier, *The Rwanda Crisis, 1959–1994: History of a Genocide* (London: Hurst, 1995).

65. These factors are woven together in Helen M. Hintjens, "Explaining the 1994 Genocide in Rwanda," *The Journal of Modern African Studies* 7, no. 2 (1999): 241–86.

66. Alison Des Forges presents an uncritical view of the RPF. Alison Des Forges, *Leave None to Tell the Story: Genocide in Rwanda* (New York: Human Rights Watch, 1999).

67. Kuperman, "Genocide Provocation."

68. Ibid., 61.

69. Ibid., 78.

70. Mahmood Mamdani, *When Victims Become Killers: Colonialism, Nativism, and the Genocide in Rwanda* (Princeton, NJ: Princeton University Press, 2001), 212.

71. Gerard Prunier, *Africa's World War: Congo, the Rwandan Genocide and the Making of a Continental Catastrophe* (New York: Oxford University Press, 2009).

72. Ibid., 15.

73. Ibid., 19.

74. Mamdani, *When Victims Become Killers,* 189.

75. The Hamitic Hypothesis is discussed in Robert Melson, "Modern Genocide in Rwanda: Ideology, Revolution, War, and Mass Murder in an African State," in *The Specter of Genocide: Mass Murder in Historical Perspective*, ed. Robert Gellately and Ben Kiernan (New York: Cambridge University Press, 2003).

76. Straus, *The Order of Genocide,* 196.

77. Ibid., 197.

78. Mamdani, *When Victims Become Killers,* 233.

79. Chris Simpson, "Accusations over Rwandan Plane Crash," *BBC News,* March 3, 2000, http://news.bbc.co.uk/2/hi/africa/664863.stm. (accessed June 24, 2008).

80. Fergal Keane, "Rwanda Leader Defiant on Killing Claim," *BBC News*, January 25, 2007, http://news.bbc.co.uk/2/hi/africa/3170451.stm (accessed June 24, 2008).

81. "France Took Part in 1994 Genocide: Rwandan Report" Http://afp.google.com/article/ALeqM5jOlufsBxNXIw5nXaUj6N_f1QVvuQ

82. Gregory Viscusi, "France Says Rwandan Government Accusations 'Unacceptable.'" *Bloomberg News*, August 6, 2008, http://www.bloomberg.com.

83. Scott Straus, *The Order of Genocide*.

84. Ibid., 45.

85. Dallaire, *Shake Hands with the Devil*. 358.

86. This chapter does not address the issue of whether U.S. or other external intervention would have been desirable. See the exchange between Kuperman and Alison Des Forges in *Foreign Affairs*, May/June 2000.

87. Samantha Power, *A Problem from Hell: America in the Age of Genocide* (New York: Basic Books, 2002).

88. The Arusha Accords are discussed in Straus, *The Order of Genocide*.

89. Philip Gourevitch, *We wish to inform you that tomorrow we will be killed with our children: Stories from Rwanda* (New York: Farrar, Straus & Giroux, 1998).

90. Ibid., 94.

91. Mamdani, *When Victims Become Killers*.

92. Power, *A Problem from Hell*, 337–38.

93. Gourevitch, *We wish to inform you*, 97.

94. Ibid., 98.

95. Linda Melvern, *A People Betrayed: The Role of the West in Rwanda's Genocide* (London: Zed Books, 2000).

96. Linda Melvern, *Conspiracy to Murder: The Rwandan Genocide* (London: Verso, 2006).

97. Ibid., 43.

98. Ibid.

99. Paul Rusesabagina and Tom Zoellner, *An Ordinary Man: An Autobiography* (New York: Viking, 2006).

100. Because of his belief that Kagame was stonewalling in the investigation of the downing of the presidential plane, Rusesabagina wrote the Queen of England asking her not meet with Kagame on his visit to the United Kingdom in 2006. See the letter in "Hero of Hotel Rwanda Calls Kagame a War Criminal," www.Taylor-Report.com (accessed July 14, 2008).

101. The November 15, 2006 letter to chief ICTR prosecutor Hassan Bubacar Jallow at www.Taylor-Report.com (accessed July 14, 2008). It is listed as "Hotel Rwanda Manager Calls for the Arrest of Kagame."

102. James Cowan, "Movie Sparks Public Feud," *National Post of Canada*, April 25, 2008.

103. The leader of the Democratic Green Party, which had been prevented from running in the elections, was found beheaded in Butare in July, 2010. See Peter Beaumont, "Deadly Attacks on Rwandan Opposition Spark Warning

by U.N," *The Observer,* July 18, 2010, http://www.guardian.co.uk/world/2010/jul/18/attacks-rwandan-opposition-un-warning (accessed October 15, 2010).

104. The RPF government has also been attacked by the lawyers for defendants in the ICTR courts at Arusha. Kagame and his cohorts are often depicted as tools of the United States. See for example, Peter Erlinder, "The Great Rwanda Genocide Coverup," *Third World Traveler,* February 20, 2008, http://www.thirdworldtraveler.com/East_Africa/Rwanda_Genocide_Coverup.html (accessed October 14, 2010).

105. See Stephen R. Shalom, "The Rwandan Genocide," http://power.consumercide.com/rwanda_genocide.html/ (accessed August 2, 2009). Shalom notes that French president Mitterand referred to two genocides in Rwanda.

106. Deborah Lipstadt, "Rwanda: A New Form of Genocide Denial," *Deborah Lipstadt's Blog,* November 20, 2007, http://lipstadt.blogspot.com/search/label/Genocide%3A%20Rwanda/.

107. Edward S. Herman and David Peterson, "Rwanda and the Democratic Republic of Congo in the Propaganda System," *Monthly Review,* http://www.monthlyreview.org/100501herman-peterson.php. (accessed January 15, 2011). Herman and Peterson present their argument in much greater detail in Edward S. Herman and David Peterson, *The Politics of Genocide* (New York: Monthly Review Press, 2009). For a less ideological perspective that argues that at least 100,000 Tutsi were killed by the Hutu government in a campaign of genocide and that the RPF was directly involved in many massacres in a conflict that resulted in up to a million deaths, see Christian Davenport and Allan C. Stam, "What Really Happened in Rwanda?" *Miller-McCune,* http://www.miller-mccune.com/politics/what-really-happened-in-rwanda-3432/ (accessed January 9, 2011).

108. Gunter Lewy, *The Armenian Massacres in Ottoman Turkey: A Disputed Genocide* (Salt Lake City: University of Utah Press, 2005), 17.

109. Akçam, *A Shameful Act,* 204–05.

110. Alan J. Kuperman, "Suicidal Rebellions and the Moral Hazard of Humanitarian Intervention," *Ethnopolitics* 4, no. 2 (2005): 149–73.

111. Ibid., 160.

112. For a brief 2010 overview of the political and economic status update that reports on the absence of political freedom in Rwanda, see "Divisionists Beware," *The Economist,* March 6, 2010, 65.

113. On the Gersony Report and other actions against Hutus by the RPF, see Prunier, *Africa's World War.*

7 FINAL THOUGHTS

1. On Yuschenko's view of the famine and his emphasis of it during a visit to Canada in 2008, see Mitch Potter, "President Starts Visit at Ottawa's Holodomor Memorial," *Toronto Star,* May 25, 2008, www.thestar.com (accessed January 9, 2011).

2. Olivia Ward, "Yuschenko Gets Hero's Welcome in Toronto," *Toronto Star*, May 29, 2008, www.thestar.com (accessed January 9, 2011).

3. The case that the famine was a direct attempt to kill Ukrainians is argued succinctly by Yaroslav Bilinsky in "Was the Ukrainian Famine of 1932–1933 a Genocide?" *Journal of Genocide Research* 1, no. 2 (1999): 147–56.

4. Ibid., 155–56.

5. Barbara B. Green, "Stalinist Terror and the Consequence of Genocide: The Great Famine," in *Is the Holocaust Unique? Perspectives on Comparative Genocide*, 3rd ed., ed. Alan S. Rosenbaum (Boulder, CO: Westview Press, 2009), 175–200.

6. Timothy Snyder, *Bloodlands: Europe between Hitler and Stalin* (New York: Basic Books, 2010).

7. Ten million is at the very highest end of the estimates of Ukrainians who died in 1932–1933, http://www.holodomoreducation.org/ (accessed August 6, 2010).

8. Snyder, *Bloodlands.*

9. "At the Forefront of Ukrainian Issues: Holodmor Awareness, http://www.lucorg.com/block.php/block_id/15/ (accessed August 5, 2009).

10. Pamphlet entitled *Holodomor Education,* sponsored by the League of Ukrainian Canadians, in the possession of the author.

11. See the general survey of deaths that resulted from Stalin's policies in Ben Kiernan, *Blood and Soil: A World History of Genocide and Extermination from Sparta to Darfur* (New Haven, CT: Yale University Press, 2007).

12. Peter Novick, *The Holocaust in American Life* (New York: Houghton Mifflin, 1999).

13. Ibid., 223.

14. Catherine Belton and Roman Olearchyk, "Medvedev Ultimatum to Ukraine Leadership," *Financial Times*, August 12, 2009, 1. The Russian naval lease at Sevastopol, due to expire in 2017, was renewed for at least 25 additional years in a 2010 treaty negotiated by the newly elected Yanukovich government, which is perceived by many observers as far more pro-Russian than was the regime of President Yuschenko.

15. Tzvetan Todorov, *Facing the Extreme: Moral Life in the Concentration Camps* (New York: Henry Holt, 1997). 253.

BIBLIOGRAPHY

Ahmad, Feroz. *The Making of Modern Turkey*. New York: Routledge, 1993.

Akçam, Taner. *From Empire to Republic: Turkish Nationalism and the Destruction of the Ottoman Armenians*. London: Zed Books, 2004.

———. *A Shameful Act: The Armenian Genocide and the Question of Turkish Responsibility*. New York: Henry Holt, 2007.

Akmam, Wardatul. "Atrocities against Humanity during the Liberation War in Bangladesh: A Case of Genocide." *Journal of Genocide Research* 4, no. 4 (December 2002): 543–59.

Alvarez, Alex. *Governments, Citizens, and Genocide: A Comparative and Interdisciplinary Approach*. Bloomington: Indiana University Press, 2001.

Amin, Samir. *Imperialism and Underdevelopment*. Sussex, UK: Harvester Press, 1977.

Anam, Tahmima. *A Golden Age*. New York: Harper Collins, 2007.

Arendt, Hannah. *Eichmann in Jerusalem*. New York: Viking Press, 1963.

Art, David. *The Politics of the Nazi Past in Germany and Austria*. Cambridge: Cambridge University Press, 2007.

Balakian, Peter. *The Burning Tigris: The Armenian Genocide and America's Response*. New York: HarperCollins, 2003.

Barron, John, and Anthony Paul. *Murder in a Gentle Land: The Untold Story of a Communist Genocide*. New York: Thomas Y. Crowell, 1977.

Bartlett, Robert. *The Making of Europe: Conquest, Colonization, and Cultural Change, 950–1350*. Princeton, NJ: Princeton University Press, 1993.

Becker, Elizabeth. *When the War Was Over: Cambodia and the Khmer Rouge Revolution*. New York: Public Affairs, 1998.

Bilinsky, Yaroslav. "Was the Ukrainian Famine of 1932–1933 a Genocide?" *Journal of Genocide Research* 1, no. 2 (1999): 147–56.

Bloxham, Donald. *Genocide on Trial: War Crimes, Trials and the Formation of Holocaust History and Memory*. Oxford: Oxford University Press, 2001.

———. *The Great Empire Game of Genocide: Imperialism, Nationalism, and the Destruction of the Ottoman Armenians*. New York: Oxford University Press, 2007.

———. *The Final Solution: A Genocide*. New York: Oxford University Press, 2009.

Brass, Paul R. "The Partition of India and Retributive Genocide in the Punjab, 1946–47: Means, Methods, and Purposes." *Journal of Genocide Research* 5, no. 1 (2003): 71–101.

Browning, Christopher R. *Ordinary Men: Police Battalion 101 and the Final Solution in Poland*. New York: Harper Collins, 1992.

———. *The Path to Genocide: Essays on Launching the Final Solution*. Cambridge: Cambridge University Press, 1992.

———. *The Origins of the Final Solution: The Evolution of Nazi Jewish Policy, September 1939–March 1942*. Lincoln: University of Nebraska Press, 2004.

Burr Bukey, Evan. *Hitler's Austria: Popular Sentiment in the Nazi Era*. Chapel Hill: University of North Carolina Press, 2000.

Burleigh, Michael. *The Third Reich: A New History*. New York: Hill & Wang, 2000.

Caserani, David. *Becoming Eichmann: Rethinking the Life, Crimes, and Trial of a Desk Murderer*. New York: Da Capo Press, 2007.

Caldwell, Malcolm. "Revolutionary Violence in a Peoples' War." *Social Scientist* 3 (1975): 43–52.

Casey, Leo. "Questioning Halabja: Genocide and the Expedient Political Lie." *Dissent* (Summer 2003): 61–65.

Chandler, David. *Brother Number One: A Political Biography of Pol Pot*. Boulder, CO: Westview Press, 1992.

———. Review of Ben Kiernan, *The Pol Pot Regime: Race, Power and Genocide in Cambodia under the Khmer Rouge, 1975–1979*. *Journal of Asian Studies* 44, no. 4 (1996): 1063–64.

———. *Voices from S-21: Terror and History in Pol Pot's Secret Prison*. Berkeley: University of California Press, 2000.

Chang, Iris. *The Rape of Nanking*. New York: Penguin, 1998.

Charney, Israel W., and Daphna Fromer, "Denying the Armenian Genocide: Patterns of Thinking as Defence-Mechanisms." *Patterns of Prejudice* 32, no. 1 (1998): 39–49.

Chaudhuri, Kalvan. *Genocide in Bangladesh*. Bombay: Orient Longman, 1972.

Chomsky, Noam, and Edward S. Herman. *After the Cataclysm: Postwar Indochina and the Reconstruction of Imperial Ideology*. Boston: South End Press, 1979.

———. "Distortions at Fourth Hand." *The Nation*, June 6, 1977, 789–94.

Chorbajian, Levon, and George Shirinian, eds. *Studies in Comparative Genocide*. Basingstoke: Macmillan and New York: St Martin's Press, 1999.

Churchill, Ward. *A Little Matter of Genocide: Holocaust and Denial in the Americas*. San Francisco, CA: City Lights Books, 1998.

———. "Forbidding the G-Word: Holocaust as Judicial Doctrine in Canada." *Other Voices* 2, no. 1 (February 2000), http://www.othervoices.org/2.1/churchill/denial.html (accessed January 18, 2011).

———. *Some People Push Back: On the Justice of Roosting Chickens* http://www.kersplebedeb.com/mystuff/s11/churchill.html (accessed January 18, 2011).

Clare, George. *Before the Wall: Berlin Days, 1946–1948*. New York: Dutton, 1989.

Clymer, Kenton. "Jimmy Carter, Human Rights and Cambodia." *Diplomatic History* 27, no. 2 (April 2003): 245–78.

Cole, Tim. *Selling the Holocaust: From Auschwitz to Schindler: How History is Bought, Packaged, and Sold*. New York: Routledge, 1999.

Collins, Larry, and Dominique Lapierre. *Freedom at Midnight*. New York: Simon & Schuster, 1975.

Crawford, Timothy W., and Alan J. Kuperman, eds. *Gambling on Humanitarian Intervention: Moral Hazard, Rebellion, and Civil War*. New York: Routledge, 2006.

Dadrian, Vahakn H. *The History of the Armenian Genocide: Ethnic Conflict from the Balkans to Anatolia to the Caucasus*. Providence, RI: Berghan Books, 1995.

Dallaire, Romeo. *Shake Hands with the Devil: The Failure of Humanity in Rwanda*. Toronto: Random House Canada, 2003.

Daniel, Robert L. "The Armenian Question and American-Turkish Relations." *The Mississippi Valley Historical Review* 46, no. 2 (September 1959): 252–75.

Davenport, Christian, and Allan C. Stam. "What Really Happened in Rwanda?" *Miller-McCune*, http://www.miller-mccune.com/politics/what-really-happened -in-rwanda-3432/ (accessed January 9, 2011).

Davies, Norman. *Europe: A History*. Oxford: Oxford University Press, 1996.

Des Forges, Alison. *Leave None to Tell the Story: Genocide in Rwanda*. New York: Human Rights Watch, 1999.

Duffy, Peter. *The Bielski Brothers: The True Story of Three Men Who Defied the Nazis, Built a Village in the Forest, and Saved 1,200 Jews*. New York: Harper Perennial, 2004.

Dwork, Deborah, and Robert Jay Van Pelt. *The Holocaust: A History*. New York: W. W. Norton, 2002.

El Fadl, Khaled Abu. *The Place of Tolerance in Islam*. Boston: Beacon Press, 2002.

Elkins, Caroline. *Imperial Reckoning: The Untold Story of Britain's Gulag in Kenya*. New York: Henry Holt, 2005.

Evans, Richard J. *In Hitler's Shadow: West German Historians and the Attempt to Escape from the Nazi Past*. New York: Pantheon, 1989.

———. *Lying About Hitler, History, Holocaust and the David Irving Trial*. New York: Basic Books, 2002.

———. *The Third Reich in Power*. New York: The Penguin Press, 2005.

Finkelstein, Norman. *The Holocaust Industry: Reflections on the Exploitation of Jewish Suffering*. London: Verso, 2000.

Frank, Andre Gunder. *Capitalism and Underdevelopment in Latin America: Historical Studies of Brazil and Chile*. New York: Monthly Review Press, 1967.

Fritzsche, Peter. *Life and Death in the Third Reich*. Cambridge, MA: Harvard University Press, 2008.

Goldhagen, Daniel Jonah. *Hitler's Willing Executioners: Ordinary Germans and the Holocaust*. New York: Vintage, 1996.

Gourevitch, Philip. *We wish to inform you that tomorrow we will be killed with our children: Stories from Rwanda*. New York: Farrar, Straus & Giroux, 1998.

Green, Barbara B. "Stalinist Terror and the Question of Genocide: The Great Famine." In *Is the Holocaust Unique? Perspectives on Comparative Genocide*, edited by Alan S. Rosenbaum. Boulder, CO: Westview Press, 2001.

Gunter, Michael M. *Pursuing the Just Cause of their People: A Study of Contemporary Armenian Terrorism*. New York: Greenwood Press, 1986.

Guttenplan, D. D. *The Holocaust on Trial*. New York: W. W. Norton, 2002.

Hancock, Ian. "Responses to the Porrajamos: The Romani Holocaust." In *Is the Holocaust Unique? Perspectives on Comparative Genocide*, edited by Alan S. Rosenbaum. Boulder, CO: Westview Press, 2001.

Hansen, Anders Bjorn. "The Punjab 1937-1947: A Case of Genocide?" In *Genocide: Cases, Comparisons and Contemporary Debates*, edited by Steven L. B. Jensen. Copenhagen: Danish Center for Holocaust and Genocide Studies, 2003.

Heder, Stephen. "Racism, Marxism, Labeling and Genocide in Ben Kiernan's *The Pol Pot Regime*." *South East Asia Research* 5, no. 2 (1997): 101–53.

———. "Hun Sen and Genocide Trials in Cambodia: International Impacts, Impunity, and Justice." In *Cambodia Emerges from the Past: Eight Essays*, edited by Judy Ledgerwood. DeKalb, IL: Southeast Asia Publications, 2002.

Herman, Edward S., and Noam Chomsky. *Manufacturing Consent: The Political Economy of Mass Media*. New York: Pantheon, 2002.

Herman, Edward S., and David Peterson. *The Politics of Genocide*, New York: Monthly Review Press, 2009.

———. "Rwanda and the Democratic Republic of Congo in the Propaganda System." *Monthly Review* (May 2010), http://www.monthlyreview.org/100501herman -peterson.php. (accessed January 15, 2011).

Hering, Bob, and Ernst Utrecht, eds. *Malcolm Caldwell's Southeast Asia*. Townsville, Australia: Committee of South-East Asian Studies, James Cook University of North Queensland, 1979.

Hilberg, Raul. *The Destruction of the European Jews*, 3rd ed., 3 vols. New Haven and London: Yale University Press, 2003.

———. *The Politics of Memory: The Journey of a Holocaust Historian*. Chicago: Ivan R. Dee, 2002.

Hintjens, Helen M. "Explaining the 1994 Genocide in Rwanda." *The Journal of Modern African Studies* 7, no. 2 (1999): 241–86.

Hinton, William. *Fanshen: A Documentary of Revolution in a Chinese Village*. New York: Vintage, 1966.

Hitchens, Christopher. *The Trial of Henry Kissinger*. London and New York: Verso, 2001.

Hochschild, Adam. *King Leopold's Ghost: A Story of Greed, Terror, and Heroism in Colonial Africa*. Boston: Houghton Mifflin, 1998.

Hovanissian, Richard G. "The Armenian Genocide and Patterns of Denial." In *The Armenian Genocide in Perspective*, edited by Richard G. Hovanissian. New Brunswick, NJ: Transaction Publishers, 1997.

———. "The Critics View: Beyond Revisionism." *International Journal of Middle East Studies* 9 (1978): 379–88.

Huttenbach, Henry R. "The Psychology and Politics of Genocide Denial: A Comparison of Four Case Studies." In *Studies in Comparative Genocide*, edited by Levon Chorbajian and George Shirinian. Basingstoke: Macmillan and New York: St Martin's Press, 1999.

Jahan, Rounaq. "Genocide in Bangladesh." In *Century of Genocide: Eyewitness Accounts and Critical Views*, edited by Samuel Totten, William S. Parsons, and Israel W. Charney, 291–316. New York: Garland Publishing, 1997.

Kershaw, Ian. *Hitler: 1936–1945: Nemesis*. New York: W. W. Norton, 2000.

Kiernan, Ben. Review of *Brother Number One: A Political Biography of Pol Pot*, by David P. Chandler. *Journal of Asian Studies* 52, no. 4 (1993): 1076–77.

———. *The Pol Pot Regime: Race, Power, and Genocide in Cambodia under the Khmer Rouge*. New Haven, CT: Yale University Press, 1996.

———. "Cover up and Denial of Genocide: Australia, the USA, East Timor and the Aborigines." *Critical Asian Studies* 34, no. 2 (June 2002).

———. "The Demography of Genocide in Southeast Asia: The Death Tolls in Cambodia, 1975–1979 and East Timor, 1975–1980." *Critical Asian Studies* 35, no. 4 (2003).

———. *How Pol Pot Came to Power: Colonialism, Nationalism, and Communism in Cambodia, 1930–1975*. New Haven, CT: Yale University Press, 2004.

———. *Blood and Soil: A World History of Genocide and Extermination from Sparta to Darfur*. New Haven, CT: Yale University Press, 2007.

Kissinger, Henry. *The White House Years*. Boston: Little, Brown, 1979.

Kuper, Leo. *Genocide: Its Political Use in the Twentieth Century*. New Haven, CT: Yale University Press, 1982.

Kuperman, Alan J. "Provoking Genocide: A Revised History of the Rwandan Patriotic Front." *Journal of Genocide Research* 6, no. 1 (2004): 61–84.

———. "Suicidal Rebellions and the Moral Hazard of Humanitarian Intervention." *Ethnopolitics* 4, no. 2 (2005): 149–73.

Kux, Dennis. *The United States and Pakistan, 1947–2000: Disenchanted Allies*. Washington, D.C.: Woodrow Wilson Center Press, 2001.

Langer, William. *The Diplomacy of Imperialism: 1890-1902, Volume 1*. New York: Alfred A. Knopf, 1935.

Levene, Mark. "Creating a Modern Zone of Genocide: The Impact of Nation and State Formation on Eastern Anatolia, 1878–1923." *Holocaust and Genocide Studies* 12 (1998): 393–433.

———. "The Chittagong Hill Tracts: A Case Study in the Political Economy of 'Creeping' Genocide." *Third World Quarterly* 20, no. 2 (1999): 339–69.

———. *Genocide in the Age of the Nation State: The Meaning of Genocide*. London: I. B.Taurus, 2005.

———. *Genocide in the Age of the Nation State, Volume 2: The Rise of the West and the Coming of Genocide*. London: I. B. Taurus, 2005.

Lewis, Bernard. *The Emergence of Modern Turkey*. New York: Oxford University Press, 1961.

Lewy, Gunter. *The Nazi Persecution of the Gypsies*. New York: Oxford University Press, 2001.

———, *The Armenian Massacres in Ottoman Turkey: A Disputed Genocide*. Salt Lake City: University of Utah Press, 2005.

Lifschultz, Lawrence. *Bangladesh: The Unfinished Revolution*. London: Zed Press, 1979.

Lifton, Robert Jay. *The Nazi Doctors: Medical Killing and the Psychology of Genocide*. New York: Basic Books, 1986.

Linenthal, Edward T. *Preserving Memory: The Struggle to Create America's Holocaust Museum*. New York: Viking Press, 1995.

Lipstadt, Deborah. *Denying the Holocaust: The Growing Assault on Truth and Memory.* New York: Plume, 1994.

———. *History on Trial: My Day in Court with David Irving.* New York: Ecco, 2005.

Lowry, Heath W. "The U.S. Congress and Adolf Hitler and the Armenians." *Political Communication and Persuasion* 3, no. 2 (1985).

MacMillan, Margaret. *Paris, 1919: Six Months that Changed the World.* New York: Random House, 2001.

Maguire, Peter. *Facing Death in Cambodia.* New York: Columbia University Press, 2005.

Malkasian, Mark. "The Disintegration of the Armenian Cause in the United States, 1918–1927." *International Journal of Middle East Studies* 16 (1984): 349–65.

Mamdani, Mahmood. *When Victims Become Killers: Colonialism, Nativism, and Genocide in Rwanda.* Princeton, NJ: Princeton University Press, 1984.

———. *Saviors and Survivors: Darfur, Politics, and the War on Terror.* New York: Doubleday. 2009.

Mann, Michael. *The Dark Side of Democracy: Explaining Ethnic Cleansing.* Cambridge: Cambridge University Press, 2005.

Margolin, Jean Louis. "Cambodia, the Country of Disconcerting Crimes." In *The Black Book of Communism: Crimes, Terror, Repression,* edited by Stéphane Courteois et al. Cambridge, MA: Harvard University Press, 1999.

Mascarenhas, Anthony. *The Rape of Bangla Desh.* New Delhi: Vikas Publications, 1971.

———. *Bangladesh: A Legacy of Blood.* London: Hodder & Stoughton, 1986.

Mayer, Arno. *Why Did the Heavens Not Darken? The Final Solution in History.* New York: Pantheon, 1990.

McCarthy, Justin. *Death and Exile: The Ethnic Cleansing of the Ottoman Muslims, 1821-1922.* Princeton: Darwin Press, 1995.

———. *The Ottoman Turks: An Introductory History to 1923.* London: Addsion, Wesley, Longman Limited, 1997.

———. *The Ottoman Peoples and the End of Empire.* London: Arnold, 2001.

———. *The Armenian Rebellion at Van.* Salt Lake City: University of Utah Press, 2006.

Mearsheimer, John J., and Stephen M. Walt. *The Israel Lobby and U.S. Foreign Policy.* New York: Farrar, Straus & Giroux, 2007.

Melson, Robert. *Revolution and Genocide: On the Origins of the Armenian Genocide and the Holocaust.* Chicago: University of Chicago Press, 1992.

———. "Modern Genocide in Rwanda: Ideology, Revolution, War, and Mass Murder in an African State." In *The Specter of Genocide: Mass Murder in Historical Perspective,* edited by Robert Gellately and Ben Kiernan. Cambridge: Cambridge University Press, 2003.

Melvern, Linda. *A People Betrayed: The Role of the West in Rwanda's Genocide.* London: Zed Books, 2000.

———. *Conspiracy to Murder: The Rwandan Genocide.* London: Verso, 2006.

Metzl, Jamie Frederic. *Western Responses to Human Rights Abuses in Cambodia, 1975–1980*. New York: St. Martin's, 1996.

Midlarsky, Manus I. *The Killing Trap: Genocide in the Twentieth Century*. Cambridge: Cambridge University Press, 2005.

Morris, Benny. *Righteous Victims: A History of Arab-Zionist Conflict, 1880–2001*. New York: Vintage, 2001.

Morse, Arthur. *While Six Million Died: A Chronicle of American Apathy*. New York: Random House, 1968.

Muhith, A. M. A. *Bangladesh: Emergence of a Nation*. Dhaka: University Press, 1992.

Naimark, Norman. *Fires of Hatred: Ethnic Cleansing in Twentieth Century Europe*. Cambridge, MA: Harvard University Press, 2002.

Nalbandian, Louise. *The Armenian Revolutionary Movement: The Development of Armenian Political Parties through the Nineteenth Century*. Berkeley and Los Angeles: University of California Press, 1967.

Nasrin, Taslima. *Shame: A Novel*. New York: Prometheus Books, 1997.

Novick, Peter. *The Holocaust in American Life*. Boston: Houghton Mifflin, 1999.

Nussbaum, Martha C. "The Gujarat Massacre." *Dissent* (Summer 2003): 15–23.

Oldenburg, Philip. " 'A Place Insufficiently Imagined': Language, Belief, and the Pakistan Crisis of 1971." *Journal of Asian Studies* 44, no. 4 (1985): 711–33.

Papazian, Dennis R. "Modern Genocide: The Case of the Nation State and Ideological Political Parties: The Armenian Case." *Idea: The Journal of Social Issues* 7, no. 1 (2002): 8.

———. "Useful Answers to Frequent Questions about the Armenian Genocide," http://www.umd.umich.edu/dept/Armenians/facts/answers/html (accessed January 10, 2011).

Ponchaud, Francois. *Cambodia: Year Zero*. New York: Henry Holt, 1978.

Prunier, Gerard. *Africa's World Wars: Congo, the Rwandan Genocide, and the Making of a Continental Catastrophe*. New York: Oxford University Press, 2008.

Quataert, Donald. "The Massacres of the Ottoman Armenians and the Writing of Ottoman History." *Journal of Interdisciplinary History* 27, no. 2 (2006): 249–59.

———. *The Ottoman Empire, 1700-1922*. 2nd ed. Cambridge: Cambridge University Press, 2005.

Orwell, George. "Notes on Nationalism." In *The Collected Essays, Journalism and Letters of George Orwell. Vol. 3: As I Please, 1943 1945*, edited by Sonia Orwell and Ian Angus. New York: Harcourt Brace Jovanovich, 1968.

Payne, Robert. *Massacre: The Tragedy of Bangladesh and the Phenomenon of Mass Slaughter throughout History*. New York: Macmillan, 1973.

Pohl, J. Otto. *Ethnic Cleansing in the USSR, 1937–1949*. Westport, CT: Greenwood Press, 1999.

Porter, Gareth, and George C. Hildebrand, *Cambodia: Starvation and Revolution*. New York: Monthly Review Press, 1976.

Rahman, Tariq. "Language and Politics in a Pakistan Province: The Sindhi Language Movement." *Asian Survey* 35, no. 11 (November 1995): 1005–16.

Riaz, Ali. *God Willing: The Politics of Islamism in Bangladesh.* Lanham, MD: Rowman & Littlefield, 2004.

Sousa, Ashley Riley. "They Will Be Hunted Down like Wild Beasts and Destroyed: A Comparative Study of Genocide in California and Tasmania." *Journal of Genocide Research* 6, no. 2 (2004): 193–209.

Roseman, Mark. *The Villa, The Lake, The Meeting: Wannsee and the Final Solution.* London: Allen Lane, 2002.

Rosenbaum, Alan S., ed. *Is the Holocaust Unique?* 3rd edition. Boulder, CO: Westview Press, 2008.

Rosenfeld, Gavriel. "The Politics of Uniqueness: Reflections on the Recent Polemical Turn in Holocaust and Genocide Scholarship." *Holocaust and Genocide Studies* 13, no. 1, 28–61.

Rossino, Alexander B. *Hitler Strikes Poland: Blitzkrieg, Ideology, and Atrocity.* Lawrence: University Press of Kansas, 2003.

Rubenstein, William. *The Myth of Rescue: Why the Democracies Could Not Have Saved More Jews from the Nazis.* London: Routledge, 1997.

Rummel, R. J. *Death by Government.* New Brunswick, NJ: Transaction Publishers, 1997.

Rusesabagina, Paul, and Tom Zoellner. *An Ordinary Man: An Autobiography.* New York: Viking, 2006.

Said, Edward. *Orientalism.* New York: Vintage, 1979.

Salik, Siddiq. *Witness to Surrender.* Karachi: Oxford University Press, 1978.

Satloff, Robert. *Among the Righteous: Lost Stories from the Holocaust's Long Reach into Arab Lands.* New York: Public Affairs Books, 2006.

Schlink, Bernhard. *The Reader.* New York: Vintage, 2008.

Secretariat of the International Commission of Jurists. *The Events in East Pakistan, 1971. A Legal Study.* Geneva: International Commission of Jurists, 1972.

Segev, Tom. *The Seventh Million: Israelis and the Holocaust.* Translated from Hebrew by Haim Watzman. New York: Henry Holt, 2000.

Shaw, Stanford J., and Ezel Kural Shaw. *History of the Ottoman Empire and Modern Turkey: Volume II: Reform, Revolution and Republic: The Rise of Modern Turkey, 1808–1975.* Cambridge: Cambridge University Press, 1977.

———. "The Authors Respond." *International Journal of Middle East Studies* 9 (1978): 388–400.

Shawcross, William. *Sideshow: Nixon, Kissinger, and the Destruction of Cambodia.* New York, Simon & Schuster, 1979.

———. *The Quality of Mercy: Cambodia, Holocaust and Modern Conscience.* New York: Simon & Schuster, 1984.

Sisson, Richard, and Leo E. Rose. *War and Secession: Pakistan, India, and the Creation of Bangladesh.* Berkeley: University of California Press, 1990.

Smith, Roger W., Eric Markusen, and Robert Jay Lifton. "Professional Ethics and the Denial of the Armenian Genocide." *Holocaust and Genocide Studies* 9, no. 1 (1995): 1–22.

Snyder, Timothy. *Bloodlands: Europe between Hitler and Stalin*. New York: Basic Books, 2010.

Solzhenitsyn, Aleksandr I. *A World Split Apart: Commencement Address Delivered at Harvard University, June 8, 1978*. New York: Harper & Row, 1978.

————. *The Gulag Archipelago: An Experiment in Literary Investigation, I-II*. New York: Harper & Row, 1973.

Stannard, David E. *American Holocaust: The Conquest of the New World*. New York: Oxford University Press, 1993.

————. "Uniqueness as Denial: The Politics of Genocide Scholarship." In *Is the Holocaust Unique? Perspectives on Comparative Genocide*, edited by Alan S. Rosenbaum. Boulder, CO: Westview Press, 2001.

Stohl, Michael. "Outside of a Small Circle of Friends: States, Genocide, Mass Killing and the Role of Bystanders." *Journal of Peace Research* 24, no. 2 (June 1987): 151–66.

Straus, Scott. *The Order of Genocide: Race, Power and War in Rwanda*. Ithaca, NY: Cornell University Press, 2006.

Sysyn, Frank. "The Ukrainian Famine of 1932-3: The Role of the Ukrainian Diaspora in Research and Public Discussion." In *Studies in Comparative Genocide*, edited by Chorbajian, Levon and George Shirinian. Basingstoke: Macmillan and New York: St Martin's Press, 1999.

Talbot, Ian. *Punjab and the Raj, 1849-1947*. New Delhi: Manohar Publications, 1988.

————. *Pakistan: A Modern History*, revised edition. London and New York: Palgrave Macmillan, 2005.

Tec, Nehama. *Defiance: The Bielski Partisans*. New York: Oxford University Press, 2008.

Thion, Serge. "Genocide as a Political Commodity." In *Genocide and Democracy in Cambodia*, edited by Ben Kiernan, 163-190. New Haven: Yale University Southeast Asia Studies, 1993.

Thomas, Lewis V. and Richard N. Frye. *The United States and Turkey and Iran*. Cambridge: Harvard University Press, 1951.

Todorov, Tzvetan. *Facing the Extreme: Moral Life in the Concentration Camps*. New York: Henry Holt, 1997.

Van Hollen, Christopher. "The Tilt Policy Revisited: Nixon-Kissinger Geopolitics and South Asia." *Asian Survey* vol. 20, no. 4, April (1980): 339-61.

Vickery, Michael. *Cambodia: 1975–1982*. Boston: South End Press, 1984.

Weitz, Eric. *A Century of Genocide: Utopias of Race and Nation*. Princeton, NJ: Princeton University Press, 2003.

Wolpert, Stanley. *A New History of India*. New York: Oxford University Press, 1977.

Wyman, David S. *The Abandonment of the Jews: America and the Holocaust, 1941–1945*. New York: Pantheon, 1984.

Ziring, Lawrence. *Bangladesh: From Mujib to Ershad: An Interpretive Study*. Karachi and Oxford: Oxford University Press, 1992.

Index